The Homeric Battle of the Frogs and Mice

Greek Texts series

The Homeric Battle of the Frogs and Mice

Joel P. Christensen and Erik Robinson

BLOOMSBURY ACADEMIC
LONDON · NEW YORK · OXFORD · NEW DELHI · SYDNEY

BLOOMSBURY ACADEMIC
Bloomsbury Publishing Plc
50 Bedford Square, London, WC1B 3DP, UK
1385 Broadway, New York, NY 10018, USA

BLOOMSBURY, BLOOMSBURY ACADEMIC and the Diana logo
are trademarks of Bloomsbury Publishing Plc

First published 2018
Paperback edition first published 2019

Cover illustration by: Ch'en-Ling

A catalogue record for this book is available from the British Library.

Library of Congress Cataloging-in-Publication Data
Names: Christensen, Joel (Joel P.), editor. | Robinson, Erik (Classicist), editor.
Title: The Homeric Battle of the frogs and mice / Joel P. Christensen and Erik Robinson.
Other titles: Battle of the frogs and mice. | Battle of the frogs and mice. English. 2018. |
Greek texts (Bloomsbury (Firm)) ; 54.
Description: New York ; London : Bloomsbury Academic, 2018. |
Series: Greek texts ; 54
Identifiers: LCCN 2017031927| ISBN 9781350035942 (hardback) |
ISBN 9781350035966 (epub)
Subjects: LCSH: Battle of the frogs and mice—Commentaries.
Classification: LCC PA4023 .B3 2018 | DDC 883/.01—dc23
LC record available at https://lccn.loc.gov/2017031927

ISBN: HB: 978-1-3500-3594-2
PB: 978-1-3501-2497-4
ePDF: 978-1-3500-3595-9
ePub: 978-1-3500-3596-6

Typeset by RefineCatch Limited, Bungay, Suffolk

To find out more about our authors and books visit
www.bloomsbury.com and sign up for our newsletters.

Magistris discipulisque nostris

Contents

Preface

This commentary developed out of an interest in making students and casual readers aware of some of the less well-known works of ancient Greek literature. We first set out to prepare a translation but found ourselves drawn into a discussion of various manuscript problems, the poem's unclear relationship with other literature, and the absence of modern reference tools to assist in reading it. Thus, in its early stages our work was designed as a commentary for students setting out with just a bit of Greek to read something a little different.

The Homeric *Batrakhomuomakhia* ("Battle of Frogs and Mice") is a parody of Greek epic, attributed to Homer during the Roman Imperial period (around first century CE). It tells the story of a war between frogs and mice set off by the death of a lone mouse who dared to take a ride on a frog's back in a marsh. The battle—and the scenes preparing for it—are steeped in Homeric conventions of assemblies, arming sequences, divine councils, and a slaughter of absurd extent. Along the way, we find humorous depictions of Athena, the brief aristeia of a mouse, and the intervention of Zeus, aided by a battalion of armored crabs. The poem was very popular in the Byzantine era where it was used as a school text, "a short and entertaining introduction to Homer" (West 2003: 235).

The *Batrakhomuomakhia* presents the reader with numerous textual problems; it received extensive commentary at the end of the nineteenth century (Ludwich 1896) followed by shorter treatments almost a century later in German (Glei 1984) and Italian (Fusillo 1988). Certain issues relating to the text's author and date remain intractable: in the last generation, scholars have dated it as early as the fifth century BCE (e.g. Bliquez 1977) and as late as the second century CE (West 2003). Despite the publishing of a similar, fragmentary "beast epic" in the 1980s (the "Battle of Weasel and Mice"; Schibli 1983) and recent re-publication with translation (West 2003) alongside literary interest (e.g.

Kelly 2009; Hosty 2014; a panel dedicated to the poem at the UK's Classical Association Annual Meeting in 2015), the poem has not received a commentary in English. Our understanding of the poem stands to benefit, additionally, from scholarly advances since Ludwich's *magnum opus* and the later commentaries, including studies in oral-formulaic poetry, monumental scholarship on the fable in the ancient world (van Dijk 1997; Adrados 1998) and literary theory. In addition, the last few decades have seen a steady increase in interest and publication on non-canonical works and "post-classical" authors (e.g. the award winning work of Whitmarsh 2014).

This commentary seeks to fill this void partially by offering an introduction, text, translation, and commentary. Our comments focus especially on the poem's character in terms of Homeric language, the language of parody, and the conventions of fable. In addition, we have focused on preparing a text that would primarily serve students and scholars unfamiliar both with the traditions that influenced the *Batrakhomuomakhia* and the history of problems which attend the poem. In this way, the resulting work is an ideal fit for intermediate and early-advanced reading of Greek (from the secondary to graduate level) or for readers who are working on their own.

The introduction is divided into sections that (1) discuss the manuscript tradition and the editing of the text; (2) introduce the genres of fable and parody; (3) present the basic features of epic meter and language; and (4) prepare the reader for engaging with the text with a summary of structure and content. Although we present a basic argument for the poem's dating in the introduction, the commentary provides readers with the evidence necessary for developing their own opinions. As such, the notes provide a range of information for a reader with only a few semesters of Greek, such as forms and vocabulary not included in primary grammars; assistance with confusing syntax; discussion with some of the significant variants for the text; and references to scholarship on subjects that relate to the poem.

We have attempted to show where and how the text relates to other traditions of Greek literature while also trying to frame some of the ways in which the parody is sophisticated in its engagement with literary traditions. Finally, we have commented on the historical character of the poem's language, signaling aspects of diction and form that help us to situate this poem and its language in time. Our conclusions about the sophistication and origin of this poem, then, are spread throughout the comments that helped to influence them.

Through the introduction and the commentary, we emphasize the trans-generic quality of the poem through its parallels with tragedy, comedy, parody, and fable (as well as epic). This discussion is also appropriate for readers who are less interested in the Greek language and more concerned with the history of literature. For this reason, especially, we have included a mostly literal translation of the poem retaining the same line numbers as our Greek text.

Acknowledgments

*"As soon as the opportunity arrives, give yourself over to your
studies or to leisure"*

ut primum fuerit occasio, relinque teque studiis vel otio trade
Pliny *Letters*, 1.9

A few years ago, we sat down to read the *Commentary to the* Iliad by
Eustathius, the Archbishop of Thessaloniki, and before reading
more than a few words, we ended up starting on the Homeric
Batrakhomuomakhia. Our path to this commentary was far from
planned or direct—we just kept moving in the direction of what we did
not understand. The final product emerged out of weekly meetings,
nightly scribblings, and the posting of passages and comments online.
We are fortunate to have been afforded the *otium* to pursue and
complete this project; but we have had considerable help along the way.

In the preparation of this commentary we have been assisted by the
efforts of the UTSA Library's Interlibrary Loan Staff; the excellent
library at the Center for the Anthropology of the Ancient World at the
University of Siena; and financial resources provided by Brandeis
University. This project would not have seen print without the fine
editorial guidance of Alice Wright and the exemplary work of Lucy
Carroll at Bloomsbury and our anonymous referees. Angela Hurley, in
addition, was invaluable in copy-editing and preparing the index.
Finally, we are deeply indebted to advice and encouragement of friends.
Portions of the translation and commentary were originally shared on
our website sententiaeantiquae.com and were improved by the reactions
of anonymous and named correspondents, among whom Paul
McKenna merits special thanks for careful reading and insightful
suggestions. We received helpful guidance *viva voce* from William S.
Duffy, Zachary Elliott, and graduate students at the University of Texas
at Austin including Cassandra M. Donnelly, William C. Shrout, Collin
MacCormack, and Aaron Cogbill.

Introduction

Date and authorship

Ancient biographical traditions attribute the "Battle of Frogs and Mice" to "Homer." Almost no one today supports such a claim. One reason for such divergent ascriptions emerges from modern conceptions of "Homer" as a poetic tradition (rather than a traditional poet); but another derives from a process that began in antiquity of restricting works attributed to Homer to the *Iliad* and the *Odyssey* alone. Our task in this introduction is not to contribute to the Homeric question, but rather to explain what features of this epic parody have caused it to be attributed (or not) to the author of the *Iliad* and the *Odyssey*.[1] As we will discuss below, there is an ancient tradition crediting "lighter" fare to the serious epic poet.

The Homeric *Batrakhomuomakhia* (hereafter, *BM*) has been dated as early as Archaic Greece and as late as Imperial Rome (and was immensely popular during the Byzantine period).[2] In recent years, more scholars place the poem's origins in the first centuries BCE/CE.[3] Our earliest evidence of the poem is subsequent to this period and appears clustered in the second–third centuries CE. For example, scholars have pointed to Plutarch's *Life of Agesilaos* (15.5)—where Alexander refers to a battle with Darius a "mouse-war"—as proof that the *BM* was in circulation as early as the fourth century BCE.[4] Similar evidence does not point

---

[1] On the idea of Homer in the ancient world and the incremental narrowing of attributions to the *Iliad* and the *Odyssey*, see Graziosi 2002; Graziosi and Haubold 2005.

[2] See Ludwich 1896; Rzach 1913 for the sixth century BCE, Bliquez 1977 for the fifth century BCE. See Kirk 1976 and Sens 2005 for the Hellenistic period.

[3] Wackernagel 1916; Wölke 1978: 46–60; Glei 1984: 34–6; and West 2003.

[4] Plut. *Vit. Ages.* 15.5: Ἔοικεν, ὦ ἄνδρες, ὅτε Δαρεῖον ἡμεῖς ἐνικῶμεν ἐνταῦθα, ἐκεῖ τις ἐν Ἀρκαδίᾳ γεγονέναι μυομαχία ("Men, when we were defeating Darius there, it was like a Mouse-battle in Arcadia"). Some scholars accept *c.* 330 BCE as a *terminus ante quem* for a *BM*, but not necessarily the same poem as ours.

to Homer: The Pseudo-Plutarchean *de Malignitate Herodoti* (around second century CE?) attributes the poem to Pigres the Carian, dating it then to the fifth century BCE based on that figure's appearance in Herodotus.[5] Additional support for an early date has been offered in the form of a relief of Homer by Archaelaus of Priene which allegedly depicted a picture of a mouse sitting at the feet of Homer.[6]

These types of evidence are circumstantial and problematic: frogs do not appear in the Plutarchean mouse-war, nor in the relief image of Homer. The earliest accurately dateable testimonia that connect the *BM* with Homer come from the Roman poets Martial and Statius, near the end of the first century CE. Martial's *Epigram* 14.183, *Perlege Maeonio cantatas carmine ranas / Et frontem nugis solvere disce meis* ("Read the frogs sung in Maeonian song / or my trifles to smooth out your brow") is read as attributing the *BM* to Homer with the patronymic adjective *Maeonio*. Similarly, in his prefatory epistle to the first book of *Silvae*, Statius evaluates the *BM* as a literary work: *sed et Culicem legimus et Batrachomachiam etiam agnoscimus, nec quisquam est inlustrium poetarum qui non aliquid operibus suis stilo remissiore praeluserit* (8–10: "But we read the *Culex* and we know the *Batrachomachia* too, and there is no famous poet who has not toyed in style more relaxed than in his other works"). Statius here uses the *BM*, along with the Pseudo-Vergilian *Culex*, as a stock type, the "light poem by a serious author."[7]

These two references conform to a general treatment in the Homeric *Lives* (dated to the Roman Imperial Period and later). Of the ancient *Vitae Homeri*, the *Vita Herodotea*,[8] *Vita Plutarchea*, and *Vita Homeri V*

---

[5] Plut. *De Herod. Mal.* 873f3: τέλος δέ, καθημένους ἐν Πλαταιαῖς ἀγνοῆσαι μέχρι τέλους τὸν ἀγῶνα τοὺς Ἕλληνας, ὥσπερ βατραχομαχίας γινομένης, ἣν Πίγρης ὁ Ἀρτεμισίας ἐν ἔπεσι παίζων καὶ φλυαρῶν ἔγραψε ("And last of all, [he made] the Greeks who were stationed at Plataia ignorant of the contest right up to the end of it, as if there were a Frog-War going on, the kind of thing Pigres wrote while playing around nonsensically in epic verse.") the *Suda* (a Byzantine encyclopedia) repeats much of this information.

[6] Most scholars now dismiss this evidence; Bliquez 1977 does not.

[7] For the use of mock-epic as preparation for serious epic in Vergil see Harrison 2007 (chapter 5).

[8] The dating of the *Vita Herodotea* is problematic. Some (see Graziosi, 2002: 73–4) would place it in the Hellenistic period, in which case the date of the *BM*'s composition would be pre-Hellenistic.

mention the *BM* in conjunction with other Homeric works.[9] While these accounts differ in their particulars, they present the *BM* as either playful diversion (παίγνια) or a mental/poetic exercise (γυμνασίας καὶ παιδείας ἕνεκα, τῆς φύσεως καὶ τῆς δυνάμεως ἕνεκα).[10] By the second century CE, the *BM* had a specific tradition among the intellectual elite of the Roman Empire as one of the "lesser" poems of "Homer". Ancient authors appear to accept the poem as Homeric play, mental exercise, or an educational text for learners.[11] Although Martial and Statius may refer to *a* Batrakhomuomakhia (and not the one we possess or that attributed by the *Vitae* to Homer), a recently published papyrus (P. Oxy. 4668) with lines shared by our poem dates to the second or third century CE.[12] There is, of course, quite a distance in time and culture, between the ascription to Homer or Pigres in the fifth century BCE and the Roman Empire. And, indeed, as Jakob Wackernagel (1916) argued, and as we will investigate in this introduction and throughout the commentary, the poem's internal evidence (language, meter, etc.) betrays significant influence from the Hellenistic and Roman periods.

---

[9] "The Khian man possessed children around the same age. They were entrusted to Homer for education. He composed these poems: the *Kekropes*, *Batrakohmuomakia*, *Psaromakhia*, *Heptapaktikê*, and *Epikikhlides* and as many other poems as were playful." ἦσαν γὰρ τῷ Χίῳ παῖδες ἐν ἡλικίῃ. τούτους οὖν αὐτῷ παρατίθησι παιδεύειν. ὁ δὲ ἔπρησσε ταῦτα· καὶ τοὺς Κέρκωπας καὶ Βατραχομυομαχίαν καὶ Ψαρομαχίην καὶ Ἑπταπακτικὴν καὶ Ἐπικιχλίδας καὶ τἆλλα πάντα ὅσα παίγνιά ἐστιν. (*Vita Herodotea* 332–4); "He wrote two poems, the *Iliad* and the *Odyssey* and, as some say, though not truthfully, he added the *Batrakhomuomakhia* and *Margites* for practice and education." ἔγραψε δὲ ποιήματα δύο, Ἰλιάδα καὶ Ὀδύσσειαν, ὡς δέ τινες, οὐκ ἀληθῶς λέγοντες, γυμνασίας καὶ παιδείας ἕνεκα Βατραχομυομαχίαν προσθεὶς καὶ Μαργίτην. (*Vita Plutarchea* 1.98–100); "Some also say that two school poems were attributed to him, the *Batrakhomuomakhia* and the *Margites*." τινὲς δ᾽ αὐτοῦ φασιν εἶναι καὶ τὰ φερόμενα δύο γράμματα, τήν τε Βατραχομυομαχίαν καὶ τὸν Μαργίτην (*Vita Quinta*, 22–4).

[10] This sentiment is echoed in the *Greek Anthology*, Exhortatory Epigrams 90.1–2: ῞Ομηρος αὐτοῦ γυμνάσαι γνῶσιν θέλων, / τῶν βατράχων ἔπλασε καὶ μυῶν μῦθον ("Because he wanted to exercise his mind / Homer made up the tale of frogs and mice").

[11] The scholia of the *BM*, ἁρμόζει μείραξιν ἁπαλοῖς ἐπτοημένοις περὶ τὰ παίγνια, ὅσους δηλαδὴ ἔτι ἐγκύκλιος παίδευσις γαλακτοτροφεῖ ("[Homer] adapted epic for young children who were especially excited for games [*paignia*], those whom a general education still milk-fed").

[12] See Wouters 2005: 105. On the MSS traditions in general see Ludwich 1896 and Glei 1984.

The manuscript tradition

The textual tradition of the *BM* has presented numerous metrical anomalies, an abundance of *variae lectiones* ("variant readings"), and several (longer) passages which seem hopelessly confused. Because our text of the *BM* is not conceived *in usum editorum* (for the purpose of establishing an authoritative text), we include only a brief outline of the textual tradition of the poem. For the most extensive discussion, readers should consult Ludwich's edition (which is in German with Latin notes).

The *BM* enjoyed a wide popularity in the Middle Ages. The oldest surviving MS, Baroccianus 50 (housed at Oxford) comes from the tenth century CE. Ludwich notes that this manuscript contains few marginal glosses, but shows significant signs of correction or alteration by a later hand. Due to limited access, Ludwich himself was not able to thoroughly inspect this copy (readers may consult the Oxford Classical Text (*Homeri Opera* Vol. V, 1912 and 1946) of T.W. Allen who was able to conduct a more complete review of it). The recent papyrus find discussed above indicates some continuity between a text available during the second/third centuries CE and this manuscript.

Ludwich numbers twenty major MSS hailing from the tenth through fifteenth centuries CE. The poem enjoyed a burst of popularity in the fifteenth century, to which forty-seven copies of the major MSS date. One of the central points upon which the MSS are divided and grouped is the inclusion of the interpolated lines 42–52 (see the discussion in the notes). A majority of the MSS include these lines, which are widely thought to be a Byzantine interpolation; however, a great number of the earlier MSS (including Baroccianus 50) have also included them.

We have not undertaken a new collation of the poem's manuscript readings. Our text is formed primarily from a comparison of the Oxford Classical Text of T.W. Allen and Ludwich's (with consultation of Glei 1984 and Wölke 1978). We have included the majority of the longer suspect passages in our text. It is our hope that by including many of the problematic passages we will encourage readers to consider them in depth and make some of their own editorial selections. In addition, a more inclusive text recognizes the importance of the poem's reception among various audiences. Just as Byzantine—and presumably earlier—editors were engaged in fashioning a *BM* based on their tastes and assumptions about foregoing literary traditions, so too may modern readers.

Our poem

We will discuss the character of the poem in the following sections and in the commentary. As a preface to our literary and stylistic contextualizations, it is worthwhile to summarize the contents of the poem. We break the poem up into the following sections (we present brief introductions to each section in the commentary):

1–8	The Proem
9–99	The *Casus Belli*: Meeting of Frog and Mouse; Death of Mouse
100–31	Mouse Assembly and Arming
132–67	Frog Assembly and Arming
168–97	Divine Council on the War
198–259	Alternating Battle Sequence
260–69	The Aristeia of Meridarpax
270–83	Divine Council
284–92	Divine Intervention in the Battle
293–302	The Arrival of the Crabs

The action is roughly as follows. Following an introduction that draws on epic motifs for beginning poems, the narrator proceeds in fable mode with "once there was a mouse." The mouse meets a frog and brags about his fine dining under the feet of human beings; the frog invites the mouse for a ride on his back across a marsh to visit his own home. While they are traveling, a water-snake appears and the frog dives. The mouse perishes. When the mouse's father hears the tale, he gathers the mice in assembly and exhorts them to war; a comic arming scene ensues as the mice gird themselves with needles and other objects to be found on the ground and floor. After the mice have announced their intentions, the frogs assemble as well and the culprit amphibian denies his culpability. The frogs arm in gear appropriate to their environment. Then, the two sides advance to meet in war.

Before they join battle, however, the scene moves to Olympus where the gods look down in anticipation. Athena refuses to lend aid to either side since the mice gnawed a hole in her robe and the frogs keep her awake at night. The gods resolve to watch the battle where the mice and frogs slaughter each other until the aristeia of a single mouse warrior signals doom for the frogs. Again, the gods comment on the action and this time Zeus enters the fray: he throws lightning bolts and sends in crabs to mutilate the mice when they will not retreat.

It is probably obvious from this summary that a good deal of the humor of the poem relies on the basic concept: a heroic battle fought by rather small and unheroic creatures. More difficult to convey in summary (and translation) is the extent to which this humor is pursued with creative naming (of mice and frogs) and its adaptation of Homeric language and integration of features from other genres. These issues will be covered throughout the commentary, but we will offer some general cultural and literary frameworks in the following sections.

The tradition of fable

The *BM* displays engagement with a wide array of genres both in its diction and its content. Noteworthy among its influences is the Greco-Roman fable, a complex tradition that spans many different genres and eras.[13] Cross-cultural comparison reveals similar traditions dating back to Ancient Mesopotamia, Egypt, and ancient India. Scholars have emphasized continuities in structure and content among these traditions, arguing in turn for their influence on the Greek tradition from the Ancient Near East.

---

[13]   For overviews of fable, see van Dijk 1997 and Adrados 1998.

In Archaic and Classical Greece, it is difficult to ascertain to what extent the fable was an independent genre instead of conventional content in other genres. For the most part, discussions of "genre" in Ancient Greece and Rome rely on structural elements like meter, contextual venues for performance, or the tone/aims of a particular type of composition.[14] The fable is exceptional for its inter-generic character. For instance, poetic genres like epic (the Hawk and Nightingale in Hesiod's *Works and Days*, 202–12), lyric (Archilochus fr. 174 [Fox and Eagle] and 185 [Ape and Fox]; Semonides fr. 9 [Heron, Eel, and Buzzard]), tragedy (e.g. Aeschylus' *Agamemnon* [Lion Cub and Man, 717–36]), and comedy (e.g. Aristophanes' *Wasps* [Mouse and Weasel, 1182]) contain examples of the fable.[15] Nearly all Classical Greek prose genres contain fables of some kind including philosophy, historiography, and oratory.

Foremost among the difficulties of defining the fable is the language used to describe it.[16] Hence, the term *fable* itself—from Latin *Fabula*—indicates in part the long and confusing history of the genre. In early Greek poetry, the terms *logos*, *ainos*, and *muthos* all introduce what we now recognize as a fable.[17] Though definitions of the fable are nearly as variable as the category itself, a basic description suffices: fables are stories set in the past which are almost always metaphorical (or allegorical), believed by their audiences to be fictitious.[18]

Most of the fables we have today can be traced to a few collections made during antiquity. The peripatetic philosopher Demetrius of Phaleron is credited with collecting fables in verse and translating them into prose in Athens during the fourth century BCE. This collection is likely the antecedent of the collection now referred to as the Augustana (dated by some to the middle Hellenistic period). The early Byzantine

[14] For a recent discussion of genre and a bibliography, see Rotstein 2012.
[15] Van Dijk 1997: 124–382 gives a full catalogue of fables in ancient genres.
[16] For a survey of modern theories regarding the fable, see van Dijk 1997: 5–37.
[17] For these terms see van Dijk 1997: 79–88; and Adrados 1998: 4–13.
[18] Van Dijk (1997: 113) a "fictitious, metaphorical narrative."

era preserves a nearly as old tradition of Anonymous Fables and variations transmitted in the Vindobonensis and Accursiana manuscripts. In addition to these, we also have the Rylands Papyrus, probably hailing from the late first century BCE.

During this process of transmission, fables remained in part what they always had been, a type of literary exercise with a guise of simplicity and an intrinsic sense of humor. Plato's Socrates liked the fable for its clear morals (Diogenes Laertius' *Vita Phil.* 2.5.45); Aristotle echoes this in classifying the fable as a type of exemplum (*Rhet.* II.20). Scholars tend to agree on the persuasive and exemplary nature of fables as well as their intrinsically comic character. By the time of Quintilian (*Inst.* 1.9.1–3), fables were regularly used for both moral instruction and practice in composition, but they were also still ripe for jest (as in the work of the early imperial poet Phaedrus), literary exercise, and competition, for Babrius and the Babrian tradition, or both, as in the case of the late Roman Avianus.

What exactly a fable contained, of course, was always transforming as well. A common notion of the Aesopic fable is that it deals primarily with animals.[19] There are lots of animal tales, true, but many fables also deal with people. As Adrados (1998: 32–3) argues, what distinguishes a fable from myth is as much its "closed" nature—fables express their "moral" directly—as well as shorter length and structure. Fables tend to put two characters into a conflict (an *agôn*), sometimes with help or replacements should they perish, in a specific situation the resolution of which leaves one character the victim and the other a victor (sometimes with divine help; often with surprising outcomes). Fables often include dialogue and end with a moral.

Even from the brief summary above, it is obvious that the *BM* adheres to some—though not all—of these characteristics—less clear is how we should conceive of the relationship between the *BM* and the fable which most closely resembles it. The "Frog and Mouse" tale is found in the *Life of Aesop*, separate from the other collections of fables.

---

[19] For a brief discussion of Aesop and the Aesopic tradition, see van Dijk 1997: 98–104.

This *Life* is thought to be later than some of the dates argued for the *BM*.[20] For this reason, there has been some debate over whether the parody draws on this specific fable or whether the fable is based on the parody (see Adrados 1998: 144). Of course, there is a middle ground where we can imagine an early fable which influenced both, but the evidence for this is uncertain.

By the Hellenistic period, "Aesopic Fable" was taken largely to mean animal fable, and the received tradition of animal tales can give us some guidelines for evaluating the *BM*.[21] The characterization of animals tends to be fairly standard. In fables, foxes are clever, lions are strong, and monkeys make fools of themselves. The message concerning frogs and mice is a little less clear. In Aristophanes' reference to "Mice and Weasels" (on which, see below) mice perish in part because they are ostentatious. But in other tales a grateful mouse frees a lion from a trap. In fables, frogs are devoured by kites, they absurdly seek a king from a serpent, and they bake in the sun. Adrados (1998: 174–5), however, sees the "Mouse and Frog" story as a special case similar to the "Eagle and Fox" where the weak animal prevails due to the intervention of a divinity (even though there is no divine intervention in the Fable below). The conflict between a mouse and a frog is not as paradigmatic as a hare being bested by a tortoise or the mice struggling against weasels. As the *BM* points out, these animals are really from different worlds, they belong to separate kinds of tales.

If we can suspend the question of derivation—along with the curious nature of its exceptionality—it is useful to consider the "Frog and Mouse" fable (Aesop, *Fabula* 302):

There was a time when all the animals spoke the same language. A mouse who was on friendly terms with a frog invited him to dinner

---

[20] While Adrados implies that the fable is derivative, e.g. 1998, 469, 655, he proposes that the prototype of the *Vita Aesopi* was in the Hellenistic fables. Van Dijk asserts "The mock heroic *Batrachomyomachia* is based upon, but does not allude to, a Frog-Mouse fable" (1997: 137). West (2003: 232) believes that "the author took his starting point from another Aesopic fable."

[21] See Adrados 1998: 398–402 for a catalogue of fables.

and led him into a storehouse of his wealth where he kept his bread, cheese, honey, dried figs and all of his precious things. And he said "Eat whatever you wish, Frog." Then the frog responded: "When you come visit me, you too will have your fill of fine things. But I don't want you to be nervous, so I will fasten your foot to my foot." After the frog bound his foot to the mouse's and dragged him in this way, he pulled the tied-up mouse into the pond. While he drowned, he said "I am being killed by you, but I will be avenged by someone still alive!" A bird who saw the mouse afloat flew down and seized him. The frog went aloft with him too and, thus, the bird slaughtered them both.

A malicious plan between friends is thus a danger to them both.

ΜΥΣ ΚΑΙ ΒΑΤΡΑΧΟΣ

ὅτε ἦν ὁμόφωνα τὰ ζῷα, μῦς βατράχῳ φιλιωθεὶς ἐκάλεσεν αὐτὸν εἰς δεῖπνον καὶ ἀπήγαγεν αὐτὸν εἰς ταμιεῖον πλουσίου, ὅπου ἦν ἄρτος, τυρός, μέλι, ἰσχάδες καὶ ὅσα

ἀγαθά, καί φησιν „ἔσθιε, βάτραχε, ἐξ ὧν βούλει." ὁ δὲ βάτραχος ἔλεγε· „ἐλθὼν οὖν καὶ σὺ πρὸς ἐμὲ ἐμπλήσθητι τῶν ἀγαθῶν μου. ἀλλ᾽ ἵνα μὴ ὄκνος σοι γένηται, προσαρτήσω τὸν πόδα σου τῷ ποδί μου." δήσας οὖν ὁ βάτραχος τὸν πόδα τοῦ μυὸς τῷ ἑαυτοῦ ποδὶ ἤλατο εἰς τὴν λίμνην ἕλκων καὶ τὸν μῦν δέσμιον. ὁ δὲ πνιγόμενος ἔλεγεν· „ἐγὼ μὲν ὑπό σου νεκρωθήσομαι, ἐκδικήσομαι δὲ ὑπὸ ζῶντος." λούπης δὲ θεασάμενος τὸν μῦν πλέοντα καταπτὰς ἥρπασεν. ἐφέλκετο οὖν σὺν αὐτῷ καὶ ὁ βάτραχος καὶ οὕτως ἀμφοτέρους διεσπάραξεν.

ὅτι ἡ τῶν φίλων πονηρὰ συμβουλὴ καὶ ἑαυτοῖς κίνδυνος γίνεται.

Variant from the *Life of Aesop* G.

Once when all the animals spoke the same language, a mouse who was friends with a frog invited him to dinner and led him into a storehouse of his wealth where he kept every type of bread, meat, cheese, olive and dried figs. Then he said "eat." Since he was so well received, the frog said "come also and dine with me so that I might treat you well." He led him to the pond and said "Swim" and the mouse responded "I don't know how to swim" and the frog said "I will teach you." Then, after binding his foot to the mouse's foot with cord he dragged the mouse. And the mouse while drowning said "I will get vengeance on you still living when I am a corpse." While he said these things, the frog went under and drowned him. As the mouse lied in the water and the frog swam on, a crow snatched the mouse who was still bound to the frog. After he ate the mouse, he killed the frog. This is how the mouse got vengeance on the frog. In the same way, when I die, I will be the death of you. For the Lydians, the Babylonians and nearly the rest of Greece will harvest the fruit of my death.

"ὅτε ἦν τὰ ζῷα ὁμόφωνα, μῦς φιλιάσας βατράχῳ ἐκάλεσεν αὐτὸν ἐπὶ δεῖπνον καὶ εἰσήγαγεν αὐτὸν εἰς ταμιεῖον πλούσιον πάνυ, ἐφ' ᾧ ἦν ἄρτος, κρέας, τυρός, ἐλαῖαι, ἰσχάδες· καί φησιν 'ἔσθιε.' καλῶς ληφθεὶς ὁ βάτραχός φησιν 'ἐλθὲ καὶ σὺ παρ' ἐμοὶ δειπνήσων, ἵνα σε καλῶς λάβω.' ἀπήγαγεν δὲ αὐτὸν εἰς λίμνην καί φησιν 'κολύμβησον.' ὁ δὲ μῦς· 'κολυμβῆσαι οὐκ ἐπίσταμαι.' ὁ βάτραχος· 'ἐγώ σε διδάξω.' δήσας τε λίνῳ τὸν πόδα τοῦ μυὸς πρὸς τὸν ἴδιον πόδα [ἔδησεν] <ἥλατο εἰς τὴν λίμνην> καὶ τὸν μῦν ἔσυρεν. ὁ δὲ μῦς πνιγόμενος εἶπεν 'νεκρὸς ὢν ζῶντά σε ἐκδικήσω.' ταῦτα εἰπόντος αὐτοῦ καταδὺς ὁ βάτραχος ἔπνιξεν αὐτόν. κειμένου δὲ αὐτοῦ ἐπὶ τοῦ ὕδατος καὶ ἐπιπλέοντος, κόραξ ἥρπασεν τὸν μῦν σὺν τῷ βατράχῳ συνδεδεμένον, καταφαγὼν δὲ τὸν μῦν ἐδράξατο καὶ τοῦ βατράχου. οὕτως ὁ μῦς τὸν βάτραχον ἐξεδίκησεν. ὁμοίως κἀγώ, ἄνδρες, ἀποθανὼν ὑμῖν μόρος ἔσομαι· καὶ γὰρ Λύδιοι, Βαβυλώνιοι, καὶ σχεδὸν ἡ Ἑλλὰς ὅλη τὸν ἐμὸν καρπίσονται θάνατον."

This tale and the *BM* share several plot elements.[22] The mouse speaks at length about the quality of his food; the frog invites him for a swim; the mouse drowns and curses the frog while dying. Lexical ties between the fable and the poem (discussed in the commentary) imply some type of relationship.[23] But the differences are also important: the *BM* leaves out anything about the binding of the foot; and the bird which kills the frog is completely absent as well. It is easy to imagine a parodist taking his

[22] See also Wölke 1978:91–178; Glei 1984: 22 and 116–17; Fusillo 1988: 32, and 89–90.
[23] E.g. the use of the non-Homeric verb ἀποπνίγω at line 119 (τοῦτον ἀπέπνιξεν Φυσίγναθος ἐς βυθὸν ἄξας) and 158 (πνίξαντες) may echo the Fable's ὁ δὲ πνιγόμενος; likewise, the rare ἀκολύμβους ("unable to swim," line 158) recalls the Fable's "I do not know how to swim" (κολυμβῆσαι οὐκ ἐπίσταμαι).

cue from the meeting of the animals and building an interspecies war over the death of the mouse, excising the avenging bird in favor of divine intervention and the all-too-comic battalion of crabs that ends the poem. But it is somewhat less easy to conceive of a fable based on the *BM* leaving out divine interest (since fables often involve gods in animal affairs).[24] In addition, the snake which features so prominently in the *BM* would be a natural component of an animal fable.

Epic parody

While the *BM* shares some similarities with both the conventions of fable and the fable passed down as "Frog and Mouse," the exact nature of this relationship is unclear. The language of the poem, moreover, attests to broad engagement with lyric and comic poetry in addition to epic. Although we have no clear fables *within* extant Homeric epic, late ancient writers attribute fable-use to Homer.[25] But another genre attached to Homer is parody. In ancient testimonies, the *BM* is often paired with a composition called the *Margites* as belonging to Homer.[26] In his *Poetics*, Aristotle mentions one of these works (1448b28–1449a3):

> We aren't able to say anything about this kind of poem before Homer— but it is likely there were many—but we must start from Homer who leaves us the *Margites* and other works of this sort. It is fitting that among these works he also developed the iambic meter—for this is the very reason that *iambos* is called this today, since men are always mocking each other in that meter. Some of the ancient poets wrote heroic poetry, others wrote iambic. Just as Homer was the exceptional

---

[24] The scholarly consensus holds that the fable is based on the BM; see van Dijk 1997: 126.
[25] Theon, *Prog.* 3; Pseudo-Diogenian *Praef.*; Philostratus, *Im.* 1.3: see van Dijk 1997: 442–3.
[26] Earliest account: Plutarch's *On the Malice of Herodotus*; it is likely that the testimony in Proclus' *Chrestomathia* (67), the various *Vitae Homeri*, Eustathius (Comm. Ad *Il.* II.6.28) and the Suda all draw on this. For issues of authorship and the poems attributed to Homer in antiquity, see Graziosi 2002.

poet in serious matters—for he didn't only do it well in other ways but he also made his representations dramatic—in the same way he was the first to display the character of comedy in dramatizing something funny, not reproachful. And his *Margites* completes an analogy for us: just as the *Iliad* and the *Odyssey* are to tragedy, so to the *Margites* is to comedy."

τῶν μὲν οὖν πρὸ Ὁμήρου οὐδενὸς ἔχομεν εἰπεῖν τοιοῦτον ποίημα, εἰκὸς δὲ εἶναι πολλούς, ἀπὸ δὲ Ὁμήρου ἀρξαμένοις ἔστιν, οἷον ἐκείνου ὁ Μαργίτης καὶ τὰ τοιαῦτα. ἐν οἷς κατὰ τὸ ἁρμόττον καὶ τὸ ἰαμβεῖον ἦλθε μέτρον—διὸ καὶ ἰαμβεῖον καλεῖται νῦν, ὅτι ἐν τῷ μέτρῳ τούτῳ ἰάμβιζον ἀλλήλους. καὶ ἐγένοντο τῶν παλαιῶν οἱ μὲν ἡρωικῶν οἱ δὲ ἰάμβων ποιηταί. ὥσπερ δὲ καὶ τὰ σπουδαῖα μάλιστα ποιητὴς Ὅμηρος ἦν (μόνος γὰρ οὐχ ὅτι εὖ ἀλλὰ καὶ μιμήσεις δραμαικὰς ἐποίησεν), οὕτως καὶ τὸ τῆς κωμῳδίας σχῆμα πρῶτος ὑπέδειξεν, οὐ ψόγον ἀλλὰ τὸ γελοῖον δραματοποιήσας· ὁ γὰρ Μαργίτης ἀνάλογον ἔχει, ὥσπερ Ἰλιὰς καὶ ἡ Ὀδύσσεια πρὸς τὰς τραγῳδίας, οὕτω καὶ οὗτος πρὸς τὰς κωμῳδίας.

Following Aristotle, discussion of ancient Greek genre has often focused on form (i.e. meter) and content/tone. Thus, Aristotle separates the *Margites* from the other Homeric epics using both criteria: it has a different meter (iambic and dactylic hexameter) and a different tone— rather than being serious (τὰ σπουδαῖα) it is funny (τὸ γελοῖον), but not in the character of personal reproach (οὐ ψόγον).[27] In addition, this type of poetry is "Homeric" to the extent that it is also *dramatic* (δραματοποιήσας). It is attractive to imagine that in referring to other poems of this type (τὰ τοιαῦτα), Aristotle leaves room for compositions like the *BM* (which is *funny* and *dramatic*), but such an assertion ignores both the context (namely that τὰ τοιαῦτα means other iambic poems) and the wide array of poems attributed to Homer in the ancient world, including many other epics in addition to the *Iliad* and the *Odyssey*.

The attribution of the *Margites* to Homer and the later pairing of the two poems gives us sufficient justification, however, to ask what that

---

[27] See Rotstein 2010 for the relationship between the *Margites* and iambic poetry.

poem might be able to tell us about the *BM*. A handful of lines survive (fr. 1–4a):

> Some old man, a divine singer, came to Kolophon,
> An assistant of the Muses and Apollo
> Holding a sweet-singing lyre in his dear hands.
> The gods didn't make him an excavator or a ploughman
> Nor wise in anything at all: he screwed up every kind of craft:
> He knew many matters, but he knew all of them badly.

> ἦλθέ τις ἐς Κολοφῶνα γέρων καὶ θεῖος ἀοιδός,
> Μουσάων θεράπων καὶ ἑκηβόλου Ἀπόλλωνος,
> φίλῃς ἔχων ἐν χερσὶν εὔφθογγον λύρην.
> τὸν δ᾽ οὔτ᾽ ἄρ σκαπτῆρα θεοὶ θέσαν οὔτ᾽ ἀροτῆρα
> οὔτ᾽ ἄλλως τι σοφόν· πάσης δ᾽ ἡμάρτανε τέχνης.
> πόλλ᾽ ἠπίστατο ἔργα, κακῶς δ᾽ ἠπίστατο πάντα.

Aristotle is right to divide this poem from Homer's other epics for its tone. It also has certain characteristics that we might identify in the fable, including the generalizing character of the opening line (ἦλθέ τις) and the continuing participle in line 3 (ἔχων).[28] And according to ancient accounts, the rest of the poem's contents would not have been at home in ancient epic. Part of Margites' ignorance extended to carnal acts (from Dio Chrys. Or. 67.5, *On Reputation*): "He would be much more foolish than Margites, who was ignorant about what to do with a woman after being married." (Πολύ γε ἂν εἴη τοῦ Μαργίτου μωρότερος, ἀγνοοῦντος ὅ, τι χρὴ γήμαντα χρῆσθαι τῇ γυναικί).[29]

In addition to the fragments above, the *Margites* is also often said to have included the famous animal maxim attributed to Archilochus that "the fox knows many things but the hedgehog knows one big thing" (πόλλ᾽ οἶδ᾽ ἀλώπηξ, ἀλλ᾽ ἐχῖνος ἓν μέγα, fr. 201). So, from the perspective

---

[28] For these qualities, see the commentary section for lines 1–7.
[29] Hesychius (an Alexandrian Lexicographer, fifth/sixth century CE) adds another detail: Margites' wife told him she had been bitten in her genitals by a scorpion and that she needed "treatment." The Byzantine Archbishop Eustathius (*Comm ad Od.* 1.395, twelfth century CE) repeats this anecdote.

of ancient scholars, an animal story seemed apt to a poem like the *Margites*. Nevertheless, for comparison to the *BM*, Aristotle's formal distinction remains. The *Margites* may share in epic language—as does much of lyric and elegiac poetry—but it is not entirely in the epic meter. For Aristotle, form and content separate the *Iliad* from the *Margites*. The *BM* crosses these lines.

Parodic epic

Aristotle does, however, offer an important comparandum for understanding the *BM*. Just as comedy relies in part on the poetic and performance conventions of tragedy, so parody also depends upon the conventions established by "serious" epic. Here, too, Aristotle gives us a clue: earlier in the *Poetics* he writes that "Hegemon of Thasos was the first to write parodies" (1448a12), although he does not tell us much more about who Hegemon was or what (he thinks) parody is.

If we weigh the ascription of the *Margites* to Homer as evidence of the antiquity of *a* Homeric tradition of humorous material paired with the serious, we can trace the origins of parody before the appearance of Hegemon in Athens (dated to the Peloponnesian War—accounts have him entertaining Athenians *c.* 416 BCE). Generic boundaries did not prevent Greek poets from using a shared language in different treatments of the same ideas. Tyrtaeus, for example, uses the same register as Homer to describe the contemporary Messenian Wars among the Spartans;[30] Archilochus uses martial language to evoke an anti-martial ethic;[31] Sappho, Alcaeus, and Mimnermus similarly use "Homeric" phrases for erotic topics.

The analogy of Athenian comedy developing alongside and in response to tragedy is helpful. As several authors have emphasized (e.g. Bliquez 1977; Olson and Sens 1999), Athenaeus' *Deipnosophists*

[30] See Steinbock 2013: 78.
[31] See Barker and Christensen 2006.

preserves fragments of a scholar named Polemon (*c.* third century BCE)
who searched for the "inventor of Parody," concluding that it was none
other than Hipponax (mid-sixth century BCE).[32] Given the pervasiveness
of epic in the Archaic and Classical periods, it is likely that poets of all
types were engaged with mockery of myth and the epic genre using its
diction and meter. The mockery of comedy and parody was likely
connected as well to the essentially agonistic character of Greek
poetry.[33] Even within the epic genre, there was probably more variety
and play than Homer and Hesiod might indicate. The poet Panyassis
(fifth century BCE), for example, sets his epic in sympotic contexts,
which result in a lexicon that differs from that of Homer and Hesiod.
Similarly, the ethnographic and fantastic poetry of Aristeas (sixth
century BCE?) uses diction and formulae distinct from both Homer
and Panyassis.

Here, too, ancient testimony provides hints but no precise answers.
Scholars have introduced inscriptional evidence on the Island of Euboea
attesting to parodic competitions at the Artemisian Games (IG XII 9
189, *c.* 340 BCE; see Degani 1983 and Rotstein 2012; cf. Olson and Sens
1999). Since these later games seem to have been modeled on the festival
known as the Greater Panathenaea where many believe the Homeric
epics were performed, similar parodic performances in Athens may
have occurred prior to the mid-fourth century BCE.[34] Following this
period, as Olson and Sens (1999) show, there was a flourishing of epic
parody leaving us poems by Archestratos of Gela (who wrote a catalogue
of the best food and drink, *c.* 390–350 BCE), Euboeus of Paros (*c.* mid-
fourth century BCE), Hipparchos (undated, but with a gastronomic
"Egyptian *Iliad*") and Matro of Pitane (early fourth century BCE).

---

[32] Epic parodies are attributed to old comic poets like Cratinus and Hermippus.
Aristophanes may have been in on the parodic game as well: he toys with Homeric
images frequently and plays games with Homeric lines in his *Peace* (1282-3).

[33] For the pervasiveness of competition and rivalry in early Greek poetry, see Griffith
1990; cf. Barker and Christensen 2006.

[34] The same ancient scholar who identified Hipponax as the "founder of parody" records
that Hegemon of Thasos won a prize of fifty drachmas in the parodic competition with
his version of the *Gigantomachy* (Ath. *Deip.* 15.698b–699d).

These poets—along with Hegemon mentioned above—share some important similarities. First, their remaining fragments are clearly engaged with Homeric language, combining distinct phrases with non-epic subjects (frequently food and topics similar to those of old comedy) and adapting conventional formulae. But, as far as we can tell from what we know of their poems, their subjects were not animals. In addition, we do not have any clear information about performance context. The level of parody implies a fairly thorough familiarity with Homeric precedents—and an audience who "get" the joke in some way or another.

To understand some of the expectations that might have attended a parody like the *BM*, it is worthwhile to consider the fragments of the early parodic exemplars, Hipponax and Hegemon, for their style and engagement with Homer. Hipponax leaves us four lines: (fr. 128; see Olson and Sens 1999: 5).

Muse, tell me the tale of the sea-swallowing
Stomach-slicing, son of Eurymedon, who eats without order—
How he died a terrible death thanks to a vile vote
in the public council along the strand of the barren sea.

Μοῦσά μοι Εὐρυμεδοντιάδεα τὴν ποντοχάρυβδιν,
τὴν ἐν γαστρὶ μάχαιραν, ὃς ἐσθίει οὐ κατὰ κόσμον,
ἔννεφ᾽, ὅπως ψηφῖδι < κακῇ> κακὸν οἶτον ὀλεῖται
βουλῆι δημοσίηι παρὰ θῖν᾽ ἁλὸς ἀτρυγέτοιο.

In the passage (*Deipn.* 15.55) where Athenaeus introduces this fragment, he quotes the earlier Polemon as commending the parodists Boiotos and Euboios for their double-meaninged play with words (τὸ παίζειν ἀμφιδεξίως). Hipponax, he explains, was an iambic poet (τὸν ἰαμβοποιόν) who founded a genre (εὑρετὴν μὲν οὖν τοῦ γένους). Several features of the fragment stand out as indicative of the ways in which parody might engage with the Homeric tradition.[35] Note the characteristic invocation of the Muse with some poetic play—the invocation starts

---

[35] For a discussion of the genre and language of this fragment, see Faraone 2004 (who argues that the poem is a curse rather than a parody).

line 1 (Μοῦσά μοι) but the verb is left until the third line (ἔννεφ'). The first line is filled out by a lengthy—and therefore probably mocking—patronym followed by an odd compound (ποντοχάρυβδιν). The final three lines end with common Homeric formulae begun with more contemporaneous images (e.g. ψηφῖδι, βουλῆι δημοσίηι).[36]

In the same discussion, Athenaeus pursues Polemon's subsequent citation of Hegemon: (fr. 1; p. 52 Brandt):[37]

> "When I arrived in Thasos they struck with missiles made of shit
> And then someone stood near me and said:
> "Dirtiest of all men, who persuaded you to mount
> this pristine stage with feet like yours?"
> I answered them all with this wise word:
> "Fame persuaded me as an unwilling old man to climb here."
> And poverty, which compels many a Thasian, dirty men with fine hair,
> To board a trading ship, men who both kill and die,
> Men who right now recite bad songs badly there.
> I too gave in to them because I need food terribly.
> But I will not again travel abroad for profit, but among the Thasians
> I will hand out glorious silver and cause no one pain,
> Lest any of the Achaean women find fault with me at home.
> When my wife kneads the ritual bread in an unseemly way,
> And some one might say when she sees the small cheese-cake:
> "What is this, woman? After your husband sang for the Athenians
> And won fifty drachmas, you bake so small a cake?"
> Pallas Athena appeared next to me as I considered these things
> While holding her golden staff, she hit me and said:
> "Suffering as much as you have, Dirty Lentil-soup, enter the contest."
> And thus emboldened, I sang even louder."

---

[36] κατὰ κόσμον occurs over a dozen times in the Homeric poems, ending the line at *Od.* 20.281. For the phrase κακὸν οἶτον ὀλεῖται in Homer, we find the phrase κλέος οὔ ποτ' ὀλεῖται in Homer (e.g. *Il.* 7.91) more than once, with the combination κακὸν οἶτον in the same metrical position (πάντες ἔσαν· τῶ σφεων πολέες κακὸν οἶτον ἐπέσπον, *Od.* 3.134) and a form of the verb with the same phrase (οἵ κεν δὴ κακὸν οἶτον ἀναπλήσαντες ὄλωνται. *Il.* 8.465). For παρὰ θῖν' ἁλὸς ἀτρυγέτοιο, see *Il.* 1.316; this phrase occurs in other genres, including the New Archilochus fragment, see Christensen and Barker 2006

[37] The Greek text is based on Kaibel's Teubner (1890; 1966) with some emendations adopted from Olson's Loeb edition of Athenaeus (2012).

Ἐς δὲ Θάσον μ' ἐλθόντα μετεωρίζοντες ἔβαλλον
πολλοῖσι σπελέθοισι, καὶ ὧδέ τις εἶπε παραστάς·
'ὦ πάντων ἀνδρῶν βδελυρώτατε, τίς σ' ἀνέπεισεν
καλὴν ἐς κρηπῖδα ποσὶν τοιοῖσδ' ἀναβῆναι;'
τοῖσι δ' ἐγὼ πᾶσιν πυκινὸν³⁸ μετὰ τοῦτ' ἔπος εἶπον·
'μνῆ μ' ἀνέπεισε γέροντα καὶ οὐκ ἐθέλοντ' ἀναβῆναι
καὶ σπάνις, ἢ πολλοὺς Θασίων εἰς ὁλκάδα βάλλει
εὐκούρων βδελυρῶν, ὀλλύντων τ' ὀλλυμένων τε
ἀνδρῶν, οἳ νῦν κεῖθι κακῶς κακὰ ῥαψῳδοῦσιν·
οἷς καὶ ἐγὼ σίτοιο μέγα χρῄζων ἐπίθησα.'
αὖθις δ' οὐκ ἐπὶ κέρδος ἀπείσομαι, εἰς Θασίους <δὲ>;
μηδένα πημαίνων κλυτὸν ἄργυρον ἐγγυαλίξω,
μή τίς μοι κατὰ οἶκον Ἀχαϊάδων νεμεσήσῃ,
πεσσομένης ἀλόχου τὸν ἀχαῖνον ἄρτον ἀεικῶς,
καί ποτέ τις εἴπῃ σμικρὸν τυροῦντ' ἐσιδοῦσα·
'ὡς φίλη, ὡνὴρ μὲν παρ' Ἀθηναίοισιν ἀείσας
πεντήκοντ' ἔλαβε δραχμάς, σὺ δὲ μικρὸν ἐπέψω;'
   Ταῦτά μοι ὁρμαίνοντι παρίστατο Παλλὰς Ἀθήνη
χρυσῆν ῥάβδον ἔχουσα καὶ ἤλασεν εἶπέ τε φωνῇ·
'δεινὰ παθοῦσα Φακῆ βδελυρή, χώρει 'ς τὸν ἀγῶνα'.
καὶ τότε δὴ θάρσησα καὶ ἤειδον πολὺ μᾶλλον.

This passage shows a much smaller percentage of Homeric formulae than we find in Hipponax (although both samples are small). Where there are resonances with Homer, they seem knowingly playful, as when Hegemon describes his speech before introducing it as a πυκινόν … ἔπος (or, according to the more recent edition, a "small word," μικρόν). In Homer's *Iliad*, the combination πυκινὸν ἔπος is used always together and within direct speech to describe a plan immediately described afterwards (e.g. 24.75).³⁹ Here, Hegemon breaks the words apart, uses them in a speech introduction, begins with a lament, and only eventually describes a previous plan he has already enacted (if his tale can be

---

38 Olson (2012) prints μικρὸν instead of πυκινὸν for τοῖσι δ' ἐγὼ πᾶσιν μικρὸν μετὰ τοῦτ' ἔπος εἶπον.

39 ὄφρά τί οἱ εἴπω πυκινὸν ἔπος, ὥς κεν Ἀχιλλεὺς / δώρων ἐκ Πριάμοιο λάχῃ ἀπό θ' Ἕκτορα λύσῃ, 24.75–6. Cf.*Il*.7.375, 11.788, and 24.744).

considered a plan). If we accept instead the reading μικρόν, we still retain a sense of play: Homeric heroes never give speeches described as slight or small! Thus, Hegemon's toying with Homeric language and convention is complex and requires a fairly sophisticated audience to "get." Thematically, the poem is especially concerned with food, money, and performance, all elements echoed in the *BM*. In addition, note the prominence of Athenians and the goddess Athena. Elements of the poem recall other parodies we have discussed. While the age of the singer—an old man—is partly comic (old men were stock figures in Attic Comedy) it also recalls the traveling old Margites from his poem.

Despite the similarities we have identified, one further comparison illustrates the extent to which the *BM* may be anomalous in the tradition of parody. The "Attic Dinner Party" by Matro of Pitane is also preserved in Athenaeus' *Deipnosophists* and it is dated to the late fourth century BCE (see Olson and Sens 1999). Its interest in food is also comic and clearly surpasses that of the *BM*, but it is also engaged with the Homeric tradition from a consciously literary perspective. A large number of the poem's lines are made of Homeric parallels or surprising adaptations— partial lines and recognizable phrases are combined with new material throughout to create a comic effect. Not only does this poem show more rigorous and extensive use of this trope, but it also uses similes (which the *BM* does not) and metapoetic tropes as when the speaker declares that he could not resist the divine cake "even if he had ten hands and ten mouths / and his stomach unbreakable and his heart bronze" (οὐδ' εἴ μοι δέκα μὲν χεῖρες, δέκα δὲ στόματ' εἶεν / γαστὴρ δ' ἄρρηκτος, χάλκεον δέ μοι ἦτορ ἐνείη).[40] In this adaptation, Matro has replaced one word in each line. Where the Homeric narrator denies his ability to recount faithfully before he performs the catalog of ships, Matro's speaker adapts the lines *after* he has already presented an

---

[40]   These lines are based on famous lines from the *Iliad* introducing the catalog of ships where the narrator denies the ability to name everyone who came to Troy (οὐδ' εἴ μοι δέκα μὲν γλῶσσαι, δέκα δὲ στόματ' εἶεν / φωνὴ δ' ἄρρηκτος, χάλκεον δέ μοι ἦτορ ἐνείη, 2.489–90).

impressive catalog of dishes. Furthermore, he does this as he protests his inability to eat anymore, a gesture of comic satiety to contrast with the fact that the Homeric narrator is just beginning. The *BM* offers no adaptations that seem so clearly playful and specifically allusive. Although a formulaic analysis shows that the *BM*'s variations on Homeric language are structurally similar (see below and Camerotto 1992: 15–16), the tone and ostentatious quality differ. Like later imitators of Homeric epic such as Nonnus (fourth or fifth century BCE), the author of the *BM* likely wants the poem to appear archaic.

As we saw above, the contents of Hegemon's poem—his reference to a performance and victory at Athens—coupled with a much later inscription, provide the evidence for a contest of parody in Athens. But, just as in the *BM*, to what degree should we credit what the narrator of this poem (which appears to be an introduction to a longer one) says about the performance of the poem? He refers to a past performance and victory (which may be fictitious). Greek poetry was highly competitive—Hesiod mentions traveling to Aulis and winning a victory in poetry in the *Works and Days* (652–60)[41]—but contest was both a context and trope in the poems themselves. No real-world contest is necessary for a poem to be influenced by the cultural poetics of rivalry. The *BM*, in fact, is imagined by later authors to be part of Homer's competition with Hesiod in the *Contest of Homer and Hesiod*. According to this account, Homer and Hesiod competed at Chalcis; the former was cheered by the audience but the latter was awarded the prize for the content of his poem.[42]

The theme of traveling to contests may also be important for considering possible performance contexts for the *BM*. Note that the predominant number of the parodists—with the exception of the authors from Old Comedy—are from outside of Athens—Syracuse, Thasos, Paros, Pitane. The world outside the poems of parody is the

---

[41]   On the confusion between this contest and Hesiod's tale in the poem, see West 1978: 319–21. On the fiction of the contest in antiquity, see Graziosi 2002.
[42]   West (2003: 298) traces this back to a sophist named Alcidamas from the fourth century BCE.

larger Greek world, indicating perhaps the genre flourishing within the power of Athenian influence (both before the fall of Athens in 404 BCE and after with its secondary flourishing during the fourth century) or a later period (e.g. the Hellenistic) when Greek culture was also international and when authors in places like Alexandria were copying Athenian texts and composing their own versions of Classical genres.

The *BM* does stand distinct from these traditions as well for the basic fact that it is an animal parody. Byzantine testimony points to a tradition of animal epics dated to the sixth through fourth centuries BCE or later (the Suda lists "Battle of the Cranes," *Geranomakhia*; and "Battle of the Spiders," *Arakhnomakhia*; fragments remain of a "Weasel and Mouse War," on which see Schibli 1983; West 2003: 259). The fragments of the *Galeomakhia*, on a papyrus from the end of the second century BCE, provide some interesting parallels. The "Battle of the Weasel and the Mice" (hereafter, *GM*) is "more Homeric" in that it uses a higher proportion of clearly Homeric parallels. Its tone is also more reserved: where the *BM* is clearly more engaged with comedic and tragic traditions in its language and its topics, the *GM* is humorous in its situation but more staid in its execution. Some comic strategies are shared by the two poems, such as humorous names: the doomed mouse at the beginning of the *GM* is called "Squeak" (Τρίξος, line 3); his wife is called the "daughter of Smokey" (Κν]ισέωνος θ[υ]γάτη[ρ], line 8) and an elder leader is called "Miller" (Μυ[λ]εύς).

Structurally, the *GM* bears similarities to the *BM*: a proem and an initial death of a mouse which sends his widow out to rouse the mice to war (5–10). It also features divine action (Hermes, at least, is present), depicts the gods as watching the scene, and provides the weasel with his own speech (26–30) and multiple speeches including a lament by a widowed mouse. The fragment consists of 60 or so lines (many incomplete) and does not tell the whole story which West (2003: 231) argues contained a triumph of the mice over the weasel, anticipated at line 128 of the *BM*. If the poem does go on to provide a clash between the species, divine engagement, and a resolution, it still might not be as long as the *BM*. But this is pure speculation.

The *BM* does not have any true peers. Perhaps, if we had additional examples of animal parody, the story would be different; but the category itself is not well represented in ancient testimony. We are left, then, to read and evaluate this poem on its own generic merits and based on its engagement with other genres.

Homeric language and meter

The Homeric dialect developed over a long duration of time.[43] As such, Homeric language is a composite of several different layers of different Greek dialects (including Ionic, Aeolic, and some Doric) with some correspondences in Mycenaean Greek (see Horrocks 1997: 196–9). Our picture of the relationship among these dialects and the final period for the formation of the Homeric dialect is complicated by analogical formations and artificial archaisms. To aid in reading this text for those familiar primarily with Attic Greek prose, we have included the following sections on meter and formulaic language. Both categories also help to inform our understanding of the *BM*'s relationship to the Homeric tradition and its likely dates.

Greco-Roman meter is based on syllable *quantity* (the length of the vowel sound) rather than syllable *quality* (where the accent falls).[44] The development of the early Greek dialect resulted in the selection of many morphological options and word spellings for metrical utility. Greco-Roman metrical rules, in addition, allow for variation in word pronunciation. Syllables may be long by *nature* (diphthongs, *eta*, *omega*, and select *alphas*, *iotas*, and *upsilons*) or long by *position* (before doubled consonants, before multiple consonants or, at times, before complex consonants like *zeta*). In most cases, a rough breathing does not act as a consonant and cannot make a previous syllable long. A consonantal stop followed by a liquid (ρ, λ) can at times be preceded by a short

---

[43] For features of the Homeric dialect see Horrocks 1997 and Russo 1997.
[44] For Greek meter in general, see West 1982. For Homeric meter, see West 1997.

syllable. Sometimes words that begin with σκ- or ζ- do not make the previous vowel long.

Dactylic hexameter—the meter of epic poetry—consists of six metrical "feet"; each foot contains either a spondee (two long syllables) or a dactyl (a long syllable followed by two short syllables) with the exception of the final two feet, which are almost always a dactyl followed by a spondee.

1	2	3	4	5	6	

$$- \cup\cup\mid\ -\cup\cup\mid\ -\cup\cup\mid\ -\cup\cup\mid\ -\cup\cup\mid\ -\ X$$

Spondee: |- -|
Dactyl: |- ∪∪|
Anceps: X = long or short syllable

Example 1: The first lines of Hesiod's *Theogony*

|- -|- ∪∪ |- ∪∪ |- -|- ∪∪ | - ∩

      Μουσάων Ἑλικωνιάδων ἀρχώμεθ' ἀείδειν,

|- ∪∪ |- ∪∪ |- ∪∪ |- ∪∪|- ∪∪ | - ∩
αἵ θ' Ἑλικῶνος ἔχουσιν ὄρος μέγα τε ζάθεόν τε,

|- ∪∪ |- -|- ∪∪ |- ∪∪|- ∪∪ | - ∩
καί τε περὶ κρήνην ἰοειδέα πόσσ' ἀπαλοῖσιν

|- - |- - |- ∪∪ |- ∪∪|- ∪∪ | - ∩
ὀρχεῦνται καὶ βωμὸν ἐρισθενέος Κρονίωνος·

Word or phrase breaks in the line called *caesurae* help to separate phrases and provide regular end and start points for formulae (regular, repeated phrases of similar metrical shape). Caesurae occur in the middle of a metrical foot. If a caesura occurs after a long syllable, it is considered *strong* (also called "masculine"); if it occurs after a short syllable (in-between *two* short syllables) it is considered *weak* (feminine). While caesurae primarily function to emphasize the sense of a line, the diaeresis is a conventional metrical pause that does not always correspond with the line's meaning. The bucolic diaeresis is a conventional pause between the fourth and fifth foot of a Homeric line.

Such pauses help to break a line of dactylic hexameter up into smaller rhythmic units (*cola*) that often correspond to sense units.

Example 2: The proem to the *Iliad* (1.1–7) with caesurae and diaereses

|– ∪∪ |– ∪∪ |– || – |– ∪∪|– ∪∪ | – ∩
Μῆνιν ἄειδε θεὰ ‖ Πηληϊάδεω ᾿Αχιλῆος

|– ∪∪ |– || – |– ∪∪ |– –|¦ – ∪∪ | – ∩
οὐλομένην‖, ἣ μυρί᾿ ᾿Αχαιοῖς ;¦ ἄλγε᾿ ἔθηκε,

|– – |– – |– – |– || ∪∪|– ∪∪ | – ∩
πολλὰς δ᾿ ἰφθίμους ψυχὰς ‖ ῎Αϊδι προΐαψεν

|– – |– || – |– ∪∪ |– ∪∪|¦– ∪∪ | – ∩
ἡρώων ‖, αὐτοὺς δὲ ἑλώρια ¦τεῦχε κύνεσσιν

|– – |– ∪∪ |– ∪ || ∪ |– ∪∪|– ∪∪ | – ∩
οἰωνοῖσί τε πᾶσι‖, Διὸς δ᾿ ἐτελείετο βουλή,

|– – |– – |– || ∪∪ |– –|– ∪∪ | – ∩
ἐξ οὗ δὴ τὰ πρῶτα ‖ διαστήτην ἐρίσαντε

|– ∪∪ |– ∪∪|– || – |– || – |¦– ∪∪ | – ∩
᾿Ατρείδης τε ἄναξ ‖ ἀνδρῶν‖ καὶ ¦ δῖος ᾿Αχιλλεύς.

Caesurae (marked with ‖) and diaereses (marked with ¦)

If there is no caesura, the cola are said to have a "bridge." Hermann's Bridge (named after Gottfried Hermann) is the tendency of Homeric poetry to avoid word end between two short syllables in the fourth foot. Similar are the Three Laws of Wilhelm Mayer (all broken by the first line of the *Iliad*). First Law: Words that begin in the first foot do not end between the shorts of the second foot or at the end of that foot. Second Law: Disyllables of the shape short-long do not occur before the caesura. Third Law: Avoidance of word end after the third or fifth princeps (the first syllable of the foot). These rules are broken with some frequency by Homer; but they become rather rigidified by the Hellenistic period.

Example 3: The Proem to the *Batrakhomuomakhia* with caesurae and diaereses

|– ∪∪ |– || – |– ∪∪ |– || ∪∪|¦– ∪∪ | – ∩
᾿Αρχόμενος|| πρώτης σελίδος|| χορὸν¦ ἐξ ῾Ελικῶνος

|– – |– || ∪∪| – ∪ ∪|– ∪ ∪ |¦ – ∪∪ | – ∩
ἐλθεῖν εἰς|| ἐμὸν ἦτορ ἐπεύχομαι ¦ εἵνεκ᾿ ἀοιδῆς,

|– ∪∪ |– || – |– ∪ ∪| – || ∪ ∪ |¦ – ∪∪ | – ∩
ἣν νέον ἐν ||δέλτοισιν ἐμοῖς || ἐπὶ ¦γούνασι θῆκα,

|– ∪∪ |– ∪∪| – || ∪ ∪| – ∪ ∪ |¦ – ∪∪ | – ∩
δῆριν ἀπειρεσίην, || πολεμόκλονον ¦ἔργον ῎Αρηος,

|– ∪∪ |– || ∪ ∪| – ∪ ∪| – ∪ ∪|¦ – ∪∪ | – ∩
εὐχόμενος || μερόπεσσιν ἐς οὔατα ¦πᾶσι βαλέσθαι

|– ∪∪ |– || ∪ ∪| – ∪ ∪| – –| – ∪ ∪ | – ∩
πῶς μύες ἐν || βατράχοισιν ἀριστεύσαντες ἔβησαν,

|– ∪∪ |– || – | – – | – ∪ ∪|¦ – ∪∪ | – ∩
γηγενέων || ἀνδρῶν μιμούμενοι ¦ἔργα Γιγάντων,

|– ∪∪ |– || – | – ∪ ∪ | – || – | – ∪∪ | – ∩
ὡς λόγος ἐν|| θνητοῖσιν ἔην·|| τοίην δ᾿ ἔχεν ἀρχήν.

The extent to which the *BM* adheres to these metrical conventions may be instructive for establishing its period of composition. Although several scholars have dismissed metrical evidence,[45] a metrical analysis of the *BM* supports the basic picture of a late poem striving to match earlier practices. For example, Hellenistic poets tend to observe word-end after an uncontracted fourth biceps at a higher percentage than Homer: the Homeric poems observe it at a rate around 47 percent, poets like Callimachus and Apollonius exhibit higher rates (57 percent

---

[45] Wölke (1978: 70–84) presents metrical analysis as inconclusive; cf. Vine 1986: 385 n. 10. Bliquez summarizes metrical analyses of the poem as "futile" (1977: 12). Janko (1982: 38–9) notes that the frequency of breaches of Meyer's First Law in the *BM* is much less than in the Homeric epics and more similar to Callimachus.

and 63 percent respectively).[46] The *BM* observes this "bucolic diaeresis" around 52 percent of the time.[47]

Formulaic language[48]

Homeric language is a distinct artistic dialect that draws on forms from the history of the Greek language and from different dialectical regions. This language developed alongside the meter; as a result, singers who were trained in the dialect were able to compose in performance. A secondary result is that Homeric language appears to be composed of repeated noun-adjective combinations, phrases, and even whole lines (many of these fitting naturally between the caesurae). Although such features were attributed to epic's oral background in antiquity, Milman Parry and his students first codified the term *formula* to describe such repeated phrases. Many decades of debate on how to define formula and what its implications were for the interpretation of the epics followed.

Parry's early definition—"an expression, regularly used, under the same metrical conditions to express an essential idea" (1971: 13)—was challenged both for its semantic limits and its implications for the meaning available in Homeric poetry. For instance, Parry argued that the Homeric language had one noun-epithet combination ready-made for syntactical need in any given position in the line. In addition, Parry suggested that the entire Homeric dialect exhibited tendencies towards thrift (economy) and thus away from synonymy. Subsequent scholars examined the linguistic system, adjusting definitions and focusing on variety and flexibility. J.B. Hainsworth, for example, reduced the definition of a formula to a "repeated word group" and along with others

---

[46] See West 1982: 154; see Barnes 1986 for Homeric cola and caesurae.

[47] This includes suspect lines. Wölke insists that there are many violations of Alexandrian tendencies (1978: 84; see 78–9 for the summary). These, however, are largely those that separate the *BM* from *all other* Greek poems: metrical features of proper names, diction shared with Greek fable, and unique literary adaptations.

[48] This is based largely on Christensen (forthcoming). See also Hainsworth 1968; Parry 1971; Russo 1997; and Garner 2011.

examined how phrases transformed (expanded, contracted, separated, otherwise adapted) for contextual (i.e. metrical, syntactical, or expressive) reasons.

Homeric meter, when broken into smaller units (cola) along the caesurae, preserves evidence of the flexibility and adaptability of epic diction. Formulae (following Hainsworth 1968) can move, expand, separate, or rearrange their parts, or generate alternatives with different case-forms or suffixes. Such flexibility has necessarily impacted notions of *how formulaic* Homeric poetry is. Analyses have shown the poems as made up of as much as 60–66 percent repeated phrases.[49] Other studies have shown that in the *Iliad* words that occur only once in Homer appear every 9.4 lines whereas in the *Odyssey* they occur every 11.8.[50]

Example 4: Formulaic Epithets For Hector (Cf. Christensen and Barker, 2013:23)

Subject (Nominative)	Object (Accusative)
Héktôr / Priamí/dês - /- ⏑ ⏑/ - ⏑ ⏑ / - -	*Héktora/ díon ⏑ / - ⏑ ⏑ / - ⏑ ⏑ / - ⏑ ⏑ /- -*
Héktôr / Priamí/dês broto/loigôi/ísos Arêi	*Héktora/ d'ainon ⏑ / - ⏑ ⏑ / - ⏑ ⏑ / - ⏑ ⏑ /- -*
Héktôr/ Pria/moio pá/is phlogí/ eíkelos/alkên	*Héktora/ Priamí/dên ⏑ ⏑ / - ⏑ ⏑ / - ⏑ ⏑ /- -*
- Hék/tôr méga/thumos ⏑ / - ⏑ ⏑ / - ⏑ ⏑ / - -	*- ⏑ ⏑ / - ⏑ ⏑ / - thrasún/ Héktora/*
- - / - Priá/moio pá/is koru/thaíolos / Héktôr	*- ⏑ ⏑ / - ⏑ ⏑ / - ⏑ ⏑ / Héktora/díon ⏑ /- -*

---

[49]   For 60 percent, see Finkelberg 1989; for 66 percent, see Dee 2010. Some distinguish between formular density (lines that are mostly formulaic) and formulaic percentage (the total number of lines that exhibit some kind of formula). According to Pavese and Boschetti (2003: 50) the *Theogony* has a formular density of 51.11 percent and a formulaic percentage of 79.26 percent whereas the *Works and Days* is 36.7 percent and 69.91 percent respectively. These should be compared with the formular density of the Homeric epics of 57.29 percent (*Il.*) and 60.23 percent (*Od.*) and formulaic percentages of 83.87 percent and 84.66 percent (51).

[50]   See Edwards 1997: 270.

- U U / - U U / - U *mél/gas* *koru/thaíolos/Héktôr* - U U / - U U / - U U / - *koru/thaíolos/Héktôr* - U U / - U U / - U U / - U U / *phaídimos/ Héktôr* - U U / - U U / - U U / - U U / *óbrimos/ Héktôr*	- U U / - U U / - U U / - U U / *Héktora/dîon* - U U / - U U / - U U / *Héktora/* *poiména/ laôn* - U U / - U U / - U U / *Héktora/* *khalkoko/rustén* - *huí/on Príam/oio da/íphronos/* *Héktora/dîon*
Of/From (Genitive)	**To/For (Dative)**
Héktoros/androphó/noio U / - U U / - U U /- - - U U / - U U / - U U / *Héktoros/androphó/noio* - U U / - U U / - U U / *Héktoros/hippodá/moio*	*Héktora/ Priamí/dê* U U / - U U / - U U /- - - U U / - U U / - U U / - U U / *Héktora/díô* - U U / - U U / - U U / *Héktora/* *khalkoko/rustê*

Descriptions of the shape of this linguistic system have often been paired with hypotheses about function: early assertions that conventional epithets served less to describe a noun at a specific moment than aid in the metrical shape of the line evolved during Parry's and Lord's comparative studies in South Slavic epic (see Lord 1960). Their observations indicated that formulaic language has a *compositional* function. In other words, performers possess a knowledge of an entire language system—phrases of various metrical shape fit to the needs of their specific song type—and re-create each song anew during performance rather than simply reciting memorized sequences.

Broader debates concerning the formula, however, have explored whether repeated phrases can have both compositional function and contextually relevant meaning. Much of this dialogue resulted from an assumption that Parry's original identifications were prescriptive rather than descriptive. In his early work, Parry asserted that the Homeric epithet may have generalized or particularized meaning but is largely void of contextually derived relevance. Both literary-minded scholars who objected to this interpretive limitation and later oralists have succeeded in showing that epithets can have compositional functions, traditional connotations, and new context-specific meanings all at the same time. As later scholars like John Miles Foley and Egbert J. Bakker have argued, oral-poetic dialects function like actual languages: meter is a part of their fabric and "speakers" conceive of their utterances in phrases and groupings ("intonation units," corresponding to the cola mentioned above) rather than single words.

For a work like the *BM*, understanding the formulaic character of the epic tradition helps us to evaluate how *Homeric* it should be considered. The formulaic character of the *BM* affects whether we envision the poem as coming out of a performance context or a more literary one (the two of course are not to be completely opposed) just as it can also give us hints for where the poem should be dated. In the *BM*, clearly Homeric formula tend to be collocated at the end of the line. The battle portion of the poem, moreover, shows a much greater proportion of formulaic language. No portion of the poem indisputably demonstrates the clearly self-conscious formulaic manipulation of a parody like Matro's *Attic Dinner Party* or the appearance of formulaic dependence in our fragments of the "Battle of Weasel and Mice."

A formulaic analysis of the *BM* yields fairly clear evidence that the poem's derivation is literate rather than oral. In examining brief passages, G.S. Kirk characterizes the poem as a literary pastiche (1976: 188–90) while Albert Lord suggests (based on five lines, 197–201) that it was an imitation of oral poetry. According to the full analysis performed by Camerotto (1992: 6) the *BM* has a formular density of 32.36 percent and a formulaic percentage of 76.36 percent (total number of lines exhibiting formulae). Such a density is comparable to the later *Homeric Hymns* (39, 30, 36). Pavese and Boschetti (2003: 51) comment that "the formular density on one hand is rather low for an oral poem and rather high for a literary poem, while the formulaic density on the other hand seems rather high for an oral poem and just suitable for a traditional one: both of these facts are due to the parodic imitation of formular heroic diction as practised by the poet." The authors point out that the epic has a large number of "equivalent formulae" (those that introduce variations that violate principles of economy, which are clear adaptations of earlier precedents).

Statistical analyses like those of Richard Janko (1982; 2012), seek to establish the antiquity of Greek poems relative to one another.[51] Several aspects of the *BM* support a date later than the poems of Hesiod and Homer. These include the masculine a-stem genitive singular which appears at a ratio of 1:80 lines in the *Iliad* and 1:124 lines in the *Hymn to Demeter* (Janko 2012: 29) whereas the two appearances in the *BM* (28 and 104 for the same patronym) provide a ratio of 1:151 lines. Similarly, the *BM* shows a diminished ratio of genitive plural in –αων (only one instance (291) for a ratio of 1:303 vs. 1.71 for the *Iliad* and 1:85 for the *Theogony*); fewer instances of a genitive singular in –οιο (12 for a ratio of 1:25 vs. 1:7.5 lines for the *Iliad* and 1:6.62 for the *Works and Days*); twelve occurrences of dative plural in -οισι/ηισι/αισι (a ratio of 1:25 lines vs. 1:8.77 for the *Iliad* or 1:5.14 for the *Theogony*); and no instances of οισ'/αισ' instead of οις/αις (which occurs over 80 percent of the time in the *Iliad* though only 36 percent of the time in the *Works and Days*).[52] One telling exception in the *BM* is the use of γαῖα instead of γῆ. Where Homeric and Hesiodic poetry prefers the former at percentages above 80, the *BM* uses it exclusively (though only on four occasions: 60, 84, 95 and 229). This seems to be a clear example of a false archaism.

While formulaic and linguistic analyses indicate a later date for the poem, some features imply a more complicated situation. In the *BM*, the particle ἄρα—extremely common in Homer (over 1,800 times between the two epics for a relative frequency near 1:15; see Denniston 1954: 33)—occurs nineteen times in 303 lines for a frequency of 1:15.9.[53] *Where* the particle appears in the *BM* is interesting as well: many of its occurrences are in the formulaic speech conclusion Ὣς ἄρ' ἔφη (65, 177, 197, 277, 285) and most (twelve) are in the last 100 lines of the

---

[51] See Janko 2012: 26–9 for graphs of gradual change.

[52] Cf. Janko 1982: 35–6 for the *BM*'s use of hiatus and lengthening as suggesting "literary influence or interference." All of the figures for Homer and Hesiod are based on Janko 2012.

[53] Hesiod's *Theogony* exhibits a ratio of the same particle at 1:20.86; *Works and Days*' ratio is a surprising 1:69 (see Zarecki 2007: 11). The particle occurs 167 times in Apollonius Rhodes' *Argonautica* (a ratio of 1:34.9); at a rate of 1:20.63 in the Homeric *Hymn to Demeter* and 1:34.11 in the *Hymn to Hermes*.

poem during the rather "Homeric" battle scene (Σευτλαῖον δ' ἄρ, 209;
cf. 226; ὠργίσθη δ' ἄρ', 239; cf. 239). Hence, in the last 106 lines of the
poem the particle occurs twelve times for a ratio of 1:8.83 which well
exceeds that of either the *Iliad* or the *Odyssey*. (And this also leaves the
ratio of the first 196 lines at 1:28.)

The lower percentages of recognized formulae in the *BM* are not,
however, completely determinative. Early epic fragments we have
mentioned earlier (e.g. Panyassis and Aristeas) are also less "formulaic"
(in the sense of exhibiting a preponderance of Homeric parallels), but
they do bear more features common to oral traditions. At the same time,
while formulaic parallels can indicate derivation from oral traditions or
engagements with the Homeric traditions, they are not entirely
diagnostic: even though we have over 30,000 lines of epic poetry from
the Archaic and Classical ages, this must represent only a small percentage
of the production of hexameter poetry over centuries before *and after*
the classical age. It is, however, the *character* of the *BM*'s formulae that
establishes its origins in a literate setting: many of the formulaic variations
have clear models in the extant textual tradition of the Homeric epics;
variations within the *BM* itself speak of intentional variations.

The metrical and formulaic data available from the *BM*—even despite
its many manuscript problems—indicate a poem that does not likely
derive from an oral performance. Instead, the adaptations indicate a
literate poet imitating Homeric style at a fairly sophisticated level. The
metrical data, while also somewhat inconclusive, is nevertheless indicative
of many of the practices of the Hellenistic era. All of this information
indicates a poem composed in the third century BCE or later.

Some conclusions about date and authorship

The language of the *BM*, then, overlaps with our sketch of its generic
qualities: The poem offers a veneer of likeness to early *epic*,[54] but its style

---

[54] Most (1993: 38) argues rather convincingly that the epic displays an intimate knowledge
       ("intemir Kenntnis") both of Homeric poetry and of scholarship on Homeric poetry.

and diction belong to a later age. Its literary and cultural contents show influences from Classical, Hellenistic, and Roman periods.[55] Foremost, the *BM*'s aesthetic and poetic strategies position it between different approaches to poetry. For instance, the poem seems to avoid overt intertextuality, perhaps following the style of early Greek epic.[56] But its beginning is clearly allusive (see the discussion in the commentary on the proem). Its characteristic mixing of genres and poetic practices are common qualities of late Hellenistic and Imperial Roman poetry.[57] If we gather this material together systematically, the later Greek or "Roman" character of the *BM* is hard to ignore.

There is no absolute evidence linking the poem to Roman authorship, but certain features indicate that it is part of a broader culture spanning Greek and Roman worlds. First, the earliest extant references to the *BM* come from Roman writers in the first century CE, followed by comparatively late Greek evidence. Moreover, though the poem reflects the author's literary education, it is nevertheless marked by instances of somewhat strange Greek,[58] awkward verbal obscurity, and numerous metrical difficulties, possible indications that the author was composing in a foreign tongue.

The poem's demonstrated engagement with varied literary traditions, its contents, and its style are also typical features of the so-called Second Sophistic and later. Indeed, from the perspective of the development of the epic genre, its attempt to mimic archaic hexameter style anticipates Quintus of Smyrna (third/fourth century CE) and Nonnus (fourth/fifth century CE). Thus, from a generic perspective, the poem hails from a transitional period between the classical Alexandrian period and the

[55] For the *BM* and the tradition of Hellenistic parody, see Sens 2005; cf. Most 1993: 33; and Kelly 2009: 46 n. 12.

[56] The parodic project does depend upon "intertextual" strategies: see Most 1993: 35. Nagy (1979: 42–3) denies that in early Greek epic "a passage in any text can refer to another passage in another text," but this does not mean that poetic traditions and motifs cannot engage with one another. For recent discussions, see Burgess 2012 (who emphasizes the need for a "knowledgeable audience" (170)) and Bakker 2013: 157–69. Bakker concludes that forbidding "quotation" or "allusion" to early Greek epic imposes a "rigid oral-literacy contrast" that has "long been disproved" (168). Cf. Currie 2016.

[57] As argued by Harrison 2007 *passim*.

[58] For example, the phrase ἀριστεύσαντες ἔβησαν in line 6.

Second Sophistic. If we could date this poem with confidence to the early years of the Imperial age (i.e. under the reign of the Julio-Claudian emperors), it would provide tantalizing clues to the character of Greek literature before its later Renaissance. Such an argument has support from other sectors as well: Bruce Winter (2001), for example, has argued for continuity between Roman Alexandria and the Sophistic in the work and life of Philo. Philostratus (second/third century CE) tells the tale of the Sophist Scopelian from Clazomenae—who went on embassy to Domitian—as composing an "Epic on Giants."[59] Our analysis of the *BM* indicates that its author, like a Philo or Scopelian, worked in a center of Greek learning and culture, but lived in an increasingly "Roman" world.

Divergences from Attic Greek[60]

Letters

The following distinctions are typical of Greek hexameter poetry and appear to a certain extent in the *BM*.

> *Long α* in Attic is almost always an -η as in Ep. θαλάττη (not θάλαττα).
>
> *Vocalization*: The replacement of -ου with -ευ as in μευ instead of μου or ἔρχευ instead of ἔρχου.
>
> *Rho*: The liquid *rho* can create variations in -αρ- or -ρα- κράτος/ κάρτος καρδίη/κραδίη due to the fact that in PIE [Proto-Indo-European] *rho* was vocalized.
>
> *Doubling* of sigmas, lambdas, and the option of initial πτ as in πτόλεμος instead of π as in πόλεμος.
>
> *Digamma* (ϝ, F): Even into the classical period, some inscriptions still used the digamma, a glide-sound similar to English "w." The impact of the digamma is still felt in the Homeric epics because certain formulae and metrical patterns rely on the existence of

---

[59] Philostratus, *Vitae Sophist.* 518.27–33.
[60] For a fuller list, see Leaf and Bayfield 1959, xxv–xliii.

the sound to make metrical position or prevent elision. One example of this may occur in the *BM* (μεμφομένων δ᾽ αὐτῶν Φυσίγναθος (ϝ)εἶπεν ἀναστάς, 146).

Contraction: Following Ionic dialects, contract vowels (especially epsilons) may not contract in dactylic hexamer. Following other dialects, they may. Homeric forms may also become "distended" so a contracted form like ὁρῶντες from ὁράωντες is re-analyzed as ὁρόωντες (see Horrocks 1997: 209).

Verbs

Augments can be omitted.

Generalization of the aorist third person plural active ending –σαν.

Infinitives with -μεν and -εμεν (Aeolic), -ναι (Ionic), μεναι (Lesbian).

Sigmatic doubling in short verbal endings, see line ὄλεσσα at 112 or ἐξετέλεσσεν at 268.

Cases

Nominative: Short -α for -ης.

Genitive: Masculine genitive in -αο, -οιο, -εω and the uncontracted feminine plural -αων.

Dative: Optional sigmatic doubling in dative plurals ending in -σι (-σσι, traced to the Aeolic dialects). Dative plurals in -ησι instead of αις as in αὐτῇσι instead of αὐταῖς.

Accusative: Short α as in βασιλῆα from βασιλεύς.

Other: The case ending -φι (likely related to latin-*ibus* and the Proto-Indo-European locative ending).

Additional features

Articles: The article is optional and functions often as a demonstrative pronoun or the equivalent of a relative pronoun.

Particles: ἤν for ἐάν; κε/κεν for ἄν.

Apocope: Shortening in prepositions (πάρ instead of παρά; κάτ instead of κατά) and particles (ἄρ, or ῾ρα instead of ἄρα).

Tmesis: The separation of compound verbs, e.g. line 3 of the *BM* ἦν νέον ἐν δέλτοισιν ἐμοῖς ἐπὶ γούνασι θῆκα.

Issues of prosody

Quantative metathesis: The movement of metrical length from one syllable to another, so -ηο can become -εω.

Metrical lengthening: For dialectical and metrical reasons some words exhibit "gemmination" (the doubling of consonants) as in line 23: ἔμμεναι· ἀλλ᾿ ἄγε θᾶσσον ἑὴν γενεὴν ἀγόρευε. This form, however, is really a result of the generalization of this phenomen from verbs like ἔμμαθε (*Od.* 17.26). Classical Ionic forms like ξένος can be ξεῖνος (lines 13, 15, 57. "*Compensatory lengthening*" (making up for the loss of a syllable or vowel in the history of the lexical item) can also be seen in words like μοῦνος. Short forms like Ὄλυμπος and ἕνεκα can be lengthened to Οὔλυμπος and εἵνεκα.

Correption: The shortening of any long-vowel or diphthong before another vowel, usually at the end of a word. Similar is synizesis, when two adjacent vowels are pronounced as one long syllable as in the end of Πηληϊάδεω in the first line of the *Iliad* (phonetically: *pey-lay-e-a-deu*).

Note on translation

We have the utmost respect for authors who transform ancient poems into modern works of art. This, however, is not the aim of our translation. Instead, we have tried to convey the sense and the content of the original Greek without considerable concern for polish. For readers who are just beginning in Greek (or have not started at all) we have tried to maintain correlation between the lines of the translation and the original. Where the text is suspect or mangled, we have made some compromises but have mostly left the translation similarly "challenged." As it is, we aim for the translation to help many but please few.

Works cited in introduction and commentary

Adrados, F. R. *History of the Graeco-Latin Fable*. Leiden, 1998.

Alden, Maureen. *Homer Beside Himself. Para-Narratives in the Iliad*. Oxford, 2000.

Arend, W. *Die typischen Scenen bei Homer*. Berlin, 1975.

Bakker, E.J. *Poetry in Speech: Orality and Homeric Discourse*. Ithaca, 1997.

Bakker, E.J. *The Meaning of Meat and the Structure of the* Odyssey. Cambridge, 2013.

Barker, E.T.E. and Christensen, J.P. "Flight Club: The New Archilochus Fragment and its Resonance with Homeric Epic." *MD* 57 (2006): 19–43.

Barker E.T.E. and Christensen, J.P. *Homer: A Beginner's Guide*. London, 2013.

Barnes, H.R. "The Colometric Structure of Homeric Hexameter." *GRBS* 27 (1986): 125–50.

Beck, D. "Speech Introductions and the Character Development of Telemachus." *CJ* 94 (1998–99): 121–41.

Beck, D. *Homeric Conversation*. Washington, D.C., 2005.

Bliquez, L.J. "Frogs and Mice and Athens." *TAPA* 107 (1977): 11–25.

Burgess, J. "Intertextuality without Text in Early Greek Epic." In Andersen and Haug (2012): 168–83.

Burkert, W. *Greek Religion*. Cambridge, 1985.

Calame, C. "From Choral Lyric to Tragic Stasimon: The Pragmatics of Women's Voices." *Arion* 3 (1994–95): 136–54.

Camerotto, A. "Analisi formulare della *Batrachomyomachia*." *Lexis* 9–10 (1992) 1–54.

Campbell, D.A. *JHS* 104 (1984): 163–5.

Christensen, J.P. "First-Person Futures in Homer." *AJP* 131 (2010): 543–71.

Christensen, J.P. "Innovation and Tradition Revisited: The Near-Synonymy of Homeric AMYNΩ and AΛEΞΩ as a Case Study in Homeric Composition." *CJ* 108.3 (2013): 257–96.

Christensen, J.P. "Trojan Politics and the Assemblies of *Iliad 7*." *GRBS* 55 (2015): 25–51.

Clay, J.S. *Homer's Trojan Theater.* Cambridge, 2011.

Currie, B. *Homer's Allusive Art.* Oxford, 2016.

Dee, J.H. *Iuncturae Homericae: A Study of the Noun-Epithet Combinations in the* Iliad *and the* Odyssey. Part 1: Repertories I–III. Hildesheim, 2010.

Degani, E. *Poesia parodica greca.* Bologna, 1983.

Denniston, J.D. *Greek Particles.* London, 1954.

van Dijk, G.J. *AINOI, ΛΟΓOI, MYΘOI: Fables in Archaic, Classical and Hellenistic Greek Literature.* Leiden, 1997.

Dover, K. *Aristophanes* Frogs. Oxford, 1993.

Dowden, K. 1980. Review of Wölke 1978.

Drews, R. *Basileus: The Evidence for Kingship in Geometric Greece.* New Haven, 1983.

Edmunds, L. "Myth in Homer." In Morris and Powell (1997): 415–41.

Edwards, M.W. "On Some 'Answering' Expressions in Homer." *CP* 64 (1969): 81–7.

Edwards, M.W. "Homeric Speech Introductions." *HSCP* 74 (1970): 1–36.

Edwards, M.W. "Homeric Style and Oral Poetics." In Morris and Powell (1997): 261–83.

Edwards, M.W. "Homer and Oral Tradition: The Type Scene." *Oral Tradition* 7 (1992): 284–330.

Elmer, D. *The Poetics of Consent.* Baltimore, 2013.

Ernesti, I.A. *Homeri Operia Omnia.* Vol: 4. Lipsiae, 1764

Faraone, C.A. "The "Performative Future" in Three Hellenistic Incantations and Theocritus' Second *Idyll.*" *CP* 90 (1995): 1–15.

Faraone, C.A. "Hipponax Fragment 128W: Epic Parody or Expulsive Incantation?" *Classical Antiquity* 23 (2004): 209–45.

Fenik, B. *Typical Battle Scenes in the* Iliad. Wiesbaden, 1968.

Finkelberg, M. "Formulaic and Nonformulaic Elements in Homer." *Classical Philology* 84 (1989): 179–97

Fogelmark, S. *Studies in Pindar with Particular Reference to Paean VI and Nemean VII.* Lund, 1972.

Foley, J.M. *How to Read an Oral Poem.* Urbana, 2002.

Foley, J.M. "Epic as Genre." In *The Cambridge Companion to Homer:* R. Fowler (ed.) 171–87. Cambridge, 2004.

Fusillo. M. *La Battaglia delle rane e dei topi. Batrachomyomachia.* Milan, 1988.

Garner, R.S. *Traditional Elegy: The Interplay of Meter, Tradition and Context in Early Greek Poetry.* Oxford, 2011.

Glei, R. *Die Batrachomyomachie.* Frankfurt Am Main, 1984.

Graziosi, B. *Inventing Homer: The Early Reception of Greek Epic*. Cambridge, 2002.

Graziosi, B. and Haubold, J. *Homer: The Resonance of Epic*. London, 2005.

Griffin, J. *Homer on Life and Death*. Oxford, 1980.

Griffith, M. "Personality in Hesiod." *Classical Antiquity* 2 (1983): 37–68.

Griffith, M. "Contest and Contradiction in Early Greek Poetry." In Griffith and Mastronarde (1990): 185–207.

Gutzwiller, K.J. *Theocritus' Pastoral Analogies: The Formation of a Genre*. Madison, 1991.

Hainsworth, J.B. *The Flexibility of the Homeric Formula*. Oxford, 1968.

Harden, S. and Kelly, A. "Proemic Convention and Character Construction in Early Greek Epic." *HSCP* 107 (2014): 1–34.

Harrison, S.J. *Generic Enrichment in Vergil and Horace*. Oxford, 2007.

Heiden, B. "The Three Movements of the *Iliad*." *GRBS* 37 (1996): 5–22.

Heiden, B. "Structures of Progression in the Plot of the *Iliad*." *Arethusa* 35 (2002): 237–54.

Hinds, S. *Allusion and Intertext: Dynamics of Appropriation in Roman Poetry*. Cambridge, 1998.

Horrocks, G. "Homer's Dialect." In Morris and Powell (1997): 193–217.

Hosty, M. "The Mice of Ithaca: Homeric Models in the Batrachomyomachia." *Mnemosyne* 67 (2014) 1008–13.

How, W.W. and Wells, J. *A Commentary on Herodotus*. Oxford, 1989.

Janko, R. *Homer, Hesiod, and the Hymns*. Cambridge, 1982.

Janko, R. "The Homeric Poems as Oral Dictated Texts." *Classical Quarterly* 48 (1998): 1–48.

Janko, R. "Πρῶτόν τε καὶ ὕστατον αἰὲν ἀείδειν: Relative Chronology and the Literary History of the Early Greek Epos." In Andersen and Haug (2012): 20–43.

de Jong, I.J.F. *Narrators and Focalizers: The Presentation of the Story in the Iliad*. London, (1987) 2004.

Kirk, G.S. *Homer and the Oral Tradition*. Cambridge, 1976.

Kelly, A. "Parodic Inconsistency: Some Problems in the BATRAKHOMYOMAKHIA." *JHS* 129 (2009): 45–51.

Kelly, A. "Hellenistic arming in the *Batrachomyomachia*." *CQ* 64 (2014): 410–13

Lazenby, F.G. "Greek and Roman Household Pets." *CJ* 44 (1949): 245–52 and 299–307.

Leaf, W. and Bayfield, M.A. *The Iliad of Homer*. London, 1959.

Lefkowitz, M. *The Lives of the Greek Poets*. London, 1981.

Lohmann, D. *Die Komposition der Reden in der* Ilias. Berlin, 1970.

Lord, A. *The Singer of Tales.* Cambridge, 1960.

Lord, A. "Homer as an Oral Poet." *HSCP* 77 (1968): 1–46.

Louden, B. "Pivotal Contrafactuals in Homeric Epic." *Classical Antiquity* 12 (1993): 181–98.

Louden, B. "Eurybates, Odysseus and the Duals in Book 9 of the *Iliad.*" *Colby Quarterly* 38 (2002): 62–76

Ludwich. A. *Die Homerische Batrachommachia des Karers Pigres nebst Scholien und Paraphrase.* Leipzig, 1896.

Mackie, H. *Talking Trojan: Speech and Community in the* Iliad. Lanham, MD, 1996.

Martin, R. *The Language of Heroes: Speech and Performance in the* Iliad. Ithaca, 1989.

Meineke, A. and Bothe, F.H. *Poetarum Comicorum Fragmenta.* Zürich, 1989.

Minchin, E. "Ring-patterns and Ring-composition: Some Observations on the Framing of Stories in Homer." *Helios* 22 (1995): 23–35.

Minchin, E. *Homer and the Resources of Memory: Some Applications of Cognitive Theory to the* Iliad *and the* Odyssey. Oxford, 2001.

Morris, I. and Powell, B. (eds). *A New Companion to Homer.* Leiden, 1997.

Morris, S.P. *Daidalos and the Origins of Greek Art.* Princeton, 1992.

Morrison, J.V. "Alternatives to the Epic Tradition: Homer's Challenges in the *Iliad.*" *TAPA* 122 (1992): 61–71.

Most, G.W. "Die Batrachomyomachia als ernste Parodie." In W. Ax and R.F. Glei (eds), *Literaturparodie in Antike und Mittelalter* Trier (1993): 27–41.

Muellner, L. *The Meaning of Homeric* EYXOMAI *Through Its Formulas.* Innsbruck, 1976.

Muellner, L. *The Anger of Achilles: Menis in Greek Epic.* Ithaca, 1996.

Nagy, G. *The Best of the Achaeans: Concepts of the Hero in Archaic Greek Poetry.* Baltimore, 1979.

Nagy, G. *Homer's Text and Language.* Urbana and Chicago, 2004.

Notopoulos, J.A. "Continuity and Interconnexion in Homeric Oral Composition." *TAPA* 82 (1951): 81–101.

Olson, S.D. *The Learned Banqueters, Volume VII Book 15. General Indexes.* Loeb Classical Library 519. Cambridge, 2012.

Olson, S.D. and A. Sens. *Matro of Pitane and the Tradition of Epic Parody in the Fourth Century* BCE. Atlanta, 1999.

Palaima, T. "The Nature of the Mycenaean Wanax: Non-Indo-European Origins and Priestly Functions." In P. Rehak ed., "The Role of the Ruler in the Prehistoric Aegean." *Aegaeum* 11 (Liège 1995): 119–39.

Parry, M. *The Making of Homeric Verse: The Collected Papers of Milman Parry.* A Parry, ed. Oxford, 1971.

Pavese, C.O. and Boschetti, F. *A Complete Formular Analysis of the Homeric Poems.* Amsterdam: 2003.

Pucci, P. "Theology and Poetics in the *Iliad.*" *Arethusa* 35 (2002): 17–34.

Ready, J. "The Textualization of Homeric Epic by Means of Dictation." *TAPA* 145 (2015): 1–75.

Riggsby, A. "Homeric Speech Introductions and the Theory of Homeric Composition." *TAPA* 122 (1992): 98–114.

Rotstein, A. *The Idea of Iambos.* Oxford, 2010.

Rotstein, A. "Mousikoi Agones and the Conceptualization of Genre in Ancient Greece." *Classical Antiquity* 31 (2012): 92–107.

Russo, J. "The Formula." In Morris and Powell (1997): 238–60.

Rzach, A. "Homeridai." *RE* 8 (1913): 2170.

Schibli, H.S. "Fragments of a Weasel and Mouse War." *ZPE* 53 (1983): 1–25.

Scodel, R. 2008. "Stupid, Pointless Wars." *TAPA* 138: 219–35.

Segal, C. "The Embassy and the Duals of *Iliad* 9.182–198." *GRBS* 2 (1968): 101–14.

Sens, A. "τίπτε γένος τοὐμὸν ζητεῖς; the Batrachomyomachia, Hellenistic epic parody, and early epic." In F. Montanari and A. Rengakos (eds), *La Poesie epique grecque: metamorphoses d'un genre litteraire,* 215–48. Geneva, 2005.

Smyth, H.W. *Greek Grammar.* Cambridge, 1955.

Steinbock, B. *Social Memory in Athenian Public Discourse: Uses and Meanings of the Past.* Ann Arbor, 2013.

Stensgaard, J. "Peitho in the *Iliad*: A Matter of Trust or Obedience?" *Classicalia et Medievalia* 54 (2003): 41–80.

Stoddard, K. *The Narrative Voice in the Theogony of Hesiod.* Leiden, 2004.

Vine, B. "Towards the stylistic analysis of the Batrachomyomchia." *Mnemosyne* 39 (1986): 383–5.

Vodoklys, E. *Blame-Expression in the Epic Tradition.* New York, 1992.

Wackernagel, J. *Sprachliche Untersuchungen zu Homer.* Göttingen, 1916.

Walsh, T.R. *Fighting Words and Feuding Words: Anger and the Homeric Poems.* Lanham, MD, 2005.

West, M.L. *Hesiod:* Theogony. Oxford: Oxford University Press, 1966.

West, M.L. *Hesiod*: Works and Days. Oxford, 1978.

West, M.L. *Greek Metre.* Oxford, 1982.

West, M.L. "Homer's Meter." In Morris and Powell, 1997:218–37.

West, M.L. *Homeric Hymns, Homeric Apocrypha, Lives of Homer.* Cambridge, 2003.

West, M.L. "Towards a Chronology of Early Greek Epic." In Andersen and Haug (2012): 224–41.

Whitmarsh, T. *Beyond the Second Sophistic: Adventures in Post-classicism.* Berkeley, 2014.

Wilkins, J. *The Boastful Chef: The Discourse of Food in Ancient Greek Comedy.* Oxford, 2000.

Willcock. M.M. "Mythological Paradeigmata in the *Iliad.*" *CQ* 14 (1964): 141–51.

Willcock. M.M. "Ad Hoc Invention in the *Iliad.*" *HCSP* 81 (1977): 41–53.

Wilson, D.F. *Ransom, Revenge, and Heroic Identity in the* Iliad. Cambridge, 2002.

Winter, B.W. *Philo and Paul Among the Sophists: Alexandrian and Corinthian Responses to a Julio-Claudian Movement.* Grand Rapids, 2001.

Wölke, H. *Untersuchungen zur Batrachomyomachie.* Meisenheim am Glan, 1978.

Wouters, A.P. Oxy. 4668 [Homer,] *Batrachomyomahia* 41, 53–8. *The Oxyrhnchus Papyri,* 68. Oxford, 2005.

Zarecki, J.P. "Pandora and the Good Eris in Hesiod." *GRBS* 47 (2007): 5–29.

Text

9 pp

Ἀρχόμενος πρώτης σελίδος χορὸν ἐξ Ἑλικῶνος
ἐλθεῖν εἰς ἐμὸν ἦτορ ἐπεύχομαι εἵνεκ᾽ ἀοιδῆς
ἣν νέον ἐν δέλτοισιν ἐμοῖς ἐπὶ γούνασι θῆκα,
δῆριν ἀπειρεσίην, πολεμόκλονον ἔργον Ἄρηος,
εὐχόμενος μερόπεσσιν ἐς οὔατα πᾶσι βαλέσθαι   5
πῶς μύες ἐν βατράχοισιν ἀριστεύσαντες ἔβησαν,
γηγενέων ἀνδρῶν μιμούμενοι ἔργα Γιγάντων,
ὡς λόγος ἐν θνητοῖσιν ἔην· τοίην δ᾽ ἔχεν ἀρχήν.
Μῦς ποτε διψαλέος γαλέης κίνδυνον ἀλύξας,
πλησίον ἐν λίμνῃ λίχνον προσέθηκε γένειον,   10
ὕδατι τερπόμενος μελιηδέϊ· τὸν δὲ κατεῖδε
λιμνόχαρις πολύφημος, ἔπος δ᾽ ἐφθέγξατο τοῖον·
Ξεῖνε τίς εἶ; πόθεν ἦλθες ἐπ᾽ ἠϊόνας; τίς ὁ φύσας;
πάντα δ᾽ ἀλήθευσον, μὴ ψευδόμενόν σε νοήσω.
εἰ γάρ σε γνοίην φίλον ἄξιον ἐς δόμον ἄξω·   15
δῶρα δέ τοι δώσω ξεινήϊα πολλὰ καὶ ἐσθλά.
εἰμὶ δ᾽ ἐγὼ βασιλεὺς Φυσίγναθος, ὃς κατὰ λίμνην
τιμῶμαι βατράχων ἡγούμενος ἤματα πάντα·
καί με πατὴρ Πηλεὺς ἀνεθρέψατο, Ὑδρομεδούσῃ
μιχθεὶς ἐν φιλότητι παρ᾽ ὄχθας Ἠριδανοῖο.   20
καὶ σὲ δ᾽ ὁρῶ καλόν τε καὶ ἄλκιμον ἔξοχον ἄλλων,
σκηπτοῦχον βασιλῆα καὶ ἐν πολέμοισι μαχητὴν
ἔμμεναι· ἀλλ᾽ ἄγε θᾶσσον ἑὴν γενεὴν ἀγόρευε.
Τὸν δ᾽ αὖ Ψιχάρπαξ ἀπαμείβετο φώνησέν τε·
τίπτε γένος τοὐμὸν ζητεῖς; δῆλον δ᾽ ἐν ἅπασιν   25
ἀνθρώποις τε θεοῖς τε καὶ οὐρανίοις πετεηνοῖς.
Ψιχάρπαξ μὲν ἐγὼ κικλήσκομαι· εἰμὶ δὲ κοῦρος
Τρωξάρταο πατρὸς μεγαλήτορος· ἡ δέ νυ μήτηρ

Λειχομύλη, θυγάτηρ Πτερνοτρώκτου βασιλῆος.
γείνατο δ' ἐν καλύβῃ με καὶ ἐξεθρέψατο βρωτοῖς   30
σύκοις καὶ καρύοις καὶ ἐδέσμασι παντοδαποῖσιν.
πῶς δὲ φίλον ποιῇ με, τὸν ἐς φύσιν οὐδὲν ὁμοῖον;
σοὶ μὲν γὰρ βίος ἐστὶν ἐν ὕδασιν· αὐτὰρ ἔμοιγε
ὅσσα παρ' ἀνθρώποις τρώγειν ἔθος· οὐδέ με λήθει
ἄρτος τρισκοπάνιστος ἀπ' εὐκύκλου κανέοιο,   35
οὐδὲ πλακοῦς τανύπεπλος ἔχων πολὺ σησαμότυρον,
οὐ τόμος ἐκ πτέρνης, οὐχ ἥπατα λευκοχίτωνα,
οὐ τυρὸς νεόπηκτος ἀπὸ γλυκεροῖο γάλακτος,
οὐ χρηστὸν μελίτωμα, τὸ καὶ μάκαρες ποθέουσιν,
οὐδ' ὅσα πρὸς θοίνας μερόπων τεύχουσι μάγειροι,   40
κοσμοῦντες χύτρας ἀρτύμασι παντοδαποῖσιν.
οὐδέποτε πτολέμοιο κακὴν ἀπέφυγον ἀϋτήν,
ἀλλ' εὐθὺς μετὰ μῶλον ἰὼν προμάχοισιν ἐμίχθην.
ἄνθρωπον οὐ δέδια καί περ μέγα σῶμα φοροῦντα,
ἀλλ' ἐπὶ λέκτρον ἰὼν ἄκρον δάκτυλον δάκνω,   45
καὶ πτέρνης λαβόμην, καὶ οὐ πόνος ἵκανεν ἄνδρα,
νήδυμος οὐκ ἀπέφυγεν ὕπνος δάκνοντος ἐμεῖο.
ἀλλὰ δύω μάλα πάντα τὰ δείδια πᾶσαν ἐπ' αἶαν,
κίρκον καὶ γαλέην, οἵ μοι μέγα πένθος ἄγουσιν,
καὶ παγίδα στονόεσσαν, ὅπου δολόεις πέλε πότμος·   50
πλεῖστον δὴ γαλέην περιδείδια, ἥ τις ἀρίστη,
ἣ καὶ τρωγλοδύνοντα κατὰ τρώγλην ἐρεείνει.
οὐ τρώγω ῥαφάνους, οὐ κράμβας, οὐ κολοκύντας,
οὐ σεύτλοις χλωροῖς ἐπιβόσκομαι, οὐδὲ σελίνοις·
ταῦτα γὰρ ὑμέτερ' ἐστὶν ἐδέσματα τῶν κατὰ λίμνην.   55
  Πρὸς τάδε μειδήσας Φυσίγναθος ἀντίον ηὔδα·
ξεῖνε λίην αὐχεῖς ἐπὶ γαστέρι· ἔστι καὶ ἡμῖν
πολλὰ μάλ' ἐν λίμνῃ καὶ ἐπὶ χθονὶ θαύματ' ἰδέσθαι.
ἀμφίβιον γὰρ ἔδωκε νομὴν βατράχοισι Κρονίων,
σκιρτῆσαι κατὰ γαῖαν, ἐν ὕδασι σῶμα καλύψαι,   60
στοιχείοις διττοῖς μεμερισμένα δώματα ναίειν.
εἰ δ' ἐθέλεις καὶ ταῦτα δαήμεναι εὐχερές ἐστι·
βαῖνέ μοι ἐν νώτοισι, κράτει δέ με μήποτ' ὀλίσθῃς,
ὅππως γηθόσυνος τὸν ἐμὸν δόμον εἰσαφίκηαι.
  Ὣς ἄρ' ἔφη καὶ νῶτ' ἐδίδου· ὁ δ' ἔβαινε τάχιστα   65

χεῖρας ἔχων ἁπαλοῖο κατ' αὐχένος ἅμματι κούφῳ.
καὶ τὸ πρῶτον ἔχαιρεν ὅτ' ἔβλεπε γείτονας ὅρμους,
νήξει τερπόμενος Φυσιγνάθου· ἀλλ' ὅτε δή ῥα
κύμασι πορφυρέοισιν ἐκλύζετο πολλὰ δακρύων
ἄχρηστον μετάνοιαν ἐμέμφετο, τίλλε δὲ χαίτας,   70
καὶ πόδας ἔσφιγγεν κατὰ γαστέρος, ἐν δέ οἱ ἦτορ
πάλλετ' ἀηθείῃ καὶ ἐπὶ χθόνα βούλεθ' ἱκέσθαι·
δεινὰ δ' ὑπεστενάχιζε φόβου κρυόεντος ἀνάγκῃ.
οὐρὴν μὲν πρῶτ' ἔπλασ' ἐφ' ὕδασιν ἠΰτε κώπην
σύρων, εὐχόμενος δὲ θεοῖς ἐπὶ γαῖαν ἱκέσθαι   75
ὕδασι πορφυρέοισιν ἐκλύζετο, πολλὰ δ' ἐβώστρει·
καὶ τοῖον φάτο μῦθον ἀπὸ στόματός τ' ἀγόρευσεν·
    Οὐχ οὕτω νώτοισιν ἐβάστασε φόρτον ἔρωτος
ταῦρος ὅτ' Εὐρώπην διὰ κύματος ἦγ' ἐπὶ Κρήτην
ὡς μῦν ἁπλώσας ἐπινώτιον ἦγεν ἐς οἶκον   80
βάτραχος ὑψώσας ὠχρὸν δέμας ὕδατι λευκῷ;
    Ὕδρος δ' ἐξαίφνης ἀνεφαίνετο, πικρὸν ὅραμα
ἀμφοτέροις· ὀρθὸν δ' ὑπὲρ ὕδατος εἶχε τράχηλον.
τοῦτον ἰδὼν κατέδυ Φυσίγναθος, οὔ τι νοήσας
οἷον ἑταῖρον ἔμελλεν ἀπολλύμενον καταλείπειν.   85
δῦ δὲ βάθος λίμνης καὶ ἀλεύατο κῆρα μέλαιναν.
κεῖνος δ' ὡς ἀφέθη, πέσεν ὕπτιος εὐθὺς ἐφ' ὕδωρ,
καὶ χεῖρας ἔσφιγγε καὶ ὀλλύμενος κατέτριζε.
πολλάκι μὲν κατέδυνεν ὑφ' ὕδατι, πολλάκι δ' αὖτε
λακτίζων ἀνέδυνε· μόρον δ' οὐκ ἦν ὑπαλύξαι.   90
δευόμεναι δὲ τρίχες πλεῖον βάρος εἷλκον ἐπ' αὐτῷ·
ὕδασι δ' ὀλλύμενος τοίους ἐφθέγξατο μύθους·
    Οὐ λήσεις δολίως Φυσίγναθε ταῦτα ποιήσας,
ναυηγὸν ῥίψας ἀπὸ σώματος ὡς ἀπὸ πέτρης.
οὐκ ἄν μου κατὰ γαῖαν ἀμείνων ἦσθα, κάκιστε,   95
παγκρατίῳ τε πάλῃ τε καὶ εἰς δρόμον· ἀλλὰ πλανήσας
εἰς ὕδωρ μ' ἔρριψας. ἔχει θεὸς ἔκδικον ὄμμα
ποινήν τ' ἀντέκτισίν τ' ὀρθὴν ὅς κ' ἀποδώσει,   97a
ποινήν αὖ τείσεις σὺ μυῶν στράτῳ οὐδὲ ὑπαλύξεις
τοῖς τίσουσί σε μυῶν στρατὸς οὐδὲ ὑπαλύξεις
    Ὥς εἰπὼν ἀπέπνευσεν ἐν ὕδασι· τὸν δὲ κατεῖδεν
Λειχοπίναξ ὄχθῃσιν ἐφεζόμενος μαλακῇσιν·   100

δεινὸν δ' ἐξολόλυξε, δραμὼν δ' ἤγγειλε μύεσσιν.
ὡς δ' ἔμαθον τὴν μοῖραν, ἔδυ χόλος αἰνὸς ἅπαντας.

καὶ τότε κηρύκεσσιν ἑοῖς ἐκέλευσαν ὑπ' ὄρθρον
κηρύσσειν ἀγορήνδ' ἐς δώματα Τρωξάρταο,
πατρὸς δυστήνου Ψιχάρπαγος, ὃς κατὰ λίμνην   105
ὕπτιος ἐξήπλωτο νεκρὸν δέμας, οὐδὲ παρ' ὄχθαις
ἦν ἤδη τλήμων, μέσσῳ δ' ἐπενήχετο πόντῳ.
ὡς δ' ἦλθον σπεύδοντες ἅμ' ἠοῖ, πρῶτος ἀνέστη
Τρωξάρτης ἐπὶ παιδὶ χολούμενος, εἶπέ τε μῦθον·
    Ὦ φίλοι εἰ καὶ μοῦνος ἐγὼ κακὰ πολλὰ πέπονθα   110
ἐκ βατράχων, ἡ πεῖρα κακὴ πάντεσσι τέτυκται.
εἰμὶ δ' ἐγὼ δύστηνος ἐπεὶ τρεῖς παῖδας ὄλεσσα.
καὶ τὸν μὲν πρῶτόν γε κατέκτανεν ἁρπάξασα
υἱέα μοι πρῶτον μυοφόρβος δορπήσατο
ἔχθιστος γαλέη, τρώγλης ἔκτοσθεν ἑλοῦσα.
θὴρ μεγάλη κλονέοντα πτέρναν σιάλοιο τυχοῦσα
τὸν δ' ἄλλον πάλιν ἄνδρες ἀπηνέες ἐς μόρον εἷλξαν   115
καινοτέραις τέχναις ξύλινον δόλον ἐξευρόντες,
ἣν παγίδα κλείουσι, μυῶν ὀλέτειραν ἐοῦσαν.
ὁ τρίτος ἦν ἀγαπητὸς ἐμοὶ καὶ μητέρι κεδνῇ,
τοῦτον ἀπέπνιξεν Φυσίγναθος ἐς βυθὸν ἄξας.
ἀλλ' ἄγεθ' ὁπλίζεσθε καὶ ἐξέλθωμεν ἐπ' αὐτοὺς   120
σώματα κοσμήσαντες ἐν ἔντεσι δαιδαλέοισιν.
    Ταῦτ' εἰπὼν ἀνέπεισε καθοπλίζεσθαι ἅπαντας.
καὶ τοὺς μέν ῥ' ἐκόρυσσεν Ἄρης πολέμοιο μεμηλώς·
κνημῖδας μὲν πρῶτον ἐφήρμοσαν εἰς δύο μηρούς,
ῥήξαντες κυάμους χλωρούς, εὖ δ' ἀσκήσαντες,
οὓς αὐτοὶ διὰ νυκτὸς ἐπιστάντες κατέτρωξαν.
θώρηκας δ' εἶχον καλαμοστεφέων ἀπὸ βυρσῶν,
οὓς γαλέην δείραντες ἐπισταμένως ἐποίησαν.
ἀσπὶς δ' ἦν λύχνου τὸ μεσόμφαλον· ἡ δέ νυ λόγχη
εὐμήκης βελόνη, παγχάλκεον ἔργον Ἄρηος·   130
ἡ δὲ κόρυς τὸ λέπυρον ἐπὶ κροτάφοις ἐρεβίνθου.
    Οὕτω μὲν μύες ἦσαν ἔνοπλοι· ὡς δ' ἐνόησαν
βάτραχοι ἐξανέδυσαν ἀφ' ὕδατος, ἐς δ' ἕνα χῶρον
ἐλθόντες βουλὴν ξύναγον πολέμοιο κακοῖο.
σκεπτομένων δ' αὐτῶν πόθεν ἡ στάσις ἢ τίς ὁ θρύλλος,   135

κῆρυξ ἐγγύθεν ἦλθε φέρων ῥάβδον μετὰ χερσίν,
Τυρογλύφου υἱὸς μεγαλήτορος Ἐμβασίχυτρος,
ἀγγέλλων πολέμοιο κακὴν φάτιν, εἶπέ τε τοῖα·
    Ὦ βάτραχοι, μύες ὔμμιν ἀπειλήσαντες ἔπεμψαν
εἰπεῖν ὁπλίζεσθαι ἐπὶ πτόλεμόν τε μάχην τε.   140
εἶδον γὰρ καθ' ὕδωρ Ψιχάρπαγα ὅν περ ἔπεφνεν
ὑμέτερος βασιλεὺς Φυσίγναθος. ἀλλὰ μάχεσθε
οἵ τινες ἐν βατράχοισιν ἀριστῆες γεγάατε.
    Ὣς εἰπὼν ἀπέφηνε· λόγος δ' εἰς οὔατα πάντων
εἰσελθὼν ἐτάραξε φρένας βατράχων ἀγερώχων·   145
μεμφομένων δ' αὐτῶν Φυσίγναθος εἶπεν ἀναστάς·
    Ὦ φίλοι οὐκ ἔκτεινον ἐγὼ μῦν, οὐδὲ κατεῖδον
ὀλλύμενον· πάντως δ' ἐπνίγη παίζων παρὰ λίμνην,
νήξεις τὰς βατράχων μιμούμενος· οἱ δὲ κάκιστοι
νῦν ἐμὲ μέμφονται τὸν ἀναίτιον· ἀλλ' ἄγε βουλὴν   150
ζητήσωμεν ὅπως δολίους μύας ἐξολέσωμεν.
τοιγὰρ ἐγὼν ἐρέω ὥς μοι δοκεῖ εἶναι ἄριστα.
σώματα κοσμήσαντες ἐν ὅπλοις στῶμεν ἅπαντες
ἄκροις πὰρ χείλεσσιν, ὅπου κατάκρημνος ὁ χῶρος·
ἡνίκα δ' ὁρμηθέντες ἐφ' ἡμέας ἐξέλθωσι,   155
δραξάμενοι κορύθων, ὅς τις σχεδὸν ἀντίος ἔλθῃ,
ἐς λίμνην αὐτοὺς σὺν ἐκείναις εὐθὺ βάλωμεν.
οὕτω γὰρ πνίξαντες ἐν ὕδασι τοὺς ἀκολύμβους
στήσομεν εὐθύμως τὸ μυοκτόνον ὧδε τρόπαιον.
    Ὣς εἰπὼν ἀνέπεισε καθοπλίζεσθαι ἅπαντας.   160
φύλλοις μὲν μαλαχῶν κνήμας ἑὰς ἀμφεκάλυψαν,
θώρηκας δ' εἶχον καλῶν χλοερῶν ἀπὸ σεύτλων,
φύλλα δὲ τῶν κραμβῶν εἰς ἀσπίδας εὖ ἤσκησαν,
ἔγχος δ' ὀξύσχοινος ἑκάστῳ μακρὸς ἀρήρει,
καί ῥα κέρα κοχλιῶν λεπτῶν ἐκάλυπτε κάρηνα.   165
φραξάμενοι δ' ἔστησαν ἐπ' ὄχθαις ὑψηλαῖσι
σείοντες λόγχας, θυμοῦ δ' ἔμπλητο ἕκαστος.
    Ζεὺς δὲ θεοὺς καλέσας εἰς οὐρανὸν ἀστερόεντα,
καὶ πολέμου πληθὺν δείξας κρατερούς τε μαχητάς,
πολλοὺς καὶ μεγάλους ἠδ' ἔγχεα μακρὰ φέροντας,   170
οἷος Κενταύρων στρατὸς ἔρχεται ἠὲ Γιγάντων,
ἡδὺ γελῶν ἐρέεινε· τίνες βατράχοισιν ἀρωγοὶ

ἢ μυσὶν ἀθανάτων; καὶ Ἀθηναίην προσέειπεν·
Ὦ θύγατερ μυσὶν ἦ ῥα βοηθήσουσα πορεύσῃ;
καὶ γὰρ σοῦ κατὰ νηὸν ἀεὶ σκιρτῶσιν ἅπαντες   175
κνίσῃ τερπόμενοι καὶ ἐδέσμασι παντοδαποῖσιν.
Ὣς ἄρ' ἔφη Κρονίδης· τὸν δὲ προσέειπεν Ἀθήνη·
ὦ πάτερ οὐκ ἄν πώ ποτ' ἐγὼ μυσὶ τειρομένοισιν
ἐλθοίμην ἐπαρωγός, ἐπεὶ κακὰ πολλά μ' ἔοργαν
στέμματα βλάπτοντες καὶ λύχνους εἵνεκ' ἐλαίου.   180
τοῦτο δέ μοι λίην ἔδακε φρένας οἷον ἔρεξαν.
πέπλον μου κατέτρωξαν ὃν ἐξύφηνα καμοῦσα
ἐκ ῥοδάνης λεπτῆς καὶ στήμονα μακρὸν ἔνησα,
τρώγλας τ' ἐμποίησαν· ὁ δ' ἠπητής μοι ἐπέστη
καὶ πράσσει με τόκον· τὸ δὲ ῥίγιον ἀθανάτοισιν.   185
χρησαμένη γὰρ ἔνησα καὶ οὐκ ἔχω ἀνταποδοῦναι.
ἀλλ' οὐδ' ὣς βατράχοισιν ἀρηγέμεναι βουλήσω.
εἰσὶ γὰρ οὐδ' αὐτοὶ φρένας ἔμπεδοι, ἀλλά με πρῴην
ἐκ πολέμου ἀνιοῦσαν ἐπεὶ λίην ἐκοπώθην,
ὕπνου δευομένην οὐκ εἴασαν θορυβοῦντες   190
οὐδ' ὀλίγον καταμῦσαι· ἐγὼ δ' ἄϋπνος κατεκείμην·
τὴν κεφαλὴν ἀλγοῦσαν, ἕως ἐβόησεν ἀλέκτωρ.
ἀλλ' ἄγε παυσώμεσθα θεοὶ τούτοισιν ἀρήγειν,
μή κέ τις ὑμείων τρωθῇ βέλει ὀξυόεντι·
εἰσὶ γὰρ ἀγχέμαχοι, εἰ καὶ θεὸς ἀντίον ἔλθοι·   195
πάντες δ' οὐρανόθεν τερπώμεθα δῆριν ὁρῶντες.
Ὣς ἄρ' ἔφη· καὶ τῇ γε θεοὶ ἐπεπείθοντ' ἄλλοι,
πάντες δ' αὖτ' εἰσῆλθον ἀολλέες εἰς ἕνα χῶρον.
καὶ τότε κώνωπες μεγάλας σάλπιγγας ἔχοντες
δεινὸν ἐσάλπιγξαν πολέμου κτύπον· οὐρανόθεν δὲ   200
Ζεὺς Κρονίδης βρόντησε, τέρας πολέμοιο κακοῖο.
Πρῶτος δ' Ὑψιβόας Λειχήνορα οὔτασε δουρὶ
ἑσταότ' ἐν προμάχοις κατὰ γαστέρα ἐς μέσον ἧπαρ·
κὰδ δ' ἔπεσεν πρηνής, ἁπαλὰς δ' ἐκόνισεν ἐθείρας.
δούπησεν δὲ πεσών, ἀράβησε δὲ τεύχε' ἐπ' αὐτῷ.   205
Τρωγλοδύτης δὲ μετ' αὐτὸν ἀκόντισε Πηλείωνος,
πῆξεν δ' ἐν στέρνῳ στιβαρὸν δόρυ· τὸν δὲ πεσόντα
εἷλε μέλας θάνατος, ψυχὴ δ' ἐκ σώματος ἔπτη.
Σευτλαῖον δ' ἄρ' ἔπεφνε βαλὼν κέαρ Ἐμβασίχυτρος,

Ἀρτοφάγος δὲ Πολύφωνον κατὰ γαστέρα τύψε· 210
ἤριπε δὲ πρηνής, ψυχὴ δὲ μελέων ἐξέπτη.
Λιμνόχαρις δ' ὡς εἶδεν ἀπολλύμενον Πολύφωνον,
Τρωγλοδύτην ἁπαλοῖο δι' αὐχένος τρῶσεν ἐπιφθὰς
πέτρῳ μυλοειδέϊ· τὸν δὲ σκότος ὄσσε κάλυψε· 213a
Τρωγλήτης δ' ἄρ ἔπεφνε Βρεκαίκιγα ἐσθλὸν ἀίξας 213b
Ὠκιμίδην δ' ἄχος εἷλε καὶ ἤλασεν ὀξέϊ σχοίνῳ
οὐδ' ἐξέσπασεν ἔγχος ἐναντίον· ὡς δ' ἐνόησε 215
Λειχήνωρ δ' αὐτοῖο τιτύσκετο δουρὶ φαεινῷ
καὶ βάλεν, οὐδ' ἀφάμαρτε καθ' ἧπαρ· ὡς δ' ἐνόησε
Κοστοφάγον φεύγοντα βαθείαις ἔμπεσεν ὄχθαις.
ἀλλ' οὐδ' ὡς ἀπέληγε μάχης ἀλλ' ἤλασεν αὐτόν·
κάππεσε δ', οὐκ ἀνένευσεν, ἐβάπτετο δ' αἵματι λίμνη 220
πορφυρέῳ, αὐτὸς δὲ παρ' ἠιόν' ἐξετανύσθη,
χορδῇσιν λιπαρῇσί τ' ἐπορνύμενος λαγόνεσσιν.
Τυροφάγον δ' αὐτῇσιν ἐπ' ὄχθαις ἐξενάριξεν.
Πτερνογλύφον δὲ ἰδὼν Καλαμίνθιος ἐς φόβον ἦλθεν,
ἤλατο δ' ἐς λίμνην φεύγων τὴν ἀσπίδα ῥίψας. 225
Λιτραῖον δ' ἄρ' ἔπεφνεν ἀμύμων Βορβοροκοίτης,
Ὑδρόχαρις δ' ἔπεφνεν Πτερνοφάγον βασιλῆα,
χερμαδίῳ πλήξας κατὰ βρέγματος· ἐγκέφαλος δὲ
ἐκ ῥινῶν ἔσταξε, παλάσσετο δ' αἵματι γαῖα.
Λειχοπίναξ δ' ἔκτεινεν ἀμύμονα Βορβοροκοίτην, 230
ἔγχει ἐπαΐξας· τὸν δὲ σκότος ὄσσε κάλυψεν.
Πρασσαῖος δὲ ἰδὼν ποδὸς εἷλκυσε Κνισσοδιώκτην,
ἐν λίμνῃ δ' ἀπέπνιξε κρατήσας χειρὶ τένοντα.
Ψιχάρπαξ δ' ἤμυν' ἑτάρου περὶ τεθνειῶτος
καὶ βάλε Πρασσαῖον κατὰ νηδύος ἐς μέσον ἧπαρ, 235
πῖπτε δέ οἱ πρόσθεν, ψυχὴ δ' Ἀϊδόσδε βεβήκει.
Κραμβοβάτης δὲ ἰδὼν πηλοῦ δράκα ῥίψεν ἐπ' αὐτόν,
καὶ τὸ μέτωπον ἔχρισε καὶ ἐξετύφλου παρὰ μικρόν.
ὠργίσθη δ' ἄρ' ἐκεῖνος, ἑλὼν δ' ἄρα χειρὶ παχείῃ
κείμενον ἐν δαπέδῳ λίθον ὄβριμον, ἄχθος ἀρούρης, 240
τῷ βάλε Κραμβοβάτην ὑπὸ γούνατα· πᾶσα δ' ἐκλάσθη
κνήμη δεξιτερή, πέσε δ' ὕπτιος ἐν κονίῃσι.
Κραυγασίδης δ' ἤμυνε καὶ αὖθις βαῖνεν ἐπ' αὐτόν,
τύψε δέ οἱ μέσσην κατὰ γαστέρα· πᾶς δέ οἱ εἴσω

ὀξύσχοινος ἔδυνε, χαμαὶ δ' ἔκχυντο ἄπαντα   245
ἔγκατ' ἐφελκομένῳ ὑπὸ δούρατι χειρὶ παχείῃ·
Τρωγλοδύτης δ' ὡς εἶδεν παρ' ὄχθησιν ποταμοῖο,
σκάζων ἐκ πολέμου ἀνεχάζετο, τείρετο δ' αἰνῶς·
ἥλατο δ' ἐς τάφρους, ὅπως φύγῃ αἰπὺν ὄλεθρον.
Τρωξάρτης δ' ἔβαλεν Φυσίγναθον ἐς ποδὸς ἄκρον.   250
ἔσχατος δ' ἐκ λίμνης ἀνεδύσετο, τείρετο δ' αἰνῶς
Πρασσαῖος δ' ὡς εἶδεν ἔθ' ἡμίπνουν προπεσόντα,
καὶ οἱ ἐκέδραμεν αὖθις, ἀποκταμεναι μενεαίνων   252a
ἦλθε διὰ προμάχων καὶ ἀκόντισεν ὀξύσχοινον·
οὐδ' ἔρρηξε σάκος, σχέτο δ' αὐτοῦ δουρὸς ἀκωκή·
οὐδ' ἔβαλε τρυφάλειαν ἀμύμονα καὶ τετράχυτρον   255
δῖος Ὀριγανίων, μιμούμενος αὐτὸν Ἄρηα,
ὃς μόνος ἐν βατράχοισιν ἀρίστευεν καθ' ὅμιλον·
ὥρμησεν δ' ἄρ' ἐπ' αὐτόν· ὁ δ' ὡς ἴδεν οὐχ ὑπέμεινεν
ἥρωας κρατερούς, ἀλλ' ἔδυνε βένθεσι λίμνης
Ἦν δέ τις ἐν μυσὶ παῖς Μεριδάρπαξ ἔξοχος ἄλλων,   260
Κναίσωνος φίλος υἱὸς ἀμύμονος ἀρτεπιβούλου·   260a
μεριδάρπαξ ὄρχαμος μιμούμενος αὐτὸν ἄρηα
ὃς μόνος ἐν μύεσσιν ἀρίστευεν καθ' ὅμιλον   261b
Κναίσων μέν, βατράχοιο βέλει πληγεὶς κατὰ χεῖρα   261c
οἴκαδ' ἵεν, πολέμου δὲ μετασχεῖν παῖδ' ἐκέλευεν·
αὐτὸς δ' ἑστήκει γαυρούμενος κατὰ λίμνην
οὗτος ἀναρπάξαι βατράχων γενεὴν ἐπαπείλει·
στεῦτο δὲ πορθήσειν βρατράχων γένος αἰχμητάων   263a
ἀγχοῦ δ' ἔστηκεν μενεαίνων ἶφι μάχεσθαι
καὶ ῥήξας καρύοιο μέσην ῥάχιν εἰς δύο μοίρας   265
φράγδην ἀμφοτέροισι κενώμασι χεῖρας ἔθηκεν·
οἱ δὲ τάχος δείσαντες ἔβαν πάντες κατὰ λίμνην·
καί νύ κεν ἐξετέλεσσεν, ἐπεὶ μέγα οἱ σθένος ἦεν,
εἰ μὴ ἄρ' ὀξὺ νόησε πατὴρ ἀνδρῶν τε θεῶν τε.
καὶ τότ' ἀπολλυμένους βατράχους ᾤκτειρε Κρονίων,   270
κινήσας δὲ κάρη τοίην ἐφθέγξατο φωνήν·
  Ὢ πόποι ἦ μέγα θαῦμα τόδ' ὀφθαλμοῖσιν ὁρῶμαι·
οὐ μ' ὀλίγον πλήσσει Μεριδάρπαξ ὃς κατὰ λίμνην
ἅρπαξ ἐν βατράχοισιν ἀμείβεται· ἀλλὰ τάχιστα
Παλλάδα πέμψωμεν πολεμόκλονον ἢ καὶ Ἄρηα,   275

οἵ μιν ἐπισχήσουσι μάχης κρατερόν περ ἐόντα.
Ὣς ἄρ' ἔφη Κρονίδης· Ἄρης δ' ἀπαμείβετο μύθῳ·
οὔτ' ἄρ' Ἀθηναίης Κρονίδη σθένος οὔτε Ἄρηος
ἰσχύει βατράχοισιν ἀμυνέμεν αἰπὺν ὄλεθρον.
ἀλλ' ἄγε πάντες ἴωμεν ἀρηγόνες· ἢ τὸ σὸν ὅπλον 280
κινείσθω· οὕτω γὰρ ἁλώσεται ὅς τις ἄριστος,
ᾧ Τιτᾶνας πέφνες ἀρίστους ἔξοχα πάντων
ὥς ποτε καὶ Καπανῆα κατέκτανες ὄβριμον ἄνδρα
καὶ μέγαν Ἐγκελάδοντα καὶ ἄγρια φῦλα Γιγάντων.
Ὣς ἄρ' ἔφη· Κρονίδης δὲ βαλὼν ἀργῆτα κεραυνὸν
πρῶτα μὲν ἐβρόντησε, μέγαν δ' ἐλέλιξεν Ὄλυμπον. 285
αὐτὰρ ἔπειτα κεραυνὸν δειμαλέον Διὸς ὅπλον
ἧκ' ἐπιδινήσας. ὁ δ' ἄρ ἔπτατο χειρὸς ἄνακτος
πάντας μέν ῥ' ἐφόβησε βαλὼν βατράχους τε μύας τε·
ἀλλ' οὐδ' ὣς ἀπέληγε μυῶν στρατός, ἀλλ' ἔτι μᾶλλον
ἔλπετο πορθήσειν βατράχων γένος αἰχμητάων, 290
εἰ μὴ ἀπ' Οὐλύμπου βατράχους ἐλέησε Κρονίων,
ὅς ῥα τότ' ἐν βατράχοισιν ἀρωγοὺς εὐθὺς ἔπεμψεν.
Ἦλθον δ' ἐξαίφνης νωτάκμονες, ἀγκυλοχεῖλαι,
λοξοβάται, στρεβλοί, ψαλιδόστομοι, ὀστρακόδερμοι,
ὀστοφυεῖς, πλατύνωτοι, ἀποστίλβοντες ἐν ὤμοις, 295
βλαισοί, χειλοτένοντες, ἀπὸ στέρνων ἐσορῶντες,
ὀκτάποδες, δικάρηνοι, ἀχειρέες, οἱ δὲ καλεῦνται
καρκίνοι, οἵ ῥα μυῶν οὐρὰς στομάτεσσιν ἔκοπτον
ἠδὲ πόδας καὶ χεῖρας· ἀνεγνάμπτοντο δὲ λόγχαι.
τοὺς δὴ ὑπέδεισαν δειλοὶ μύες οὐδ' ἔτ' ἔμειναν, 300
ἐς δὲ φυγὴν ἐτράποντο· ἐδύετο δ' ἥλιος ἤδη,
καὶ πολέμου τελετὴ μονοήμερος ἐξετελέσθη.

Translation

As I start from my first page, I pray that the chorus
comes into my heart from Helikon for the sake of the song
Which I have just set down upon the tablets on my knees—
a song of limitless strife, the war-rousing work of Ares—
because I hope to sound to the ears of all mortal men   5
how the mice went forth to best the frogs,
imitating the deeds of the earth-born men, the giants,
as mortal tale goes. It has *this kind* of beginning.

Once upon a time, a thirsty mouse escaped the weasel's danger
and then lowered his greedy chin down to a pond   10
to take pleasure in the honey-sweet water. A pond-loving frog,
a big-talker, saw him and uttered something like this:

"Friend, who are you? From where have you come to our shore?
Who sired you?
Tell me everything truly so I don't think you're a liar.
If I consider you a worthy friend, I'll take you home,   15
where I will give you many fine gifts of friendship.
I am King Bellowmouth and I am honored
throughout the pond as leader of frogs for all days.
My father Mudman raised me up after he had sex
with Watermistress along the banks of the Eridanus.   20
I see that you are noble and brave beyond the rest,
and also a scepter-bearing king and a warrior in battles.
Come closer and tell me of your lineage."

Then Crumbthief answered and spoke:

"Why do you seek out my lineage? It's known   25
to all men, gods and flying things in the sky.
I am known as Crumbthief. I am the son
of great-hearted Breadnibbler and my mother Mill-licker,
who was daughter of King Hamnibbler.
She birthed me in a hidey-hole and nourished me with food
like figs and nuts and all kinds of choice sweets.   30
How could you make me your friend when our nature is so different?
Your life is in the water—but it is my custom
to nibble away at the foods of men. And I never miss out
on thrice-kneaded bread in the well-rounded basket.
Nor does a long-robed flat cake dressed out with plenty of sesame and cheese 35
ever escape me. Neither does a ham-slice, a white-robed liver
nor just-curdled cheese from sweet-milk,
nor the wholesome honey-cake which even the gods desire,
nor the things cooks carve out for mortals' feasts   40
when they season the dishes with every kind of spice.
I have never fled the dread song of war
but instead I head straight into the danger and join the forefighters.
I don't fear people, even though they have such great size;
no, I run up to their beds and bite the tip of their fingers.   45
Then I take their ham and no pain overtakes the man,
no one wakes from sleep when I bite him.
But I do really fear two things over the whole earth:
the hawk and the weasel who bring me great grief
and also the grievous mousetrap where a deceptive fate awaits me.   50
But I fear the weasel more than anything, that beast who is best
at ferreting a hole-dweller out of his hole.

I don't eat radishes, cabbage, and pumpkins;
and I don't munch on pale beets or parsley.
Such things are the delicacies of pond-dwellers like you."   55

Grinning at this, Bellowmouth responded:
"Friend, you brag too much about your belly. We also
have many marvels to see in the pond and on the shore.

Zeus gave the frogs an amphibious realm
to dance upon the earth or cover our bodies in water   60
and to inhabit homes divided doubly in parts.
If you wish to learn about these things too, it's simple.
Climb on my back, hold on tight so you don't slip
and then you can come happily to my home."

Thus he spoke and offered up his back. Crumbthief hopped on quickly,   65
holding his hands around Bellowmouth's delicate neck with a light embrace.
At first he was rejoicing as he looked upon the neighboring harbors
and delighted in Bellowmouth's swimming. But, then, when he was
splashed by the roiling waves, he poured forth a flood of tears
and reproached his useless decision. He tore at his hairs,   70
squeezed his feet around his stomach and his heart
shook at the novelty and he wished to get back to land.
He wailed dreadfully under the oppression of chilling fear.
First, he set his tail into the water as though guiding a rudder,
and prayed to the gods to make it to the shore.   75
He was splashed again by the murky water, and kept shouting out for help.
Then he made a speech like this as he proclaimed:

"Didn't the bull carry his cargo of love in this way
when he led Europa over the waves to Krete?
Such is the way this frog set out and led a mouse to his house   80
after raising his pale body on the white wave."

Suddenly, a water snake appeared, a bitter sight to both,
holding his throat up straight out of the water.
When he saw him, Bellowmouth went under water, considering not
what sort of friend he was about to abandon to death.   85
He submerged in the depth of the pond, and avoided black death.
But the mouse, as he was let go, fell backward into the water,
clenched his hands, and squeaked as he was dying.
Several times he went down below the water, and several times
he kicked and came back up. But it was not possible to ward off fate.   90
His wet hair put more weight on him,

and dying in the water, he shouted out these words:

"You won't evade the gods in doing these deceitful things,
tossing me shipwrecked from your body as if off a crag.
You rotten bastard, you were not better than me upon land   95
at fighting or wrestling or running, so you brought me to the water
and hurled me into it! God has an eye for vengeance.
You will not avoid paying a penalty and
righteous payback to the host of mice who honor me."

As he said this, he gasped in the water. And Platelicker
saw him as he sat upon the luxuriant banks.   100
Then he wailed terribly, ran, and informed the mice.
A dread wrath fell upon them as they learned his fate,
and they ordered their heralds to summon their kin
to the assembly at the home of Breadmuncher at dawn.
He was father of pitiful Crumbthief who floated on the pond   105
as a corpse facing upward, no longer struggling
on the banks but raised up in the middle of the sea.
And so they came hurrying at dawn and among them first
Breadmuncher rose enraged over his son to make this speech:

"Friends, even if I alone suffered these many evils from the frogs,   110
it would still be a vile crime against us all.
I am wretched because I have lost three children:
a most hateful weasel snatched up the first and killed him
as she dragged him from his hole.
Harsh men dragged the second to his doom   115
once they designed a wooden trick with their newfangled arts—
that thing they call the trap, the destroyer of mice.
[A mouse-eating great beast made my first son into dinner
as he chanced upon him spinning on his fat heel.]
The third was beloved to me and his prized mother,
Bellowmouth drowned him once he dragged him to the deep.
Come, let us arm ourselves and go out to face them   120
once we've arrayed our bodies in our well-worked arms."

In saying this, he persuaded everyone to arm themselves;
and so, Ares who loves war armed them.
First, they fit their greaves to their two legs,
after breaking some pale beans and fitting them well, 125
beans they nibbled clean by working on them all night.
They had chestpieces made of reed-bound hides
which they made skillfully after flaying a weasel.
Their shield was the middle-section of a lamp. And their spear
was a well-measured needle, a completely bronze work of Ares. 130
The helmet on their temples was the husk of chick pea.

And this is the way the mice were armed. When the frogs noticed
they rose up from the water: and once they gathered in the same place
they summoned a council for wicked war.
While they were examining the conflict and noise, 135
a herald approached carrying a staff in his hand:
Bowldiver, the son of great-hearted Cheeseborer,
in announcing the evil report of war said these kind of things:

"My frogs: the mice threaten you and send me
to tell you to arm yourselves for war and battle. 140
They saw Crumbthief, whom your king
Bellowmouth killed in the water. But fight,
all of you who were born best among the frogs."
He explained it, speaking in this way. The report entered all their ears
and disturbed the minds of the arrogant frogs. 145
While they were reproaching, Bellowmouth stood and said:

"Friends, I didn't kill the mouse, nor did I witness him dying.
He drowned altogether because he was playing near the shore
trying to mimic the swimming of frogs. These villains
are blaming me when I am not at fault. But let us seek 150
a plan so that we may kill those treacherous mice.
I will announce the strategy that seems best to me.
Let all of us stand after adorning ourselves in arms
on the top of the banks where the land is steep.

Whenever they come rushing against us—   155
Once we have snatched them by their helmets as each approaches—
we will throw them straight into the water with their weapons.
When we drown those unaccustomed to the water in this way,
we will happily dedicate a trophy to the murder of mice."

So speaking he persuaded everyone to arm themselves.   160
First, they covered their shins with the leaves of reeds
and they had breastplates from fine yellow beets
they fitted well the leaves of cabbage into shields
and a great sharp reed was worked as a spear for each.
The horns of polished snails covered their heads.   165
They stood on the high banks defending themselves;
and as they brandished their spears, courage filled each of them.

Zeus called the gods to starry heaven
and showed them the mass of war and strong warriors
so many, so great, carrying enormous spears   170
just as the army of centaurs or giants had once approached them.
Then, laughing sweetly, he asked who among the immortals
were supporters for the frogs or mice. And he addressed Athena:

"Daughter, won't you go forth to help the mice?
For they all continuously dance around your temple   175
Delighting in the smell and every kind of treat."
So Kronos' son asked and Athena responded:

"Father, I would never come to the aid of the distressed mice
because they have done me many evils
by ruining my garlands and lamps to get at the oil.   180
One thing they did really wears at my thoughts.
They ate up at the robe which I wore myself out weaving
from tender weft I spun myself on a great warp—
they fill it with holes. The mender waits for me
and makes me his debtor, a thing horrible for the gods.   185
For I spun it in debt and I can't pay it back.

But there is no way I want to help the frogs.
For these creatures are not of sound mind: yesterday
when I was returning from war and really worn out
and needing sleep, they did not allow me to nap even a little,   190
as they made a ruckus. And I lay there sleepless,
with a headache until the rooster crowed.
Come on, let us gods avoid helping them,
lest one of us get wounded by a sharp missile,
for they fight up close, even if a god should confront them.   195
Let's all instead enjoy watching this battle from heaven."

So she spoke and the other gods assented to her
and they all came gathered together in one spot.
Then some mosquitoes bearing great trumpets
sounded the dread song of battle. And from heaven   200
Kronos' son, Zeus, thundered the portent of wicked war.

First, Croakmaster struck Lickman with a spear
through his stomach, mid-liver, as he stood among the forefighters.
And he fell down headlong and dirtied his delicate hair.
He thundered as he fell, and his weapons clattered about him.   205
Hole-dweller next hurled at Muddy's son
and fixed a stout spear in his chest. Then black death took him
as he fell and his soul flew from his body.
Bowldiver killed Beeteater when he struck him in the heart
and Breadmuncher struck Sir Croaks-a-lot in the stomach—   210
and he then fell headlong, and his soul flew from his limbs.
When Pondlubber saw Sir Croaks-a-lot dying
he acted first in crushing Holedweller's tender neck
with a rock like a mill-stone. Then darkness covered his eyes.
Grief overtook Basilson and he drove him through with a sharp reed   215
as the other didn't raise his spear against him. When Lickman saw this,
he took aim at him with his own shining spear
and hurled it: he didn't miss his liver. Then, when he noticed
that Spice-eater was fleeing, he rushed upon the lush banks.
And he did not let up from battle, no, he ran him through.

He fell and didn't look up again: then the pond was dyed   220
with purple blood even as he was stretched out on the shore
as he tried to rise with his intestines and trailing loins.
Then he despoiled Cheesenibbler on the same banks.
When Minty saw Hamcarver he went into flight
and he was driven into the pond while rushing, after abandoning his shield. 225
Blameless Mudbedder killed Poundweight.
Watergrace killed King Hameater
after striking him with a stone on the top of his head. And his brains
dribbled from his nose and the earth was spattered with blood.

Platelicker then killed blameless Mudbedder   230
as he sprung at him with his spear. Then darkness covered his eyes.
When Greenstalk saw this, he dragged Smokehunter by the foot,
overpowered him, and drowned him in the pond as he reached out his
hand.
Crumbthief defended his dead friend
and hurled at Greenstalk through his stomach into his liver—   235
then he fell forward and his soul descended to Hades.
Cabbagetreader saw this and threw a lump of mud at him;
it smeared his face and he nearly blinded him.
When he was enraged by this, he grabbed a heavy rock
lying on the ground, a burden to the earth, with his stout hand   240
and he struck Cabbagetreader with it below the knees. His right greave
was completely shattered and he fell face-up into the dust.
Croakerson defended him and went straight at the other guy,
striking him in the middle of the stomach. The whole sharp reed
pierced into him and all of his guts poured out on the ground   245
because of the spear as it was withdrawn by the strong hand.
When Holedweller saw this from the banks of the river,
he retreated, limping from the battle to rest, since he was terribly worn out.
He rushed into the ditches in order to flee the sheer destruction.
Breadmuncher struck Bellowmouth on the top of the foot.   250
He retreated to the furthest part of the pond, terribly worn out.
And when Greenstalk saw him falling still half-alive,
again he then ran out, desiring to kill,
and he went through the champions and hurled his sharp-reed.

He didn't break the shield and the tip of the spear held fast.
Shining Oregano, as he imitated Ares himself,   255
and was the only one who prevailed through the engagement among the
frogs,
did not strike the four-measured, blameless helm
but he rushed at him. But when the frog saw him, he didn't wait for
the strong heroes, but he dived into the depths of the pond.

There was a child among the mice who stood out from all others,   260
Pieceplunder, the dear son of blameless Grater, the Bread-councilor.
He was on his way home; he had ordered the child to join in the war.
But he was threatening to eliminate the race of the frogs
as he stood nearby desiring to fight with force.
First, he split a nut along its middle into two halves   265
and set them on both his bare hands as defense,
then everyone feared him and scattered around the pond.
He would have achieved his goal since his strength was so great
if the father of men and gods had not taken note.
Kronos' son pitied the dying frogs;   270
he spoke this kind of speech as he shook his head.

"O wretches, I really see a wonder with my eyes!
Pieceplunder worries me not a little as he crosses like
a thief among the frogs. But quickly then,
let's send war-rousing Pallas or even Ares   275
to restrain him from battle, even though he is mighty."

So Zeus spoke and Ares responded with a speech:

"Son of Kronos, neither the power of Athena nor Ares
is able to ward steep destruction from the frogs.
Let's all go as allies. Or maybe you should   280
brandish your arms. Whoever is best will be caught in this way,
as when you killed the stout man Kapaneus,
great Enkelados, and the fierce tribes of the giants."

So he spoke and the son of Kronos threw down shining lightning

and thundered first and shook great Olympos.   285
Then he hurled and threw the frightening weapon of Zeus
and it flew from the master's hand
and frightened all the frogs and mice as he threw.
But the army of the mice did not let up—they even more   290
hoped to eradicate the race of spear-bearing frogs—
unless Kronos' son took pity on the frogs from Olympos
and sent helpers straight away to the frogs.

Suddenly, the armor-backed, crooked-clawed
bow-waling, twisted, scissor-mouthed, hard-shelled,   295
bone-built, broad-backed, with shining shoulders,
crooked-legged, lip-stretching, with eyes set in their chest,
eight-footed, two-headed, handless creatures who are called
crabs, went to war. They easily cut off the mice's tails with their mouths
along with their feet and hands. And their spears were bent back.
The cowardly mice were frightened of them and waited no longer   300
to turn to flight. The sun was already setting.
And the end of this war was accomplished in a single day.

Commentary

Part 1: The Proem—Epic poems, whether monumental poems like the Iliad *or* Odyssey *or shorter performance pieces like the Homeric Hymns, typically begin with "introductions," proemia which (1) invoke a deity; (2) anticipate the subjects and themes of the poem to follow; and (3) sometimes establish the authority of the narrator to sing the song in question. This proem uses language similar to other proemia but in some rather indirect ways. In addition, it is largely unformulaic in the traditional sense—its phrases and images offer few direct parallels in extant epic.*

The term "proem" comes from Greek prooimion, roughly "the thing before the oimê [song-path]." Ancient testimony identifies the term with "preludes" to longer poems. For the four parts of a proem as (1) invocation; (2) advertisement of the topic; (3) reinvocation; (4) beginning of the song, see Harden and Kelly 2014: 8. For an analysis of this proem, see Wölke 1978: 84–91; and Scodel 2008: 227–8 for its self-consciously literary character. The BM *has an indirect invocation (by calling for the chorus from Helicon, 1–2) followed by an invocation of the topic (strife, δῆριν ἀπειρεσίην) and then a delayed specification of that strife as one between the frogs and mice (line 6) before the story starts at line 9. Of particular contrast with the proemia of Homer and Hesiod, the* BM *emphasizes writing (line 3), the fame of this particular tale (lines 5 and 8) and exhibits a ring structure: it begins with* Ἀρχόμενος *(1) and ends with* ἀρχήν *(8).*

1   Ἀρχόμενος: "Beginning from, as I begin from," common in epic and hymnic poetry. Hesiod's *Theogony* offers the declaration that the narrator "begins" with the Muses (Μουσάων Ἑλικωνιάδων ἀρχώμεθ᾽

ἀείδειν, 1); similar are the remains of the lost *Epigonoi* (Νῦν αὖθ᾽ ὁπλοτέρων ἀνδρῶν ἀρχώμεθα, Μοῦσαι, 1; "Muses, let us now sing in turn of younger men"). Cf. also the Hom. *Hymn to the Muses and Apollo* (Μουσάων ἄρχωμαι ᾽Απόλλωνός τε Διός τε); and A.R, *Arg.*: ᾽Αρχόμενος σέο Φοῖβε παλαιγενέων κλέα φωτῶν (cf. Glei 1984: 112 *ad loc.*). As with Apollonius' line, the *BM* does not exhibit the performative subjunctive common to choral and performance-oriented poetry (e.g. Hesiod's ἀρχώμεθ;' see Calame 1994–95: 142–5; cf. Fogelmark 1972: 93–4; Faraone 1995: 3–11 and Christensen 2010: 1–3.). The indirect evocation of the Muses (through the mention of Helicon), seems a rather Hellenistic strategy. Perhaps this explains the origin of the variant for the next phrase πρῶτον μουσῶν, which would render this line "beginning first with the Muses, I pray that a chorus comes from Helicon into my heart."

πρώτης σελίδος: from σελίς, σελίδος (f.), translate as "page." Some texts have πρῶτον μουσῶν instead of πρώτης **σελίδος**; the phrase seems a rather bland attempt to adhere more closely to proemial norms. πρώτης σελίδος is found in Z, the oldest of our surviving MSS, which dates back to the tenth century. This σελίς is associated with Homeric poetry in later writing: cf. *Grk. Anth.* 4.2: ῎Ανθεά σοι δρέψας ῾Ελικώνια καὶ κλυτοδένδρου / Πιερίης κείρας πρωτοφύτους κάλυκας / καὶ σελίδος νεαρῆς θερίσας στάχυν ἀντανέπλεξα ...; or *Vita Homeri* (Plutarch): "double pages of heroes" (δισσὰς ἡμιθέων γραψάμενος σελίδας / ὑμνεῖ δ᾽ ἡ μὲν νόστον ᾽Οδυσσῆος πολύπλαγκτον / ἡ δὲ τὸν ᾽Ιλιακὸν Δαρδανιδῶν πόλεμον) Cf. also the lexicographer Photius (μηδ᾽ ἐς ῾Ομηρείην σελίδ᾽ ἔμβλεπε μηδ᾽ ἐλεγείην / μὴ τραγικὴν Μοῦσαν, μηδὲ μελογραφίην, 187).

Note the internal jingling of the line: 1 ᾽Αρχόμενος...σελίδος... ῾Ελικῶνος. Such sound-play is not typical of early hexameter.

χορὸν ἐξ ῾Ελικῶνος: "[I pray that a] chorus [comes] from Mt. Helicon"; for Helicon as a location of the Muses see Hes. *Th.* 1 (Μουσάων ῾Ελικωνιάδων ἀρχώμεθ᾽ ἀείδειν). *Heliconian* Muses are special to

Hesiod but not to be differentiated from the Olympian Muses. Mt. Helicon is in Thrace, but this epithet may have been extended to Olympus; see West 1966: 152. The Hellenistic scholiast and poet Moschus comments on this passage, "αὗται μὲν ἐν τῇ Πιερείᾳ γεννῶνται, ἐν δὲ τῷ Ἑλικῶνι χορεύουσιν." ("They [the Muses] were born in Pieria, but they dance on Helicon.") The use of χορός to refer to the *group* of dancers, rather than the dance itself, represents a post-Homeric semantic range; it suggests that the poem was composed subsequent to the flowering of Attic tragedy. One scholiast records a fanciful etymology from the Byzantine scholar John Tzetzes: "Ἑλικῶν δὲ κατὰ Τζέτζην αἱ βίβλοι, εἰς ἃς ἑλίσσονται καὶ συστρέφονται καὶ οἱονεὶ χορεύουσιν αἱ Μοῦσαι." ("Helicon, according to Tzetzes, refers to books, into which the Muses are twisted and collected together as though they were dancing.") The image of a chorus dancing into the poet's heart is striking (Scodel 2008: 227 calls it "disconcerting") and probably evidence of a late date of composition.

2 ἐλθεῖν εἰς ἐμὸν ἦτορ ἐπεύχομαι: introduces indirect statement, accusative subject χορόν. In Homer ἐπεύχομαι means "boast" or "threaten." Here it means more like "to pray or hope," which is also possible in Homer; see Muellner 1976: 17–67.

εἵνεκ' ἀοιδῆς: "for the sake of a song." In Homer, *aoidê* indicates the action of a performing bard. Cf. *Od.* 1.340–341. (...ταύτης δ' ἀποπαύε' ἀοιδῆς / λυγρῆς, ἥ τέ μοι αἰὲν ἐνὶ στήθεσσι φίλον κῆρ. "Stop this mournful song / which always pains the dear heart in my chest.")

Note also preponderance of ε/η sounds concentrated into one line.

3 ἣν νέον ἐν δέλτοισιν ἐμοῖς: "which I just recently wrote on my tablets." The antecedent of ἥν is ἀοιδῆς ("the song which..."). The narrator refers to the practice of writing drafts on tablets, probably covered in wax. The practice is documented in the early classical age in vase painting (most famously by Douris whose tablet-writing vase is held in Berlin). The earliest similar evidence of writing is in Aesch. *Prom. Bound*, 789: ἣν ἐγγράφου σὺ μνήμοσιν δέλτοις φρενῶν. Cf. also

Eur. *Iph.Taur.*: ἐς τήνδε δ' ὤικισ' αἶαν. αἵδ' ἐπιστολαί, / τάδ' ἐστὶ τὰν δέλτοισιν ἐγγεγραμμένα. The *BM*'s line recalls Callimachus' *Aetia* (1.21–2: καὶ γὰρ ὅτε πρώτιστον ἐμοῖς ἐπὶ δέλτον ἔθηκα / γούνασιν, ᾿Α[πό]λλων εἶπεν ὅ μοι Λύκιος· "When I first set my tablet on my knees, Lykian Apollo spoke to me"). This parallel has led some (e.g Bliquez 1977: 12) to argue that the opening lines are a Hellenistic interpolation. Others have seen this as firmly establishing a Hellenistic character for the poem, see Sens 2005: 217; cf. Wölke 1978: 58–61 and Glei 1984: 22.

νέον: neuter singular adjective used as adverb.

ἐμὸν ἦτορ ἐπεύχομαι. . .δέλτοισιν ἐμοῖς: The preponderance of first-person reference in the proem may align the *BM* with the tradition of fable. Adrados (1998: 368) suggests that fables often use the first-person to strengthen the persuasive and moralizing force.

ἐπὶ γούνασι θῆκα: Tmesis with unaugmented aorist.

4   δῆριν ἀπειρεσίην: "endless strife"; cf. *Il.* 17.158 (ἀνδράσι δυσμενέεσσι πόνον καὶ δῆριν ἔθεντο) for strife in war; cf. *Od.* 24.515: υἱός θ' υἱωνός τ' ἀρετῆς πέρι δῆριν ἔχουσι. δῆριν is line-initial at Hes. *Sc.* 251 and 306. Cf. Nicander 450 (δῆριν ἄγει γενύεσσιν ὅταν βλώσκοντα καθ' ὕλην). Camerotto (1992: 12) counts this phrase as an "equivalent formula," likely evidence of literary adaptation. In this metrical position, ἀπειρεσίην appears at *Il.* 20.58 (γαῖαν ἀπειρεσίην ὀρέων τ' αἰπεινὰ κάρηνα) and *Od.* 11.621 (εἶχον ἀπειρεσίην· μάλα γὰρ πολὺ χείρονι φωτί).

If "strife" is the theme of this poem, one might expect it a little earlier: the *Iliad* begins with its theme of wrath (μῆνις) and the *Odyssey* starts by indirectly naming its subject (ἄνδρα). Strife is announced as the topic of the fragmentary "Battle of Weasel and Mice" (line 1: Μοῦσά μοι ἔννεπ]ε νεῖκο[ς]. . .) and used later to refer to the action (μέγα νεῖκος, 27).

πολεμόκλονον ἔργον ῎Αρηος: ("the war-rousing work of Ares") a transfered epithet from Ares to the work. This epithet is applied to

Athena at *Anacreonta* fr. 55.33 (πολεμόκλονόν τ' Ἀθήνην). For this phrase as providing a *terminus ante quem* for the poem of *c.* 570–500 BCE, see Bliquez 1977: 12. πολεμόκλονον may be ironic, since Ares eventually prevents war instead of rousing it; see lines 278–9 below. Camerotto (1992: 16) believes this is analogically based on the phrase πολεμήϊα ἔργα at *Od.* 12.116.

5 εὐχόμενος μερόπεσσιν ἐς οὔατα πᾶσι βαλέσθαι: see line 2 for indirect statement introduced by εὐχόμενος.

μερόπεσσιν: "mortals" (see μερόπεσσι βροτοῖσιν, *Il.* 2.285). The term only appears in the plural and has its origins in *meromai* plus *ops* (literally "dividing the voice," meaning "articulate" or having language). In Homer, the word is only used as an adjective for *brotos* or *anthrôpos*, so this substantive use is a departure. For the imagery of sound striking the ears, see *Il.* 10.535 ἵππων μ' ὠκυπόδων ἀμφὶ κτύπος οὔατα βάλλει.

6 πῶς μύες ἐν βατράχοισιν: πῶς here is an indirect interrogative, i.e. "tell you how the mice went among the frogs." This use not common in Homer (though the direct use is). For a proem, an initial question subject is common, as in the *Iliad*'s "who of the gods set these two to battle in strife?" (Τίς τ' ἄρ σφωε θεῶν ἔριδι ξυνέηκε μάχεσθαι; 1.8). Such re-emphasis is common as transition from proemia to narrative.

ἀριστεύσαντες ἔβησαν: various MSS have the future ἀριστεύσοντες instead of the aorist particple. The form ἔβησαν is used with the aorist participle at *Od.* 5.107 where the participle clearly indicates action prior to the finite verb (εἰνάετες, δεκάτῳ δὲ πόλιν πέρσαντες ἔβησαν. "Nine-years, in the tenth they left after sacking the city"). But here the periphrasis likely has a progressive sense: "they went about triumphing among the frogs."

7 γηγενέων. . .Γιγάντων: "earth-born. . .giants"; mice live in the earth and are "born" from it, hence the epithet γηγενέων could aptly describe mice and giants. The comparison with giants (born from Gaia, "Earth") is obviously humorous. Note as well the separation: the epithet begins

the line and the "joke" (giants) ends it. The epithet may be a hyper-archaism, appearing often in Ap. Rhodes (frequently with Cyclopes, e.g. 1.510: γηγενέες Κύκλωπες ἐκαρτύναντο κεραυνῷ). But cf. early archaic Eumelus of Corinth (fr. 19: γηγενέες· φρίξεν δὲ περὶ στιβαροῖς σακέεσσι); and late fifth century Antimachus (γηγενέας τε θεοὺς προτερηγενέας Τιτῆνας). Forms of the adjective appear with some frequency among the tragedians (Aeschylus; Euripides), Aristophanes, and Plato.

Γιγάντων: For the giants, see Hes. *Th.* 185 (γείνατ᾽ Ἐρινῦς τε κρατερὰς μεγάλους τε Γίγαντας. "[And Gaia] gave birth to the strong furies and the mighty giants") and fr. 43a 65 (ἐν Φλέγρηι δ]ὲ Γίγαντας ὑπερφιάλους κατέπεφ[νε. "He killed the arrogant giants in Phlegrê"). In addition to being comedic, the comparison is also pejorative (giants were arrogant and challenged the cosmic order).

μιμούμενοι: "imitating, mimicking"; the participle does not occur in hexameter poetry.

8   ὡς λόγος: "as the story goes" *vel sim.* Some MSS have *epos* instead of λόγος (which would be more Homeric). The phrase ὡς λόγος probably draws on the language of fable. Post-classical fable traditions conventionally summarize the tale's moral with phrases like "the *logos teaches/makes clear*" etc. (ὁ λόγος δηλοῖ / διδάσκει / ἁρμόζει). Other aspects of the introduction of the tale strengthen the resonance with fable. As Adrados (1998: 383–4) demonstrates, fables are often introduced with an imperfect (e.g. ἦν γὰρ χρόνος πότε, Pl., *Protagoras*, 370c: ὅτε φωνήεντα ἦν τὰ ζῷα) combined with markers of indefinite time (e.g. πότε; see Μῦς ποτε on line 8 below) and person (τις; cf. Archilochus fr. 174: αἶνός τις ἀνθρώπων ὅδε).

ἔην: Uncontracted 3rd person singular imperfect of εἰμί.

τοίην δ᾽ ἔχεν ἀρχήν: "this sort of beginning." This creates a ring structure with the beginning of the proem (Ἀρχόμενος; on ring structures and oral poetry, see Minchin 1995; Minchin 2001: 181–202) and also the general sort of introduction that is not uncommon to the transition to the actual narrative. The use of the qualitative τοίην, rather than τήνδε, may mark the following tale as especially divorced from specific context. In addition, the indefiniteness of τοίην may complement the fabular style mentioned above on line 7. This level of indefiniteness, however, may be parodic: once the story begins in classical fable, the narration is fairly straightforward, without this type of hedging.

9–64 The poem continues with the language of fable and the meeting of a frog and mouse near the edge of a marsh. The two question each other in mock heroic style, though the mouse engages in extensive comic boasting about the superiority of his diet. The frog invites the mouse for a ride across his pond.

9 Ποτε: this indefinite temporal adverb answers both the temporal echo of the last line (Μῦς ποτε) and the interrogative πῶς (line 6), recalling the "once-upon-a time" formula common to *fabulae* (see the introduction; see van Dijk 1997: 125 for a full bibliography). For a temporal starting point in epic, consider *Il.* 1.6 ("from when those two first stood apart in strife": ἐξ οὗ δὴ τὰ πρῶτα διαστήτην ἐρίσαντε) or the *Cyp.*1.1: "there was a time when the tribes of men were always weighing down the earth" (ἦν ὅτε μυρία φῦλα κατὰ χθόνα πλαζόμεν' αἰεὶ).

γαλέης κίνδυνον ἀλύξας: Psicharpax's escape from a weasel is not wholly necessary to the story, but it facilitates the introduction of the two worst mouse-antagonists in the fabulist tradition: frogs and "weasels. (See, for example, Aesop *Fab.* 239: Ποτὲ δὲ γαλαῖ ἐμάχοντο πρὸς μύας κατατροποῦσαι αὐτοὺς καὶ ἀναιροῦσαι. "Once the weasels fought against the mice, turning them to flight and seizing them.") Moreover, Psicharpax's recent escape from death heightens the pathos of his "accidental" drowning.

ἀλύξας: Adrados (1998: 385–6) isolates an initial use of participle as characteristic of fables (and cites this line specifically).

διψαλέος: "thirsty" cf. English dipsomania. During a reading of this commentary, William C. Shrout has suggested that this should be compared to the snake in Nicander's *Theriaca* (φωλειοῦ λοχάδην ὑπὸ γωλεὰ διψὰς ἰαύῃ, 125).

γαλέης: "Weasel or Cat"; LSJ Greek Lexicon defines γαλέη as "a name given to various animals of the *weasel* kind, *weasel, marten, polecat,* or *foumart.*" Glei (*ad loc.*) suggests that the meaning of γαλέη is unclear, meaning either "weasel" or "cat." The modern sense would naturally incline to the selection of the cat as the mouse's natural enemy, but this would be anachronistic. The evidence strongly suggests that the animal in question here is, in fact, a weasel. Ludwich, in his commentary (*ad loc.*) explains that the confusion of the weasel and the cat was a product of the scholiasts in late antiquity and later interpreters of the poem; indeed, he notes that lexical appearances of "cats" as we know them are not easy to find before the fourth century CE. In ancient Greece, weasels (probably closer to our ferret) were commonly domesticated and used for rodent control. Cats (Gr. αἴλουρος, "cat," *felix domesticus* whence our *ailourophobia,* "fear of cats") became more common during the Hellenistic period and later; it is clear from the language and literature that weasels fulfilled their cultural (and poetic) roles. The overlap between the function of the animals leads to confusion: sometimes the word for weasel (γαλέη, *galea*) may actually indicate a *cat.* Cats appear in Greek imagery as early as the sixth century BCE; they are still paired with weasels by the time of Plutarch (first Century CE) and *gatta* appears in Greek by the fifth century CE. For Greek and Roman domesticated pets, see Lazenby 1949.

The *Vitae Aesopi* (both G and W) have αἴλουρος for the animal we would recognize as a cat. The *domestic* weasel appears to have been smaller than the wild one. The physician Philumenus (date uncertain) describes the shrew as <ἡ> μυγαλῆ ἀπεικάζεται μὲν κατὰ τὴν χρόαν τῇ κατοικιδίῳ γαλῇ, κατὰ δὲ τὸ μέγεθος μυΐ, ὅθεν καὶ σύνθετον τὸ ὄνομα ἔχει. "The shrew is compared in its skin to the domestic weasel, but in its size to the mouse, from which it derives its compound name." (Philumenus, *de venenatis animalibus eorumque remediis,* 33.1.)

Herodotus, in describing the wild animals of Libya (*His.* 4.192), proceeds immediately from the discussion of mice to the discussion of wild weasels. Strabo (*Geog.* 3.2.6) explains that Libyan weasels were used specifically for driving hole-dwelling animals out of their abodes. This is in accordance with the description which Troxartes later gives in the *BM* (lines 113–114) of the death of one of his sons. Cf. Phaedrus 1.24, 1 for a similar use for the domesticated weasel.

10   ἐν λίμνῃ: "in the pond, marsh"; with πλησίον the action seems overdetermined. The choice of water-body may have some conventional connection with frogs in the fifth century BCE and later. The word λίμνη has fairly extensive meanings: it refers to several different bodies of water, including lakes, ponds, swamps, and marshes. The parodist Matro even uses it to refer to the sea. Bliquez (1977) notes that this may be a reference to the Athenian neighborhood ἐν Λίμναις (his conjecture has not gained wide acceptance.)

λίχνον: "Greedy." This is not an epic word; its earliest attestation is Eur., *Hip.* 913 (ἡ γὰρ ποθοῦσα πάντα καρδία κλύειν / κἂν τοῖς κακοῖσι λίχνος οὖσ᾽ ἁλίσκεται). Note the alliteration πλησίον ἐν λίμνῃ λίχνον followed by the near homoioteleuton (quasi-rhyming) between the syllable end after λίχνον and the line final γένειον. The repeated L-sounds could be meant to mimic the sound of drinking.

γένειον: "Chin"; Homeric, often at the end of a line; cf. *Il.* 24.516 (οἰκτίρων πολιόν τε κάρη πολιόν τε γένειον).

11   τερπόμενος: "taking pleasure in." In the active this verb means "to cause delight." In the middle it is the intransitive (quasi-reflexive). Achilles is described at *Iliad* 9.187: τὸν δ᾽ εὗρον φρένα τερπόμενον φόρμιγγι λιγείῃ. Similarly so in the *Odyssey*, Odysseus is afforded the chance to delight in the song of the Sirens (12.52): ὄφρα κε τερπόμενος ὄπ᾽ ἀκούσῃς Σειρήνοιϊν.

μελιηδέϊ: "honey-sweet"; usually of wine, see *Il.* 4.346, 18.345; and grain (10.569) and fruit (18.568) but also of sleep: *Od.* 19.551.

12 λιμνόχαρις: "pond-loving"; this epithet occurs only in the *BM*. Similar compounds are readily formed in early Greek poetry. Cf. the daughters of Nereus in Hesiod's *Theogony* (240–63; e.g. "Wave-swift" Κυμοθόη, 245; "Sea-conveyer" Ποντοπόρεια, 256; and "Sandy" Ποντοπόρεια, 257). Ludwich records conjectures λιμνοκράτης or λιμνοκράτωρ in place of λιμνόχαρις.

πολύφημος: "very famous"; "much known." This epithet may recall the Cyclops of the *Odyssey* (see Sens 2005: 241–2); on that ground, this reading is to be preferred over the comparatively flat πολύφωνος. However, it is possible that an editor or copyist inserted the famous reference. However, see line 19, where Physignathos was fathered by Πηλεύς ("Muddy," and not the famous father of Achilles). This suggests that the incorporation of famous Homeric character names in novel ways is part of the parody's general poetic program. In addition (Sens 2005), the contexts of the *BM* and the *Odyssey* may have humorous apposition: Like the Cyclops, the frog is a water-boundried creature whose way of life threatens the protagonist. Diogenianus, the late paroemiographer, informs us that the frogs of Seriphos were silent: Βάτραχος Σερίφιος: ἐπὶ τῶν ἀφώνων. Οἱ γὰρ ἐν Σερίφῳ βάτραχοι οὐ φθέγγονται.

ἔπος δ᾽ ἐφθέγξατο τοῖον: "He uttered this kind of speech." A rather un-Homeric speech-introduction. The word *epos* occurs in speech introduction (e.g. *Il.* 1.361; 3.198); as does φθέγγω at *Od.* 21.192 (φθεγξάμενός σφ᾽ ἐπέεσσι προσηύδα μειλιχίοισι; cf. *Od.* 14.292), and *Il.* 21.123 (ἀνέρι εἰσάμενος, βαθέης δ᾽ ἐκ φθέγξατο δίνης) where it falls in the same position. But the combination ἔπος. . .τοῖον is odd. On speech introductions as a feature of oral-composition, see Edwards 1970 and Riggsby 1992. See also the note on line 8. Camerotto (1992: 14) compares this line to Non. *Dion.* 4.601 (παρθενικὴ δὲ πιοῦσα τόσην ἐφθέγξατο φωνήν) and Moschus 2.134 (ἀμφί ἑ παπτήνασα τόσην ἀνενείκατο φωνήν). The use of forms of τοῖος shifts the narrative into a less literal mode. Perhaps the suggestion is that no human could know exactly what a frog or mouse said, and therefore the author will not attempt to give a literal transcription, but will fashion the speeches so as to suit the speaker and occasion.

13   Ξεῖνε τίς εἶ; πόθεν ἦλθες ἐπ' ἠϊόνας; τίς ὁ φύσας; "Who are you
and where are you from and who are you parents" is formulaic, see
Od. 3.71 (=9.242: ὦ ξεῖνοι, τίνες ἐστέ; πόθεν πλεῖθ' ὑγρὰ κέλευθα) and
14.187 (τίς πόθεν εἰς ἀνδρῶν; πόθι τοι πόλις ἠδὲ τοκῆες;). These lines
may have become proverbial: Seneca the Younger has the deceased
emperor Claudius quoting the *Odyssey* at *Apocolocyntosis* 5.

φύσας: "who sowed you?" (i.e. "who is your father"); Glei (119) notes
that this is not epic usage, though it is common in tragedy. This suggests
a date of composition subsequent to the fifth century BCE. The phrase
was likely selected for the wordplay with **Φυσίγναθος**.

14   ἀλήθευσον: This verb does not appear in Homer. However, see
Plato, *Rep.* 413.a.6: ἦ οὐ τὸ μὲν ἐψεῦσθαι τῆς ἀληθείας κακόν, τὸ δὲ
ἀληθεύειν ἀγαθόν; ἦ οὐ τὸ τὰ ὄντα δοξάζειν ἀληθεύειν δοκεῖ σοι εἶναι;
("Doesn't it seem right to you that it is wrong to be deceived of the
truth, but right to hear it? And isn't it that case that to discuss this as
they really are is to speak the truth?"). For the sentiment, however,
consider the repeated line ἀλλ' ἄγε μοι τόδε εἰπὲ καὶ ἀτρεκέως
κατάλεξον ("Come, tell me this and tell it all to me truly," e.g. *Od.* 4.486)
or *Od.* 15.263 (εἰπέ μοι εἰρομένῳ νημερτέα μηδ' ἐπικεύσῃς. "Tell me
truly what I have asked and don't hide it").

μὴ ψευδόμενόν σε νοήσω: "so that I may not know you are a liar."
Negative purpose clause with a future: μή alone can signal a purpose
clause (like Latin *ne*) see Smyth §2193.

ψευδόμενον: "Liar"; more as a simple substantive than subordinating
participle.

νοήσω: This form ends the line four times in the *Iliad*. The future
indicative may appear in purpose clauses, see Smyth §2203. But there is
morphological ambiguity between the aorist subjunctive and future
indicative.

15   εἰ γάρ σε γνοίην φίλον ἄξιον ἐς δόμον ἄξω· Future more vivid
with an optative protasis with εἰ. See Smyth §2359.

γνοίην: First person aorist optative of γιγνώσκω.

ἄξιον ἐς δόμον ἄξω: Camerotto (1992: 15) compares the phrase to *Od*. 18.328 (...ἐς δόμον ἐλθών) and notes that 119 (ἐς βυθὸν ἄξας) in this poem is an ironic interplay with this line. Such variation, according to Camerotto, indicates a literary origin. The use of ἄξιον...ἄξω is more than an idle pun. The adjective ἄξιος means "worthy" by a general extension of its original verbal significance, "weighing down the scale." This latter meaning can be traced back to a very specific use of ἄγω, to "draw down in the scales..." (See LSJ, definition VI.) The pun may foreshadow Psicharpax's fate in drowning. Indeed, a suspicious reader might suspect that Physignathus intends the mouse harm all along.

16 δῶρα δέ τοι δώσω: Cognate accusatives are common in early Greek poetry (see *Od*. 4.589: καὶ τότε σ' εὖ πέμψω, δώσω δέ τοι ἀγλαὰ δῶρα. "And then I will send you off well and I will give you glorious gifts.").

ξεινήϊα: For "guest-gifts." Homer offers a shortened form (e.g. *Od*. 9.517...ἵνα τοι πὰρ ξείνια θείω) but this neuter plural appears five times in the *Iliad* and the *Odyssey* (e.g. 24.273) and twice in this metrical position (*Il*. 4.33; 24.273).

πολλὰ καὶ ἐσθλά: Hendiadys: "many fine guest-gifts." The pairing appears in this position seven times in the *Iliad* and *Odyssey* (e.g. *Od*. 2.312).

17 βασιλεύς: "king, lord." In Homer, most heroes are also *basileis*, that is, leaders of their community. Nowhere in the *Iliad* and the *Odyssey* does any hero introduce himself as *basileus*. Surely the unfolding phrase ("I am I, King Physignathos...") would sound especially humorous to those steeped in the epic tradition. For the semantic range of *basileus* and kingship before the Archaic Age, see Drews 1983; for distinctions between *basileus* and *wanax*, cf. Palaima 1995.

The issue of kingship among the frogs (and their inability to select a leader) is a topic in Aesop's *Fables*, 44: βάτραχοι λυπούμενοι ἐπὶ τῇ ἑαυτῶν ἀναρχίᾳ πρέσβεις ἔπεμψαν πρὸς τὸν Δία δεόμενοι βασιλέα αὐτοῖς παρασχεῖν. ὁ δὲ συνιδὼν αὐτῶν τὴν εὐήθειαν ξύλον εἰς τὴν λίμνην καθῆκε. καὶ οἱ βάτραχοι τὸ μὲν πρῶτον καταπλαγέντες τὸν ψόφον εἰς τὰ βάθη τῆς λίμνης ἐνέδυσαν, ὕστερον δέ, ὡς ἀκίνητον ἦν τὸ ξύλον, ἀναδύντες εἰς τοσοῦτο καταφρονήσεως ἦλθον ὡς καὶ ἐπιβαίνοντες αὐτῷ ἐπικαθέζεσθαι. ἀναξιοπαθοῦντες δὲ τοιοῦτον ἔχειν βασιλέα ἧκον ἐκ δευτέρου πρὸς τὸν Δία καὶ τοῦτον παρεκάλουν ἀλλάξαι αὐτοῖς τὸν ἄρχοντα. τὸν γὰρ πρῶτον λίαν εἶναι νωχελῆ. καὶ ὁ Ζεὺς ἀγανακτήσας κατ' αὐτῶν ὕδραν αὐτοῖς ἔπεμψεν, ὑφ' ἧς συλλαμβανόμενοι κατησθίοντο.

"The frogs, distressed by the anarchy prevailing among them, sent ambassadors to Zeus asking him to give them a king. He took note of their silliness and threw down a piece of wood into the pond. The frogs, terrified at first by the loud sound, submerged themselves in the depths of the pond. Later, when the piece of wood was still, they came back up and rose to such a height of insolence that they mounted the wood and perched upon it. Deeming this king unworthy of them, they sent messengers to Zeus, asking him to change their king, because the first one was too lazy. Zeus was irritated by this, so he sent them a snake as king, by whom they were all snatched up and eaten."

λίμνην: "pond." See above, note 10.

18 τιμῶμαι: Contract of τιμα-ομαι. Honor, *timê*, is an important indication of the social esteem held by heroes in Homer. See Wilson 2002.

ἡγούμενος: "leader"; a present participle likely functioning as a simple substanative, i.e. "I am honored as leader of the frogs."

ἤματα πάντα: "for all time" common formula for "forever." Cf. *Il.* 8.539 ("I would be deathless and ageless for all days"; εἴην ἀθάνατος καὶ ἀγήρως ἤματα πάντα).

19 Πηλεύς: "Mudman"; sounds like Achilles' father, Peleus. Using Achilles' patronym in an unexpected way may be a trope of parody. The parodist Euboeus is said by Athenaeus to have written in the *Battle of the Bathmen* (τῆς τῶν βαλανέων μάχης) when a potter argues with a barber over a woman "don't you, though so noble, rob this man, nor you, son of Peleus" (μήτε σὺ τόνδ᾽ ἀγαθός περ ἐὼν ἀποαίρεο, κουρεῦ, / μήτε σύ, Πηλείδη (*Deipn*. 699b). The frog here may also be positioned as an Achilles-character as a child of water-based mother (see "Watermistress," below) and as someone who excels all others (see ἔξοχον ἄλλων). Most (1993: 38–9) sees the rivalry between Achilles and the *Iliad*, on the one hand, with Odysseus and the *Odyssey* on the other, as possibly played out through the mouse and frog. For the meeting of the frog and mouse as echoing the meeting of Odysseus with the Cyclops, see Sens 2005: 237–44.

ἀνεθρέψατο: There is a variant ποτ᾽ εγείνατο. The form ἀνεθρέψατο does not occur in Homer, but the variant occurs in the same position at *Od*. 1.233, 4.13, and 21.172. In such cases, however, the mother is the subject of the verb εγείνατο.

Ὑδρομεδούσῃ: "Watermistress."

20 μιχθεὶς ἐν φιλότητι: Lit: "after mingling in love," the typical idiom for "having sex" (cf. *Il*. 2.232; *Th*. 823 for this position). Describing one's own conception, however, is more typical of the genealogical descriptions to be found in Hesiod and the Homeric Hymns. Cf. Hom. *Hymn to Hermes* where the god is born, creates the lyre and then sings of how Zeus and Maia conceived him (58–9). The mixing of heroic and hymnic registers would probably be clear to ancient audiences.

παρ᾽ ὄχθας Ἠριδανοῖο: The textual tradition provides ὠκεανοῖο as an alternative to Ἠριδανοῖο. The geographic location provides extra flavor. (Yet, the variant is grander.) The Eridanos is not known to Homer, but Glei (*ad loc*.) notes that in Lucian's *Dialogues of the Gods* 25.3, the water of the Eridanos became warmer after Phaethon fell into it. A scholiast suggests that this makes it optimal for frog-breeding. The identification of this location with a stream in Athens may serve to localize the poem in an Attic tradition; see Bliquez 1977: 20.

21 καλόν: Both here and at line 162, the alpha of καλόν must be taken as long in order to resolve the scansion of the line. For the line's sentiment, consider Achilles' words to Lykaon in the *Iliad*: "don't you see what kind of a man I am, both good-looking and large?" (οὐχ ὁράᾳς οἷος καὶ ἐγὼ καλός τε μέγας τε; *Il*. 21.108)

ἔξοχον ἄλλων: "beyond the rest." This phrase occurs only in line-final position in the *Iliad*, six times (6.194, 9.631, 9.641, 13.499, 17.358, 20.184) and three times in the *Odyssey*, (5.118, 6.158, 19.247).

22 σκηπτοῦχον: "scepter-bearing." Three classes of people hold the σκῆπτρον in Homer: kings, priests, and heralds. Agamemnon threatens Chryses by suggesting that his heraldic scepter will not avail him against regal rage: μή νύ τοι οὐ χραίσμῃ σκῆπτρον καὶ στέμμα θεοῖο· (*Il*. 1.28). Later, while reproaching Agamemnon, Achilles swears by his own scepter: ναὶ μὰ τόδε σκῆπτρον (*Il*. 1.234).

μαχητήν: "warrior" from μαχητής; in this position, see *Il*. 16.186 (Εὔδωρον πέρι μὲν θείειν ταχὺν ἠδὲ μαχητήν). The combination of scepter-bearing king and warrior (with adjectives from the prior line) is parodic: the frog appears to be comparing the mouse to a king (like Agamemnon) and a warrior (like Achilles).

Lines 22–3 are omitted by some MSS. See on line 27, as well as the speech of Troxartes in 110–20. Accepting these lines as interpolations requires a thematic balancing to establish Psicharpax's status among the mice. This may be the only place in which he is assigned royal lineage.

23 ἔμμεναι: Epic lengthened infinitive for εἶναι, postponed somewhat harshly from the indirect statement initiated at line 21 (καὶ σὲ δ᾽ ὁρῶ...). Cf. Hes. *Works and Days*, 272: ἔμμεναι, εἰ μείζω γε δίκην ἀδικώτερος ἕξει.

ἑήν: Homeric reflexive possessive pronoun: "his own."

ἀγόρευε: Homer does not use this verb for genealogical explication; in most instances, it refers to communication of plans or counsels, or alternatively the interpretation of omens. The parodist likely uses the verb to mark the frog's bombastic and elevated style.

24   Ψιχάρπαξ: Note the abrupt introduction the name of Psiparchax ("crumbsnatcher") before he reveals it in line 27.

ἀπαμείβετο φώνησέν τε: basically just "answer"; a typical formula in Homer. See *Od.* 7.298 (ἀπαμείβετο φώνησέν τε); cf. *Il.* 20.199. For typical answering formulas in Homer, see Edwards 1969.

25   τίπτε: τί, "why?". This line may recall the exchange between Glaukos and Diomedes in the *Iliad*. (See Glei 1984: 124; Fusillo 1988: 92–3; and Sens 2005: 235–7.) The two meet in the midst of battle and the latter has been warned not to attack any more gods (he wounded Aphrodite in book 5). Diomedes asks Glaukos his name and his parentage and Glaukos responds "son of Tydeus, why do you ask me my family history?" (Τυδείδη μεγάθυμε τί ἢ γενεὴν ἐρεείνεις; 6.145).

τοὐμόν: τὸ ἐμόν

ζητεῖς: This usage is un-Homeric. In Homer, the verb describes concrete action of actual pursuit, rather than the metaphorical "pursuit" of questioning. See *Il.* 14.258:... ἐμὲ δ᾽ ἔξοχα πάντων / ζήτει. More commonly, Homer would employ a word such as ἐρεείνεις. Consider *Il.*6.145: Τυδείδη μεγάθυμε τί ἢ γενεὴν ἐρεείνεις;

The oldest MSS read τὸ δ᾽ ἄσημον ἄπασιν in place of δῆλον δ᾽ ἐν ἄπασιν. The older reading fails to render the proper sense: Psicharpax would hardly be surprised that Physignathos must ask his name if it were indeed undistinguished among all. On this basis, Ludwich conjectured εὔσημον in place of ἄσημον.

26   οὐρανίοις πετεηνοῖς: "flying things in the sky"; periphrasis for birds. cf. Hes. *Works and Days* 277: ἰχθύσι μὲν καὶ θηρσὶ καὶ οἰωνοῖς πετεηνοῖς. The adjective in epic is more often associated with divine

creatures. E.g. *Il.* 17.195 (Πηλεΐδεω ᾿Αχιλῆος ἅ οἱ θεοὶ οὐρανίωνες) and is thus likely humorous here.

27 κικλήσκομαι: "I am called"; common in Homer with an iterative sense—cf. "My name is Nobody: my mother and father and all the rest of my companions call me Nobody" Οὖτις ἐμοί γ᾿ ὄνομα· Οὖτιν δέ με κικλήσκουσι / μήτηρ ἠδὲ πατὴρ ἠδ᾿ ἄλλοι πάντες ἑταῖροι.' (*Od.* 9.366-7).

εἰμὶ δὲ κοῦρος: Not the most common word for "son" in Homer (υἱός). But *kourê* is frequently used for daughters (cf. *Il.* 1.98: πρίν γ᾿ ἀπὸ πατρὶ φίλῳ δόμεναι ἑλικώπιδα κούρην).

The use of κοῦρος is jarring after hearing from Physignathos in line 22 that Psicharpax was manifestly a sceptre-bearing king and warrior in battle; the semantic range of κοῦρος extends from infancy to late adolescence, but it does not seem to have been used as a generic substitute for υἱός. This may be intentionally absurd; more likely, it lends some support to the omission of lines 22-3. (See also the 110-20, where no mention is made of Psicharpax's royalty.) Indeed, the possibly interpolated lines at 22-3 provide the only hint that Psicharpax is the king of the mice. It is possible Psicharpax's royal lineage was introduced to create parity with Physignathos.

28 Τρωξάρταο: This masculine genitive singular in -αο occurs nearly 200 times in the *Iliad* (see Janko 2012: 29) for an occurence rate of 1:80 lines. In the *BM*, it only occurs again with the same word, for a ratio of 1:151 (compare the *Hymn to Demeter* which shows a ratio of 1:124).

μεγαλήτορος: "Great-hearted," common in Homer. See *Il.*2.547 (δῆμον ᾿Ερεχθῆος μεγαλήτορος, ὅν ποτ᾿ ᾿Αθήνη).

29 Λειχομύλη: "Millstone licker" (λείχω + μύλη); The mice are, in general, given names which hint at their inclination to eating. Compounds in Λειχ- (cp. English "lick") occur in three mouse names:

Λειχομύλη, Λειχοπίναξ, and Λειχήνωρ. Not dissimilar is the naming of Phaiakians: the sea-faring people have a princess named Nausikaa ("excelling in ships" or "ship-burner") and forebears like Nausithoos ("swift-ship," cf. *Od.* 6.7).

Πτερνοτρώκτου: "Hamnibbler" (Πτέρνα + τρώκτος, verbal adjective from τρώγω). Πτέρνα is a mock-epic form adapted from Lat. *perna*. See LSJ *s.v.* Forms occur at 29, 37, 224. The parodist Matro uses κωλή (κωλῆν δ᾽ ὡς εἶδον, ὡς ἔτρεμον (Ξ 294)· ἐν δὲ σίναπυ). Jackob Wackernagel (1916) identifies the repeated use of πτέρν- compounds throughout the poem as evidence for a later date. As Wackernagel points out, this use of πτέρνα is entirely unattested in Greek literature prior to the *BM*. The equivalent *perna*, however, was in common use among Latin authors *c.* third century BCE.

30   γείνατο: from γίγνομαι; cf. ln. 19. which has ποτ᾽ ἐγείνατο as an alternative to ἀνεθρέψατο. The preference of ποτ᾽ ἐγείνατο in 19 is supported by the reading here.

ἐν καλύβῃ: "hidey-hole," cf. *kaluptô*, "hide." This word does not appear to be used before Thucydides. In later Greek, this term can also mean a shelter made of branches.

βρωτοῖς: Glei (*ad loc.*) suggests that this word is suspect because it effectively doubles the sense of line 31. However, there is no *prima facie* reason for suspecting a word solely because of redunancy. In Homer, βρῶσις is preferred.

31   σύκοις καὶ καρύοις: "figs and nuts."

ἐδέσμασι παντοδαποῖσιν: "all kinds of treats"; ἐδέσμα is not found as early as Homer. It rises in popularity in the fourth century BCE (appearing in Xenophon and Aristotle). Forms appear in Aesop's *Fabulae* as well. The adjective παντοδαποῖσιν is also not typical, but it appears in one fragment of Sappho (152). The mouse expatiates on his diet and may recall some of the excessive consumption used to characterize figures in comedy. For this phrase, cf. Matro of Pitane's "all kinds of food" (εἴδατα πάντα). For an exploration of the use of food in Attic comedy, see Wilkins 2000.

32 φίλον ποιῇ: Deliberative subjunctive using the second person (relatively rare, see Smyth §1805b). The abstract use of ποίειν is un-Homeric. It is also highly irregular to see φίλον used as a substantive in this way.

τόν: Functions here as a relative with με as its antecedent: "When I am not the same in nature."

φύσιν: "Nature, character." This is non-Homeric; *phúsis* seems to draw on later scientific and philosophical treatments. Cf. Aesch., *Suppl.* 496: μορφῆς δ᾽ οὐχ ὁμόστολος φύσις. Alternatively, the sense may simply mean "form." Cf. Aesop, *Fab.* 50: καὶ ἡ θεὸς ἀγανακτήσασα κατ᾽ αὐτῆς πάλιν αὐτὴν εἰς τὴν ἀρχαίαν φύσιν ἀποκατέστησεν. "The goddess was irritated with her, and changed her back to her original form." The central point of this fable was that the weasel, though changed in *appearance*, did not change in *nature* or *inner character* (described in the fable as *tropon*); this occasions Aphrodite's anger, leading her to change the weasel back to its original *form* (φύσιν). If the *BM* shares substantial lexical similarities with the fabulist tradition, this passage may help to properly explain the exact force of φύσιν here.

ὁμοῖον: "The same"; Homeric poetry uses this word to express equality more than similarity. Cf. *Il.* 2.553–4: τῷ δ᾽ οὔ πώ τις ὁμοῖος ἐπιχθόνιος γένετ᾽ ἀνὴρ / κοσμῆσαι ἵππους τε καὶ ἀνέρας ἀσπιδιώτας·

33 σοί: dative of possession with βίος.

βίος: This abstract use of βίος, "way/mode of life," is characteristic of later Greek thought but evident already in Hesiod; e.g. *Works and Days*, 42: Κρύψαντες γὰρ ἔχουσι θεοὶ βίον ἀνθρώποισιν.

ἐν ὕδασιν: "your life is in the water." Homer does not use plural forms of ὕδωρ. Apollonius Rhodes does, see 3.876: οἵη δέ, λιαροῖσιν ἐν ὕδασι Παρθενίοιο.

αὐτὰρ ἔμοιγε: The combination ἔμοιγε ends lines in Homer and αὐτὰρ often appears in the penultimate position; this particular combination does not occur.

34   ὅσσα: ὅσα, lengthened for metrical reasons. See the introduction.

ἔθος: Does not occur in Homer. The use of *ethos* + infinitive seems comparatively late. Cf. Dem., *Adversus Leptinem* 40.2.

λήθει: From λανθάνω. In Homeric usage, this verb does not mean to evade or escape literally. It often signifies that a thing or person will not escape someone's mind or notice. Cf. *Il.* 23.323-5 αἰεὶ τέρμ' ὁρόων στρέφει ἐγγύθεν, οὐδέ ἑ λήθει. ὅππως τὸ πρῶτον τανύσῃ βοέοισιν ἱμᾶσιν. This, combined with the comment of Physignathos at line 57, provides an excellent characterization of Psicharpax, begun in line 10, where he is described as having a *likhnon geneion*, a gluttonous mouth. It is perhaps significant that the king of mice is described as voracious and greedy in an oral sense, in contrast to the king of the frogs, who swells at the jaw for another reason (his croaking and bombast!).

35   ἄρτος τρισκοπάνιστος: "thrice-kneaded bread" (τρίς + κοπανίζω), a hapax legomenon; also available is δυσκοπάνιστος ("ill-kneaded bread"; cf. Glei and Wölke *ad loc.*).

ἀπ' εὐκύκλου κανέοιο: "well-woven basket." The adjective *eukuklos* modifies shields in the *Iliad* (5.453) and wagons/chariots in the *Odyssey* (cf. 6.58). The use of this adjective for basket is certainly mock-heroic. The combination of martial language and bread perhaps recalls lines like those of Archilochus fr. 2: "My kneaded bread is in my spear / Ismarian wine is in my spear / and I drink while leaning on my spear" (ἐν δορὶ μέν μοι μᾶζα μεμαγμένη, ἐν δορὶ δ' οἶνος / Ἰσμαρικός· πίνω δ' ἐν δορὶ κεκλιμένος). Where Archilochus subverts by mixing martial and sympotic language, the parodist applies epic diction to more mundane objects.

κανέοιο: -οιο an Archaic genitive singular. The uncontracted κανέοιο occurs in the *Odyssey* in connection too with bread: *Od.* 17.343-344:

ἄρτον τ᾽ οὖλον ἑλὼν περικαλλέος ἐκ κανέοιο / καὶ κρέας, ὥς οἱ χεῖρες ἐχάνδανον ἀμφιβαλόντι·

36 πλακοῦς: "flat-cake." This was often offered as part of a sacrifice or simple sacrifices to gods. In his parody, Matro of Pitane is stuffed but cannot refuse the proffered cakes: "When I saw entering the baked child of Demeter, that cake, how could I then hold back from the divine cake?" (Δήμητρος παῖδ᾽ ὀπτὸν ἐπεισελθόντα πλακοῦντα / πῶς ἂν ἔπειτα πλακοῦντος ἐγὼ θείου ἀπεχοίμην, 117–18).

τανύπεπλος: "flowing-robed," often used of female characters in Homer; here, probably humorous in describing the cake.

σησαμότυρον: "sesame-cheese." The sesame-cake was sometimes part of a wedding feast in Athens. See Aristophanes' Peace 869: ὁ πλακοῦς πέπεπται, σησαμῆ ξυμπλάττεται.

37 οὐ τόμος ἐκ πτέρνης: "slice of ham"; τόμος is from τέμνω, "to cut." In referring to food, τόμος was common in Old and Middle Comedy. See Alexis fr. 1 (Χορδαρίου τόμος ἧκε καὶ περίκομμά τι); Eubulus, fr. 15.7 (νενωγάλισται σεμνὸς ἀλλᾶντος τόμος); and Cratinus fr. 192 (ὡς λεπτός, ἤ δ᾽ ὅς, ἔσθ᾽ ὁ τῆς χορδῆς τόμος). Cf. Pherecrates fr. 45.5 and Mnesimachus fr. 4.14.

πτέρνης: "Ham"; mock-epic form adapted from Lat. perna. See LSJ s.v. See above on line 29.

οὐχ ἥπατα λευκοχίτωνα: "white-girded liver": another humorous application of feminine clothing to food. Cf. πλακοῦς τανύπεπλος, 36. The adjective is probably late.

38 νεόπηκτος: "Newly-curdled"; πήγνυμι can mean "to make chesse by curdling milk" on the parallel of stiffening limbs or materials. See LSJ s.v. III. This compound is also rather late.

ἀπὸ γλυκεροῖο γάλακτος: "from sweet-milk." This combination occurs in the Odyssey (τυροῦ καὶ κρειῶν οὐδὲ γλυκεροῖο γάλακτος, 4.88).

39　οὐ χρηστὸν μελίτωμα: "wholesome honey-cake." A scholiast to Aristophanes' *Knights* 345 cites this line: "For we call a treat 'wholesome' when it is well-made" (χρηστὸν γὰρ ἔδεσμα καλοῦμεν τὸ εὖ ἠρτυμένον. καὶ Ὅμηρος "οὐ χρηστὸν μελίτωμα, τὸ καὶ μάκαρες ποθέουσιν").

40　οὐδ' ὅσα πρὸς θοίνας: "However much the cooks prepare for a feast." Typically πρός + accusative denotes motion, but it can indicate general relation to or for, as in purpose, see Smyth §1695.3b.

μερόπων: "mortals"; on this adjective, see above on line 5.

μάγειροι: "cooks," popular figures in comedy and post-classical Greek but extant as early as Herodotus (6.60.2). For cooks in parody, cf. Matro fr. 1.8 (τῷ δὲ μάγειροι μὲν φόρεον πλῆσάν τε τραπέζας).

41　κοσμοῦντες χύτρας: "arranging/seasoning the dishes." The active of *kosméô* is not extant in Homer in participle form. The passive κοσμηθέντες occurs in both the *Iliad* and the *Odyssey*.

ἀρτύμασι παντοδαποῖσιν: "every kind of dressing/spice." See line 31 (ἐδέσμασι παντοδαποῖσιν) above.

42–53: These lines are omitted by our oldest MSS but are part of the *Prosodia Byzantina* (metrically problematic lines whose interpolation is dated to the Byzantine period). Fusillo 1988 argues there are good reasons to consider all of these lines inserted in the twelfth century. Lines 44, 45, and 47 are ametrical. We have included the lines for their stylistic difference and interest. The content is obviously satirical and a break from the culinary catalogue. Although the speech returns to the subject of food after at line 54, this contested section adds a "heroic" aspect to the characterization of Crumbthief. Martial language with Iliadic flavoring is prominent in this section.

42　ἀπέφυγον: An Attic form. ἀπὸ does not occur in compounds with φεύγω in Homer.

πτολέμοιο: πολέμου; the form is Homeric, e.g. *Il.* 7.232 (καὶ πολέες· ἀλλ' ἄρχε μάχης ἠδὲ πτολέμοιο). In the non-Byzantine segments, however, the parodist prefers the other form: e.g. 123: καὶ τοὺς μέν ῥ' ἐκόρυσσεν Ἄρης πολέμοιο μεμηλώς, which is an adaptation of a Homeric formula (13.469: βῆ δὲ μετ' Ἰδομενῆα μέγα πτολέμοιο μεμηλώς). Both spellings coexist in Homer. In this context, however, πτολέμοιο is likely a hyperarchaism.

ἀϋτήν: "Battle cry"; the language clearly draws on martial Homeric passages.

43 μετὰ μῶλον: "into the fray," often in the phrase "fray of Ares" (μῶλον Ἄρηος, 18.134). For this phrase, with the verb "to go," cf. *Il.* 18.188 πῶς τὰρ ἴω μετὰ μῶλον).

προμάχοισιν ἐμίχθην: "I have mixed among the forefighters" the sentiment is Iliadic, see 4.354: "[You will see] the dear father of Telemachus mixing among the forefighters" (Τηλεμάχοιο φίλον πατέρα προμάχοισι μιγέντα) and 13.642 for the combination with the participle (αὐτὸς δ' αὖτ' ἐξ αὖτις ἰὼν προμάχοισιν ἐμίχθη).

44 ἄνθρωπον οὐ δέδια καί περ μέγα σῶμα φοροῦντα: This line is ametrical; the last three feet scan well for dactylic hexameter (περ μέγα σῶμα φοροῦντα) but the first half does not.

δέδια: Perfect of δείδω ("to fear"). Homer has δείδια (13.49) and this poem has the lengthened περιδείδια at line 51. For δέδια, see Sophocles *Oed. Col.* 1469 (δέδια τόδ'· οὐ γὰρ ἄλιον).

φοροῦντα: "bearing," here "having" (more like ἔχοντα). For this verb as denoting a physical attribute, cf Archestratos (fourth century BCE, Sicily): ἤδη χρὴ γεραόν, πολιὸν σφόδρα κρᾶτα φοροῦντα ("an old man with a very gray head," fr. 59.2).

καί περ: This combination often signals a concessive use of the participle and typically appear separate as at *Il.* 1.577 ("I will advise mother even though she already knows herself," μητρὶ δ' ἐγὼ παράφημι καὶ αὐτῇ περ νοεούσῃ). The particle περ alone can signal concession; see Smyth §2083a.

45   ἀλλ' ἐπὶ λέκτρον ἰὼν ἄκρον δάκτυλον δάκνω: This line is also ametrical.

ἄκρον δάκτυλον: "finger tip" or "toe-tip."

46   πτέρνης: "ham"; See above on line 29.

λαβόμην: This form only occurs here. In the middle, λαμβάνω means to "keep hold of" or "to make one's own" and takes a genitive direct object.

καὶ οὐ πόνος ἵκανεν ἄνδρα: "no pain comes to the man." For πόνος as simply "pain" see Simonides fr. 15.1 (αἰῶνι δ' ἐν παύρωι πόνος ἀμφὶ πόνωι).

47   νήδυμος: "sweet"; a typical epithet of sleep (ὕπνος) in Homer, e.g. *Il.* 14.354 "Sweet sleep went to rush to the ships of the Achaeans" (βῆ δὲ θέειν ἐπὶ νῆας Ἀχαιῶν νήδυμος Ὕπνος).

δάκνοντος ἐμεῖο: Perhaps taken as a genitive absolute (i.e. "Sweet sleep never flees when I bite"); but the force of the preposition in ἀπέφυγεν (see above, line 42) might take a genitive object (i.e. "Sweet sleep never fled from my bite").

ἐμεῖο: ἐμοῦ.

48   δύω: The passage is part of Byzantine interpolation, but it introduces *two* feared opponents (the hawk and the weasel) and adds a *third* (a mousetrap). It is possible that in this "mistake" the *BM* is alluding to similar Homeric oversights as in the famous problem of the duals of *Iliad* 9 where a pair is described as going on the embassy which actually includes three people (Odysseus, Phoinix, and Ajax; plus the two heralds). For the ancient debate and a good overview on this, see Segal 1968. For more recent discussions and bibliography, see Louden 2002.

τά: The article in Homer is often used as a relative, see line 32 above.

δείδια: See on 44.

πᾶσαν ἐπ' αἶαν: αἶα ("land, earth") is Homeric. This phrase is typical, see *Il.* 23.742: (χάνδανεν, αὐτὰρ κάλλει ἐνίκα πᾶσαν ἐπ' αἶαν).

49 κίρκον: "hawk"; in Homer the hawk is described in a simile (*Il*. 17.755–759):

> As a flock of starlings or jackdaws moves on,
> They squawk constantly when they see a hawk coming on,
> Bearing murder for the small birds.
> In this way, the sons of the Achaians shrieked when they saw
> Aeneas and Hector, and they lost their battle-courage.

τῶν δ᾽ ὥς τε ψαρῶν νέφος ἔρχεται ἠὲ κολοιῶν
οὖλον κεκλήγοντες, ὅτε προΐδωσιν ἰόντα
κίρκον, ὅ τε σμικρῇσι φόνον φέρει ὀρνίθεσσιν,
ὣς ἄρ᾽ ὑπ᾽ Αἰνείᾳ τε καὶ Ἕκτορι κοῦροι Ἀχαιῶν
οὖλον κεκλήγοντες ἴσαν, λήθοντο δὲ χάρμης.

In the *Odyssey*, the hawk is a messenger of Apollo (15.526: κίρκος, Ἀπόλλωνος ταχὺς ἄγγελος· ἐν δὲ πόδεσσι).

καὶ γαλέην: "weasel"; see above on line 9 for the weasel as a mouse-antagonist.

ἄγουσιν: sc. φέρουσιν.

50 παγίδα: παγίς: "A snare, a trap" but here a "mousetrap." Forms of this noun appear as early as Aristophanes (*Birds*, 194 and 527) and Aesop, although they refer to snares for birds. An earlier noun (πάγη) overlaps in meaning; both derive from πήγνυμι ("to fix, fasten"). For the Trojan Horse as a "wooden trap," see *Grk. Anth.* 9.152.4 (αἴθε δ᾽ Ἐπειὸς / κάτθανε πρὶν τεῦξαι δουρατέαν παγίδα).

στονόεσσαν: "grievous," cf. *Il*. 24.721 (θρήνων ἐξάρχους, οἵ τε στονόεσσαν ἀοιδὴν).

δολόεις: "tricky, deceptive".

πέλε: A synonym for ἔστι. The middle form is more common in Homer. For this form, see *Il*. 19.365 (τοῦ καὶ ὀδόντων μὲν καναχὴ πέλε. . .).

51 πλεῖστον: adv. "the most, especially." This form occurs in Homer, but not at the beginning of the line.

περιδείδια: "I *really* fear." This is a Homeric form: cf. *Il.* 10.93 αἰνῶς γὰρ Δαναῶν περιδείδια. . .). Cf. above on δέδια at line 44.

ἤ τις ἀρίστη: Another Homeric phrase in a familiar position. See *Il.* 17.62. Here, however, the indefinite pronoun seems a bit forced.

52   τρωγλοδύνοντα: "hole-dweller." Cf. English "troglodyte."

ἐρεείνει: "seek out." In Homer, this verb means more frequently "to ask, inquire"; cf. "to seek" and "to ask" on line 25 above.

53   ῥαφάνους: "radish."

κράμβας: "cabbage." The cabbage was used for food and medicinal purposes in ancient Greece. Aristotle prescribes cabbage juice as a hangover cure (*Problemata* 873a–b) where in Athenaeus it is also given to women post-partum (*Deipn.* 9.369=9.10 Kaibel).

κολοκύντας: "pumpkins."

Ernesti 1764 suspects that lines 53–55 ought to come before line 40. This would collocate all of the food discussion. However, the transition from line 52 to the reply of Physignathos in line 57 ("You prattle on too much about food.") is rather abrupt.

54   οὐ σεύτλοις χλωροῖς: "pale beets."

ἐπιβόσκομαι: "to feed on"; usually used of animals in Homer and without the prefix.

σελίνοις: "parsley."

55   ἐδέσματα: See above on line 31.

κατὰ λίμνην: See above on line 17.

56   μειδήσας: "Grinning," often appears in responses to speeches in Homer, e.g. *Il.* 23.555 ("So he spoke, and shining, swift-footed Achilles grinned"; Ὣς φάτο, μείδησεν δὲ ποδάρκης δῖος Ἀχιλλεὺς). This masculine participle seems more popular in the Hellenistic period, see, e.g. Ap. Rhodes 2.61 (ἦκα δὲ μειδήσας, οἵ οἱ παρὰ ποσσὶν ἔκειντο).

ἀντίον ηὔδα: "He responded, answered back"; a typical Homeric speech introduction. See, *Il.* 3.203 (Τὴν δ' αὖτ' Ἀντήνωρ πεπνυμένος ἀντίον ηὔδα).

57   λίην: "excessively," adv.

αὐχεῖς: "You brag about your belly" with ἐπὶ γαστέρι. αὐχεῖς is not a Homeric word, but it does appear in Aeschylus (*Ag.* 1497; cf. Eur. *Her.* 31 Χο. εἰ σὺ μέγ' αὐχεῖς).

ἐπὶ γαστέρι: "on your belly" with the sense of "because of." See Smyth §1689.2c. This use not typical in Homer. The phrase appears in the *Odyssey* (7.216: οὐ γάρ τι στυγερῇ ἐπὶ γαστέρι κύντερον ἄλλο) but the sense there seems more one of addition or comparison ("there is nothing more shameful *beyond* a belly").

The charge that mice are gluttons is commonplace in Greek literature. See *Gr.Anth.* 9.86 Παμφάγος ἑρπηστὴς κατὰ δώματα λιχνοβόρος μῦς: "The all-eating, tidbit-munching mouse who crawls about the house." See also the note on line 29, above, on mouse name compounds with Λειχ-. Also, the mouse's character in the fabulist tradition is not infrequently that of the "dinner host." See, for example, the mouse and frog fable presented in *Vita Aesopi* G: ὅτε ἦν τὰ ζῷα ὁμόφωνα, μῦς φιλιάσας βατράχῳ ἐκάλεσεν αὐτὸν ἐπὶ δεῖπνον καὶ εἰσήγαγεν αὐτὸν εἰς ταμιεῖον πλούσιον πάνυ, ἐφ' ᾧ ἦν ἄρτος, κρέας, τυρός, ἐλαῖαι, ἰσχάδες· καί φησιν 'ἔσθιε.' "When animals all spoke the same language, a mouse on friendly terms with a frog called him to dinner and led him to his well-stocked store-room, where there was bread, meat, cheese, oil, and fish. And he said 'eat.'"

The enumeration of comestibles seems a stock theme in the fabulist tradition and in comedy. However, if lines 42–52 are indeed interpolation, we may suspect that the interpolator imported the long list of foods precisely because of its similarity to the sorts of catalogue found in the fables. Alternatively, the catalogue of food can be read as a parody of the long catalogues which are typical of epic and didactic poetry.

ἔστι καὶ ἡμῖν: sc. ἔξεστι ("it is possible for us to see many wonders") or "we have many wonders..."; dative of possession with subject enjambed in the next line.

58   θαύματ᾿ ἰδέσθαι: This plural (θαύματ᾿) does not occur in Homer (but does in Hesiod and Homeric *Hymns*). For the singular with this infinitive, see Hom. *Od.* 13.108: φάρε᾿ ὑφαίνουσιν ἁλιπόρφυρα, θαῦμα ἰδέσθαι. The phrase-pattern may have antiquity. Cf. the plural at Hes. *Th.* 834 (ἄλλοτε δ᾿ αὖ σκυλάκεσσιν ἐοικότα, θαύματ᾿ ἀκοῦσαι).

It is possible that the contrast between the frog and mice had allegorical force for some ancient audiences. (See Most 1993 for the contrast as an elaborate literary satire pitting proponents of the *Iliad*—the mice— against those of the *Odyssey*—the frogs.) In this first exchange of speeches, one might imagine an ethical allegory, namely that the two species represent different types of sensual indulgence. The mice are clearly stock "glutton" characters; perhaps the frogs resemble the aesthetes described in Plato's *Republic* (476b): Οἱ μέν που, ἦν δ᾿ ἐγώ, φιλήκοοι καὶ φιλοθεάμονες τάς τε καλὰς φωνὰς ἀσπάζονται καὶ χρόας καὶ σχήματα καὶ πάντα τὰ ἐκ τῶν τοιούτων δημιουργούμενα, αὐτοῦ δὲ τοῦ καλοῦ ἀδύνατος αὐτῶν ἡ διάνοια τὴν φύσιν ἰδεῖν τε καὶ ἀσπάσασθαι. "These are, in a way, fond of hearing and seeing, and they gratefully embrace beautiful sounds, colors, shapes, and all sorts of things worked up out of those things, though their minds are unable to see and embrace the nature of beauty itself." It may be useful to compare this use of τὴν φύσιν with that found earlier at line 32; in Plato, the term clearly refers to the inner "nature" of a thing, as opposed to its appearance.

59   ἀμφίβιον...νομήν: "amphibious realm"; lit. "a double-lived pasture." The "amphibious life" is rather over-elaborated over the next few lines, which has led some (such as Ernesti 1764) to suspect the lines due to their tautologous nature.

Κρονίων: "Son of Kronos," Zeus, a typical epithet in this position.

60   σκιρτῆσαι κατὰ γαῖαν, ἐν ὕδασι σῶμα καλύψαι: δίδωμι (here, ἔδωκε) often takes an infinitive (i.e. "Zeus grants that we dance upon

the earth"). But combined here with the object ἀμφίβιον...νομὴν it seems a bit forced. The chiastic structure of this line (infinitive-prepositional phrases-infinitive) is characteristic of Hellenistic play. Note possible humorous foreshadowing in "covering the body in water" (σῶμα καλύψαι).

γαῖαν: This lengthened form of γῆ (which also occurs at lines 84, 95, and 229) is common in early Greek poetry and identified by Janko 1982 an archaism (indicating a later date for the text).

61   στοιχείοις: "Parts, or elements"; from στοῖχος, "row or rank." The meaning "parts" or "elements" is common in philosophical prose; the noun appears colloquially as well, e.g. Aes. *Fab.* 32.2.9 ("The story shows that no place, no land, no sky nor any *part* of the water safekeeps murders of men," ὁ μῦθος δηλοῖ, ὅτι τοὺς φονεῖς τῶν ἀνθρώπων οὔτε γῆς οὔτε ἀέρος οὔτε ὕδατος στοιχεῖον οὔτε τόπος ἄλλος φυλάττει). The root noun was available as early as Homer, cf. "in a ranked line" μεταστοιχί (*Il.* 23.358).

Many of the old MSS, including Z, omit this line altogether. See Plato for the earliest literary attestation of the word in this way (Timaeus 48 b): ...καὶ ἕκαστον αὐτῶν λέγομεν ἀρχὰς αὐτὰ τιθέμενοι στοιχεῖα τοῦ παντός... "... and we call each of them beginnings, having established that they are the elements of everything..." Ancient philosophers, in particular the Milesians and other Pre-Socratics, were much given to speculation on questions of physics and natural history; in particular, they were fascinated by the division of the world into στοιχεῖα, "elements." Cf. Diogenes Laertius on the Egyptians: Τὴν δὲ τῶν Αἰγυπτίων φιλοσοφίαν εἶναι τοιαύτην περί τε θεῶν καὶ ὑπὲρ δικαιοσύνης. φάσκειν τε ἀρχὴν μὲν εἶναι τὴν ὕλην, εἶτα τὰ τέσσαρα στοιχεῖα ἐξ αὐτῆς διακριθῆναι, καὶ ζῷά τινα ἀποτελεσθῆναι. ("The philosophy of the Egyptians about the gods and justice was this. They said that material was the beginning of everything, and from that four elements were separated, out of which certain living things are made," *Vit. Soph.* 1.10.5.)

διττοῖς: Un-Homeric. A word such διπλόος would be more common. Theognis has the non-Attic Δισσαί (837).

δώματα ναίειν: "to inhabit homes," still governed by ἔδωκε, i.e. "Zeus has granted that we inhabit. . ." Cf. Hes. *Th.* 303: ἔνθ' ἄρα οἱ δάσσαντο θεοὶ κλυτὰ δώματα ναίειν ("The gods were alloted to inhabit famous homes") and νῆσος δενδρήεσσα, θεὰ δ' ἐν δώματα ναίει ("The forested island where the goddess inhabited her home," *Od.* 1.51).

μεμερισμένα: "divided" from μερίζω, "to divide." This participle does not occur in Homer (and is typical more of philosophy), but consider a scholion to the *Odyssey*, which says of the Aethiopians: "The Aithiopians are on the east and the west—both groups settled near the ocean. This is why they are the 'furthest of men'" (Αἰθίοπες ἀνατολικοὶ καὶ δυσμικοί. κατοικοῦσι δὲ ἀμφότεροι πρὸς τῷ ὠκεανῷ. τούτου χάριν φησὶν "ἔσχατοι ἀνδρῶν." νενέμηνται, μεμερισμένοι εἰσίν, E Schol. in *Od.* 1.23). This gives the boast of Physignathos a comic effect by extending his range between the real and semi-mythical worlds. Cf. line 20, where ὠκεανοῖο is a variant of Ἠριδανοῖο.

62   δαήμεναι: from δάω, a Homeric infinitive, "to learn," often with a genitive direct object. Cf. *Il.* 21.487 (εἰ δ' ἐθέλεις πολέμοιο δαήμεναι. . .).

εὐχερές: Lit. "ready-to-hand," i.e. "easy."

63   βαῖνέ. . .ἐν: ἐμβαίνω is often used with getting on ships.

ἐν νώτοισι: "on my back." The plural is often used metaphorically for the sea (e.g. *Od.* 17.146: οἵ κέν μιν πέμποιεν ἐπ' εὐρέα νῶτα θαλάσσης.) but this dative form appears twice for portions of meat (*Il.* 7.321; *Od.* 14.437), and elsewhere with horses (see Theognis 249: οὐχ ἵππων νώτοισιν ἐφήμενος·).

κράτει δέ με μήποτ' ὀλίσθῃς: from κρατέω (imperative singular, often confused with the 3rd person indicative κρατεῖ); "Hold me tight so you don't slip off"; κράτει has no Homeric parallels but appears with a genitive object in Sophocles (*Philokt.* 1292: πρότεινε χεῖρα, καὶ κράτει τῶν σῶν ὅπλων).

64 γηθόσυνος: "happy," a Homeric adjective, e.g. *Il.* 4.272 ("Ὣς ἔφατ', Ἀτρεΐδης δὲ παρῷχετο γηθόσυνος κῆρ). Sens (2005: 238–41) finds complex engagement here with the *Odyssey*, especially book 5 and Odysseus' shipwreck.

ὅππως. . .εἰσαφίκηαι: Uncontracted middle aorist subjunctive from ἀφικνέομαι (ὅππως—lengthened from ὅπως—object clause of effort). This is a Homeric form, though rare: μὴ καὶ ὑπὲρ μοῖραν δόμον Ἄϊδος εἰσαφίκηαι, 3.336). In Homer, object clauses may take the subjunctive or optative where Attic might use future forms, see Smyth §2217.

65–92 *The mouse climbs on the frog's back and is at first delighted at the novel experience of swimming. Then, fear sets in; the frog compares himself to Europa. And a watersnake appears! The frog dives to escape the snake, abandoning the mouse to fate. As he dies, he appeals to the gods for vengeance.*

65 "Ὣς ἄρ' ἔφη καί: A typical speech conclusion, cf. *Il.* 1.584 ("Ὣς ἄρ' ἔφη καὶ ἀναΐξας δέπας ἀμφικύπελλον).

ὁ δ': The particle δέ with a noun is frequently used to signal a subject change.

ἐδίδου: Imperfect, 3rd singular active. This form occurs once with an augment in Homer (*Od.* 11.289). Cf. *Il.* 23.895 (Ταλθυβίῳ κήρυκι δίδου περικαλλὲς ἄεθλον) for the form without an augment.

66 ἁπαλοῖο: Most manuscripts have τρυφεροῖο instead. Restored, τρυφεροῖο: recalls Iliadic battle language: ἀντικρὺ δ' ἁπαλοῖο δι' αὐχένος ἦλθ' ἀκωκή, *Il.*17.49.

κατ' αὐχένος: "around, or along the neck."

ἅμματι κούφῳ: "with a light embrace"; Some manuscripts have ἅλματι καλῷ ("beautiful brine").

67 ἔχαιρεν: Note the imperfect tense indicating continuing action.

τὸ πρῶτον: "At first", adverbial accusative.

ὅρμους: "harbors"; Some manuscripts have λίμνας instead.

68 νήξει: dative singular, related to νήχω "swim"; a post-Homeric word.

ῥα: Line-final ῥα is comparatively rare in Homer.

69 κύμασι πορφυρέοισιν: "purple or rolling waves"; a Homeric phrase, see *Il.*21.326 (πορφύρεον δ᾽ ἄρα κῦμα διιπετέος ποταμοῖο) and *Od.* 11.243 (πορφύρεον δ᾽ ἄρα κῦμα περιστάθη οὔρεϊ ἶσον). This specific phrase occurs in the Homeric *Hymn to Athena* (κύμασι πορφυρέοισι κυκώμενος, ἔσχετο δ᾽ ἄλμη, 12). Camerotto (1992: 12) argues that this line (along with 76 below) is an equivalent formula, evidence of literary adaptation of oral poetic conventions.

ἐκλύζετο: "he was splashed by"; used in conjunction with "waves" in Homer, see *Il.* 23.61 (ἐν καθαρῷ, ὅθι κύματ᾽ ἐπ᾽ ἠϊόνος κλύζεσκον).

πολλὰ δακρύων: "weeping much"; for Homer, it is heroic to cry. This line is probably based on δάκρυα λείβων (13.658); cf. Camerotto (1992: 16).

70 ἄχρηστον: "useless," from χράομαι.

μετάνοιαν: "decision, change of mind." This is post-Homeric, fairly common in Attic Greek and later. Cf. Thucydides' description of the Athenians' repentance of their decision to destroy Mytiline: καὶ τῇ ὑστεραίᾳ μετάνοιά τις εὐθὺς ἦν αὐτοῖς (3.36.4). Compounds with -νοια become popular in philosophical and technical works.

ἐμέμφετο: "to reproach, find fault with," from μέμφομαι. This verb is found only in ἐπί- compounds in Homer.

τίλλε δὲ χαίτας: "he tore his hair." Hair and clothing rending is part of a formulaic expression of grief. See *Il.* 22.406 where Hecuba tears her hair (τίλλε κόμην...)

71 ἔσφιγγεν: "he was squeezing."

ἦτορ πάλλετ': "His heart was leaping"; from πάλλω which functions like an intransitive middle (i.e. πάλλομαι) in Homer. For this phrase, see *Iliad* 22.451–2: ἐν δ' ἐμοὶ αὐτῇ / στήθεσι πάλλεται ἦτορ ἀνὰ στόμα, νέρθε δὲ γοῦνα.

72 πάλλετ' ἀηθείῃ καὶ ἐπὶ χθόνα βούλεθ' ἱκέσθαι: Some MSS omit this line.

ἀηθείῃ: "the novelty" (lit., "unaccustomedness"). Forms of this word appear in Plato, but not earlier. See Apollonius of Rhodes 2.1063–5 αὐτὰρ πασσυδίῃ περιώσιον ὄρνυτ' αὐτήν ἀθρόοι, ὄφρα κολῳὸν ἀηθείῃ φοβέωνται / νεύοντάς τε λόφους καὶ ἐπήορα δούραθ' ὕπερθεν. Cf. *Il.* 10.493 (νεκροῖς ἀμβαίνοντες· ἀήθεσσον γὰρ ἔτ' αὐτῶν).

ἱκέσθαι: from ἱκνέομαι, Homeric aorist infinitive. Some MSS have ἰδέσθαι.

73 δεινά: Adverbial, "terribly" used in the combination δεινὰ δ' ὁμοκλήσας in the *Iliad* (e.g. 20.448).

ὑπεστενάχιζε: "groan beneath"; the compound is not Homeric, but στενάχιζε is.

φόβου κρυόεντος ἀνάγκη. "Chilling fear" is a Homeric combination (*Il.* 9.2), but the full phrase "by necessity of. . ." is a little tortured. This is likely another equivalent formula, see Camerotto (1992: 12).

74 οὐρήν: "tail."

ἠΰτε κώπην: "like a rudder."

ἐφ' ὕδασιν: see above, 33.

75 This line basically repeats the same thoughts as line 72 (πάλλετ' ἀηθείῃ καὶ ἐπὶ χθόνα βούλεθ' ἱκέσθαι).

σύρων: "dragging, drawing" from σύρω.

ἱκέσθαι: see on 72 above.

76 ὕδασι πορφυρέοισιν: see above on line 69 for κύμασι πορφυρέοισιν. This particular combination does not occur in Homer. Some MSS have κύμασι instead of ὕδασι. This may be another literary adaptation of the formula, see Camerotto (1992: 16).

ἐκλύζετο: See on 69, the image is repeated.

πολλά: Adverbial accusative.

ἐβώστρει: Related to βοάω ("to shout"); rare, but in the *Odyssey* (12.124). Other MSS have the metrically weaker δ' ἐβόα.

77 καὶ τοῖον φάτο μῦθον ἀπὸ στόματός τ' ἀγόρευσεν: This line is omitted by some texts. As a speech introduction it is a bit odd. For the generic kind of speech anticipated by τοῖον, see above on note 12. Such a generalizing introduction may derive from the epic's engagement with the tradition of fables. Without this line, 78–81 should probably not be considered direct discourse, since there is speech-concluding formula. Despite the difficulty, we have elected to retain this line: the self-address might recall moments of deliberation in the *Odyssey* as when Odysseus is being tossed about after his raft is destroyed (e.g. 5.298–313).

ἀπὸ στόματος: Does not occur in Homer.

ἀγόρευσεν occurs in the *Iliad* (8.29). Without the line, subsequent lines must be read as indirect speech.

78 Οὐχ οὕτω. . .: Most editors punctuate this speech as a statement, but there is some Homeric precedent for starting a question with a negative, see *Il.* 7.448; 9.339; 15.555; and 21.108.

ἐβάστασε: "to lift up." Lines 78–81 have been identified by several scholars as alluding to Moschus' *Europa* from the Hellenistic period. See Glei 1984: 34–6; Fusillo 1988: 39–43.

φόρτον ἔρωτος: "cargo of love"; see Anacreon fr. 115.1 (φόρτον Ἔρωτος). For this phrase as providing a *terminus ante quem* for the poem of *c.* 570–500 BCE, see Bliquez 1977: 12.

79   ταῦρος ὅτ᾽ Εὐρώπην: Zeus, disguised as a bull, abducts Europa and takes her to Crete. She gives birth to Minos, Sarpedon and Rhadamanthys. See Apollodorus 3.1. In Homer, comparison to mythological examples (called *paradeigmata*) is a common motif in speeches, see Willcock 1964; Edmunds 1997; and Alden 2000. Here, the parodist imitates the Homeric style and satirizes it through inapposite (though quite amusing) comparison. One might also sense in this a subtle critique of Homeric use of *paradeigmata*—just as the mouse here makes a grand and somewhat inapposite comparison from myth, so too the Homeric heroes' comparisons may be imperfect.

80   ἁπλώσας: "To make single, unfold, spread out" as in ἱστία. Other MSS have instead ἐπιπλώσας, cf. *Il.* 3.47 ("once he sailed upon the sea after gathering his trusty companions," πόντον ἐπιπλώσας, ἑτάρους ἐρίηρας ἀγείρας). Earlier editors (e.g. Ludwich) suggested that ὑψώσας from 81 would be a better fit here, moving ἁπλώσας to its place.

ἐπινώτιον: "on the back," a rare and later word; cf. line 63 above.

81   ὑψώσας: "raise on high," from ὑψόω, a later verb.

ὠχρὸν δέμας: "pale skin"—perhaps the poet is thinking of the pale color of a frog's skin.

ὕδατι λευκῷ: This could be repunctuated as a question, but the word order is imperfect. The phrase "white water" appears in Homer (see *Od.* 23.282) in connection with bathing.

82   Ὕδρος: "watersnake."

ἐξαίφνης: "Suddenly," some MSS have ἐξαπίνης which appears in this position in Homer (e.g. *Il.* 5.91). ἐξαίφνης does occur, but less frequently (*Il.* 17.738 and 21.14 with the same participle ὄρμενον ἐξαίφνης).

ὅραμα: "sight, spectacle"; also a later word, see Demosthenes *Exordium* 55.1.7: ἀλλ᾽ ὅραμα τοῦτ᾽ ἐποιεῖθ᾽ ὁ δῆμος αὐτοῦ καλόν, ὦ ἄνδρες Ἀθηναῖοι, καὶ λυσιτελὲς τῇ πόλει.

83   ἀμφοτέροις: "a bitter sight *for them both*."

ὀρθόν: adverbial with ὑπὲρ ὕδατος "straight up above the water."
Homeric poetry tends to use the adjective in noun agreement (e.g στῆ
δ᾽ ὀρθὸς καὶ μῦθον ἐν ᾿Αργείοισιν ἔειπεν, 23.830).

τράχηλον: "throat."

84   κατέδυ: "he went under," aorist 3rd singular.

οὔ τι νοήσας: "he wasn't thinking at all about. . .οἷον ἑταῖρον."

85   οἷον ἑταῖρον: "What kind of companion," i.e. his species/ability.

ἀπολλύμενον: "who is being killed"; some MSS have the infinitive
ἀπολλύμεναι. This participle appears in Homer (δῷς; ἐπεὶ οὔ τι Τρῶας
ἀπολλυμένους ἐλεαίρεις, *Il.* 7.27) although it is more common without
ἀπό.

86   δῦ δὲ βάθος λίμνης: Unagumented aorist: "Entered the depth of
the sea" seems to be an adaptation of the Homeric αὐτὴ δ᾽ ἂψ ἐς πόντον
ἐδύσετο κυμαίνοντα (*Od.* 5.352).

κῆρα μέλαιναν: "black death," a typical Homeric phrase (e.g. *Il.* 2.859).
For this line, see *Il.* 3.360 (ἔγχος· ὃ δ᾽ ἐκλίνθη καὶ ἀλεύατο κῆρα
μέλαιναν).

ἀλεύατο: "avoid, shun, escape" from ἀλέομαι.

βάθος: βάθος is not present in Homer. Consider, however, the related
βένθος in *Il.* 18.38 (πᾶσαι ὅσαι κατὰ βένθος ἁλὸς Νηρηΐδες ἦσαν).

87   ἀφέθη: aorist passive, 3rd singular of ἀφίημι.

πέσεν ὕπτιος εὐθὺς ἐφ᾽ ὕδωρ: πέσεν ὕπτιος is a common collocation
in Homer (see *Il.* 15.647). ὕπτιος: "sprawled out; on one's back;
backward."

88   ἔσφιγγε: see on line 71 ("he was squeezing"). Line 88 is considered
suspect by several editors, but the image is appropriate.

κατέτριζε: "squeaked," according to Fusillo (*ad loc.*), a word used only of beasts.

89 πολλάκι μὲν. . . πολλάκι δ᾽ αὖτε: The single-line anaphora is clever, but un-Homeric.

90 λακτίζων: "kicking." This form appears twice in the *Odyssey* of opponents in duress (18.99 and 22.88).

ὑπαλύξαι: "avoid"; used in Homer in avoiding death. For this aorist, see *Il.* 12.327 (μυρίαι, ἃς οὐκ ἔστι φυγεῖν βροτὸν οὐδ᾽ ὑπαλύξαι).

91 δευόμεναι δὲ τρίχες πλεῖον βάρος εἷλκον ἐπ᾽ αὐτῷ: The image is probably based on the human experience of being dragged down by wet clothing. Furred animals are not so encumbered.

δευόμεναι: from δεύω, "to dip, dye."

πλεῖον βάρος: The comparative in early Greek may use a partitive genitive (e.g. Theogn. 1.606: μοίρης πλεῖον); see Smyth §1315. Some MSS have πλεῖστον which is more common as a straight modifier.

92 ἐφθέγξατο: "uttered"; the combination τοίους ἐφθέγξατο μύθους is rather generalized for a speech introduction. This is probably a literary adaptation of formulaic language, see the comments on line 12 above.

ὀλλύμενος: "perishing"; cf. *Iliad* 11.83 and above on line 85.

93 δολίως: "trickily"; many MSS have γε θεούς instead of the direct object. The verb λανθάνω takes a supplementary participle, here "you won't get away with doing these things!" The variant posits the gods as witnesses of the deeds ("you won't escape the notice of the gods"). In Homer, this verb often appears with the person deceived as an object, see *Od.* 13.393 (καὶ λίην τοι ἐγώ γε παρέσσομαι, οὐδέ με λήσεις). For λανθάνω with a participle, see *Od.* 22.198 (λήσει ἀνερχομένη χρυσόθρονος, ἡνίκ᾽ ἀγινεῖς). It would be natural to call upon the gods here, as our mouse does in line 97. The adverb δολίως is a little late and the sense seems a bit strange.

94   ναυηγόν: "shipwreck"; some MSS provide instead ἐς λίμνην με.

95   οὐκ ἄν… ἦσθα: With the past tense indicative, ἄν indicates past unreal potential, translate "you couldn't be better than me on land", *vel sim.*

κατὰ γαῖαν: "on land." See Smyth §1784.

96   παγκρατίῳ: The pankration is a post-Homeric sport. According to Herodotus (9.105), it was one in which the Athenians excelled: Ἐν δὲ ταύτῃ τῇ μάχῃ Ἑλλήνων ἠρίστευσαν Ἀθηναῖοι, καὶ Ἀθηναίων Ἑρμόλυκος ὁ Εὐθοίνου, ἀνὴρ παγκράτιον ἐπασκήσας.

πάλη: Unlike the pankration, wrestling is Homeric, see *Iliad* 23.634–5. For this whole line, cf. *Od.* 8.206 (ἢ πὺξ ἠὲ πάλῃ ἢ καὶ ποσίν, οὔ τι μεγαίρω).

εἰς δρόμον: "in the footrace," another good archaic competition see *Il.* 23.373.

97   ἔκδικον ὄμμα: "an eye for vengeance"; Zeus is often worshipped as a god of justice. The phrase is not quite archaic and it may echo what the frog says in the Aesopic tradition: ἐγὼ μὲν ὑπό σου νεκρωθήσομαι, ἐκδικήσομαι δὲ ὑπὸ ζῶντος ("I am being killed by you but I will be avenged by the living").

97–8:   These two lines are considered to be Byzantine interpolations. The sense of both is reflected in the current line 98/99.

97a   ποινήν τ ἀντέκτισίν τ᾽ ὀρθήν ὅς κ᾽ ἀποδώσει

ἀντέκτισίν: is un-Homeric and a gloss for ποινήν which is Homeric. Cf. Glei *ad loc.*; Ernesti (*ad loc.*) notes a "Christian" character to this line.

ὀρθήν: "straight" is often associated with justice in Hesiod (e.g., "let us resolve this conflict with straight judgments, which are the best things that come from Zeus " … ἀλλ᾽ αὖθι διακρινώμεθα νεῖκος / ἰθείῃσι δίκῃς, αἵ τ᾽ ἐκ Διός εἰσιν ἄρισται, *Works and Days*, 36–7).

98 τοῖς τίσουσί σε μυῶν στρατὸς οὐδὲ ὑπαλύξεις or ποινὴν αὖ τείσεις σὺ μυῶν στράτῳ οὐδὲ ὑπαλύξεις: The paying back of penalties is common in Homer but usually in exchange for harm done to honor or the like (see Wilson 2002). In the *Odyssey*, punishment for a crime is more usually marked with terms of *tisis*. Yet, in describing his treatment of the Cyclops, the narrator combines the thematic terms (23.313–14):

> ἠδ' ὅσα Κύκλωψ ἔρξε, καὶ ὡς ἀπετείσατο ποινὴν
> ἰφθίμων ἑτάρων, οὓς ἤσθιεν οὐδ' ἐλέαιρεν.

> And however many things the Kyklops did, even then he paid the exchange for my strong companions, the men he ate and did not pity.

τοῖς τίσουσί σε μυῶν στρατός: There is a noun/subject agreement problem with this phrase. While the syntax is not exactly clear, the sense is basically the same.

99 Ὣς εἰπὼν ἀπέπνευσεν ἐν ὕδασι: Note the melodramatic, extended death scene (from 88–99). In modern film, for example, this hyperbole might seem humorous. In ancient epic, however, death scenes are often drawn out and unrealistic. Consider the Homeric deaths of Patroklos and Hektor. The parodic sense is not in the length of the scene but in the character who is dying.

ἀπέπνευσεν: "to die," literally "to breathe out," a metaphor for death clearer in Pin. *Nem.* 1.47 (ψυχὰς ἀπέπνευσεν μελέων ἀφάτων); cf. *Il.* 4.524.

τὸν δὲ κατεῖδεν: "looked down upon him."

100-31 The mice learn of the death of their companion. They hold an assembly and decide to wage war against the frogs. This is followed by an arming scene. The assembly scenes are amusing for the heroic depiction of the mice (imitating conventional assembly scenes). The arming sequence combines the process of heroic arming with weapons made from material available for mice—the parody thus relies on the intrinsic humor of arming with these materials and the clever images offered therein.

100 ὄχθῃσιν ἐφεζόμενος μαλακῇσιν: "sitting on the soft banks"; the participle ἐφεζόμενος occurs in the *Iliad* (δενδρέῳ ἐφεζόμενοι ὄπα λειριόεσσαν ἱεῖσι, 3.152) where the comparison of the elders of Troy to cicadas may evoke a sense of uselessness.

[100a] καί ρα κραιπνότατος μοίρας μυσὶν ἄγγελος ἦλθεν: "and the swiftest messenger of the fate came to the mice." This variant line is also probably a Byzantine interpolation. The adjective κραίπνος is common in Homer, but the superlative does not appear.

101 δραμών: Aorist participle of τρέχω.

δεινόν: Adverbial accusative.

ἐξολόλυξε: "wailed out," a *hapax legomenon*. The root related to ululation has to do both with triumphal and mournful exclamation. In Homer, ὀλολύζω is most often associated with women and can express joy. Consider Eurkyleia's near-exultation at the death of the suitors, *Od.* 22.408 (ἴθυσέν ρ' ὀλολύξαι, ἐπεὶ μέγα εἴσιδεν ἔργον).

ἤγγειλε: 3rd person singular aorist of ἀγγέλλω. This form occurs at *Od.* 23.22 (ταῦτ' ἐλθοῦσ' ἤγγειλε καὶ ἐξ ὕπνου ἀνέγειρε).

μύεσσιν: This dative plural is lengthened for metrical reasons. The same form occurs at least once in the *Galeomuomakhia* (line 10) and is reconstructed elsewhere (line 4). Note that the shorter form appears at line 173 (μυσίν). The *GM* also displays both forms (the shorter one occurs at line 28; see West 2003: 260).

102 τὴν μοῖραν: "fate." The ametrical variant τὸν μόρον (see Glei *ad loc.*) is more Homeric semantically; in Homer μοῖρα tends to indicate "portion" or "allotment" rather than "fate" as in death.

ἔδυ χόλος αἰνός: "A dread rage came over them." Homer uses three words (*mênis*, *kholos* and *kotos*) to describe anger; χόλος is most frequently used for anger within a social group over slights and honor (and is destabilizing according to Walsh 2005). On *mênis* as denoting divine rage, see Muellner 1996.

103 κηρύκεσσιν: Lengthened for metrical reasons.

ὄρθρον: This is not the typical epic phrasing for "morning": it is probably late. See Plutarch's *Publicola*, 22.5 for a description of a foggy morning: καὶ κατὰ τύχην ὁμίχλης βαθείας ἐπιπεσούσης περὶ ὄρθρον.

104 κηρύσσειν: with κηρύκεσσιν, such figura etymologica (see above on "giving gifts," line 16) are common in early Greek poetry. Compare to *Od.* 2.7–8: αἶψα δὲ κηρύκεσσι λιγυφθόγγοισι κέλευσε / κηρύσσειν ἀγορήνδε κάρη κομόωντας Ἀχαιούς.

ἐς δώματα Τρωξάρταο: "the house of Breadnibbler"; in the *Iliad*, the Trojan assembly is held before Priam's house (2.788) and the gods also meet in Zeus' home. The Greeks meet in assembly near Odysseus' ship (see Clay 2011). The Ithakans in the *Odyssey* seem to have a specific assembly-area as do the Phaiakians (7.44). In the depiction of the Kyklopes as being uncivilized and savage, Odysseus notes that they do not have a place for assemblies and laws (τοῖσιν δ' οὔτ' ἀγοραὶ βουληφόροι οὔτε θέμιστες, 9.112).

ἀγορήνδ': here seems to be used metaphorically (i.e. "to 'assembly' before, at the home of . . .") whereas the typical Homeric use of this form implies motion to the place of assembly (Ὣς ὅ γε κοιρανέων δίεπε στρατόν· οἳ δ' ἀγορὴν δὲ / αὖτις ἐπεσσεύοντο νεῶν ἄπο καὶ κλισιάων, *Il.* 2.207–8)

105 δυστήνου: "wretched," Homeric.

ὃς κατὰ λίμνην: see above, line 17: The word λίμνη has a fairly extensive reach: It refers to several different bodies of water, including lakes, ponds, swamps, and marshes.

106 ὕπτιος: "facing up; on his back," used sometimes for falling from a distance (e.g. *Od.* 18.398) but here used instead of a floating corpse; common in descriptions of deaths.

ἐξήπλωτο: A later verb (ἐξαπλόω), "to unfold, or spread out."

οὐδὲ παρ' ὄχθαις: "nor on the banks," usually of rivers but here of the marsh/pond.

107   ἦν ἤδη τλήμων: τλήμων ("unfortunate"; "enduring"), common in tragedy but infrequent in epic (see *Il.* 10.231: ἤθελε δ' ὁ τλήμων Ὀδυσεὺς καταδῦναι ὅμιλον).

μέσσῳ δ' ἐπενήχετο πόντῳ: lit. "he was swimming upon" (from νήχω, deponent νήχομαι), but here means more like "floating in the middle of the pond." Note the hyperbolic use of *pontos* ('sea') for a pond.

108   ὡς δ' ἦλθον σπεύδοντες ἅμ' ἠοῖ: On assembly meetings, see above on 104. The phrase ἅμ' ἠοῖ ("at dawn") appears often in Homer (e.g. *Il.* 11.685).

πρῶτος ἀνέστη: "He rose first"; typical assembly turn-taking language.

109   Τρωξάρτης ἐπὶ παιδὶ χολούμενος: The participle χολούμενος does not appear in the *Iliad* or *Odyssey* but it does appear in the Homeric *H. Hermes* (308) and Hesiod's *Works and Days* (138). It does not typically take the preposition ἐπὶ + dative (instead ἀμφί is more common). The participle χωόμενος is more common in Homer in this sense.

εἶπέ τε μῦθον: "speak a speech" or simply just "speak." Combinations of this verb and noun are common in Homeric speech introductions. This specific introduction, however, is not—this is likely an adaptation of a conventional line, see Camerotto (1992: 14).

110   εἰ καί: "even if." Ancient readers may have felt the adversative sense of the conditional weak: Some MSS have ἀλλ' ἡ with πεῖρα. The combination is rather un-Homeric, where εἴ περ would be more common except where εἰ καί may have the force of αὖ as in Hom. *Il.* 16.623 (εἰ καὶ ἐγώ σε βάλοιμι τυχὼν μέσον ὀξέϊ χαλκῷ).

The force of εἰ καί without a coordinating particle (e.g. ἄν, κε, γε) in the apodosis may be harsh, motivated perhaps by the the father's emotionality or, imperfect composition.

κακὰ πολλὰ πέπονθα: from πάσχω; cf. *Od.*11.6: μάλα πολλὰ πέπονθας. This is likely another formulaic adaptation of a literary nature (rather than being a reflex of an oral tradition).

111   ἐκ βατράχων: "from the frogs." The preposition ἐκ + the genitive can express agency or origin of action in early Greek poetry.

ἡ πεῖρα κακὴ πάντεσσι τέτυκται: Other MSS have μοῖρα instead of πεῖρα, paralleled by *Il.* 3.101. But τέτυκται tends to end the line with various subjects (e.g., *Il.* 24.354). For πάντεσσι τέτυκται, cf. *Il.* 14.246. The angered mouse's use of πεῖρα as a "trial" may be humorous when used in reference to the sea-dwelling frogs. The noun πεῖρα was etymologically connected to the word pirate. Cf. a scholion to Sophokles' *Ajax* 2: "In Attic usage, *peira* means a trick or contrivance; for this reason, criminals on the sea are called *peiratai* (pirates)." (πεῖρα γὰρ Ἀττικῶς δόλος καὶ τέχνη, ὅθεν καὶ πειραταὶ οἱ κατὰ θάλατταν κακοῦργοι.)

112   δύστηνος: "ill-fated"; see above on 105.

ὄλεσσα: aorist 1st person singular of ὄλλυμι. The sigma is doubled, see the introduction.

113   This sequence begins a catalogue of mouse enemies moving from weasel, to men and culminating, humorously, in frogs.

114   γαλέη: "weasel" or "cat"; see above on line 9. The poetic tradition of a "Battle of Weasel and Mice" may be echoed here; the fragmentary poem has πρῶτον γὰρ μιν ἑλοῦσα γαλῆ ... (line 6; see West 2003: 258).

τρώγλης ἔκτοσθεν ἑλοῦσα: compare Skylla grabbing men in the *Odyssey* (οὓς ἔφαγε Σκύλλη γλαφυρῆς ἐκ νηὸς ἑλοῦσα, 12.310).

τρώγλης: Mice live in holes, even in the city. For this motif of animal fable, see the fragment of the "Battle of Weasel and Mice": "in the hole-home bed-chamber" τρ]ωγλαίωι {ἐν} θαλάμωι (line 9; West 2003: 258).

113–14: There are alternate lines in the Byzantina prosodia: υἱέα μοι πρῶτον μυοφόρβος δορπήσατο / θὴρ μεγάλη κλονέοντα πτέρναν σιάλοιο τυχοῦσα: "a big mouse-eating beast first made a meal of my son, a beast found him as he rushed after a ham-hock."

115 ἄνδρες ἀπηνέες: "harsh men." The adjective ἀπηνής is common in Homer but this uncontracted plural may be a hyper-archaism. Its earliest appearance is in Theocr., *Id.* 22.169.

εἷλξαν: "dragged" from ἕλκω.

116 καινοτέραις τέχναις: "new-fangled arts/tricks." The adjective καινός is not Homeric.

ξύλινον δόλον: "wooden trick," the phrase may recall the Trojan horse. The subsequent mention of the trap may be another allusion to Callimachus (fr. 177. 15–37; see Scodel 2008: 232).

117 Allen excises this line because it was taken from verse 50. Glei (*ad loc.*) points out that verse 50 was omitted in many MSS. Given the metrical difficulties (see below) this line is more likely corrupted than interpolated.

ἥν παγίδα κλείουσι: "which they call a trap"; see above on line 50. κλείουσι is a conjecture by Ludwich to fix metrical problems. The original MSS have καλέουσι (offering a run of short syllables in the second and third feet).

μυῶν ὀλέτειραν: "destroyer of mice"; ὀλέτειραν, cf. ὄλλυμι.

118 ὁ τρίτος: "the third son." The other two have just been described, this is the son in question.

ἀγαπητός: "beloved," used of Telemachus by Euryklea in the *Odyssey* (2.265) and of Astyanax in the *Iliad* (*Il.* 6.501).

ἐμοὶ καὶ μητέρι κεδνῇ: Dative with ἀγαπητός. Cf. *Od.* 10.8 (οἱ δ᾽ αἰεὶ παρὰ πατρὶ φίλῳ καὶ μητέρι κεδνῇ.)

119 τοῦτον ἀπέπνιξεν Φυσίγναθος ἐς βυθὸν ἄξας: The MSS have the alternate line τοῦτον ἀπέκτεινεν βάτραχος κακὸς ἔξοχος ἄλλων, "A frog who exceeds all others in wickedness killed him."

ἀπέπνιξεν: ἀποπνίγω: "to choke, suffocate, drown." This recurs at 233. The verb is not Homeric, but is frequent Aristophanes and the Attic orators. In Aesop, the Mouse speaks "while drowning" (ὁ δὲ πνιγόμενος).

ἐς βυθὸν ἄξας: ἄξας: sigmatic aorist of ἄγω; Homer uses the root-aorist ἤγαγον. This line is a play on line 15 above (ἐς δόμον ἄξω) and probably an adaptation of a traditional formula. Glei argues that this line is a holdover from the traditional fable where the former ties a rope around the mouse and drags him to his death (δήσας οὖν ὁ βάτραχος τὸν πόδα τοῦ μυὸς τῷ ἑαυτοῦ ποδὶ ἥλατο εἰς τὴν λίμνην ἕλκων καὶ τὸν μῦν δέσμιον). On the relationship between the Fable and this parody, see the Introduction.

120 ἀλλ' ἄγεθ' ὁπλίζεσθε: "But arm yourselves"; ἄγετε commonly strengthens imperatives in Homer. The form ὁπλίζεσθε does not appear in Homer. Some MSS have ὁπλισόμεσθα instead (which appears at *Od.* 12.292)

καὶ ἐξέλθωμεν ἐπ' αὐτούς: The hortatory subjunctive is often used in Homer in conjunction with imperatives.

121 This line is omitted in many MSS and by Ludwich (1896). The first half is the same as line 153 and the second half appears in Homer (cf. ἀλλ' ἄρα μιν κατέκηε σὺν ἔντεσι δαιδαλέοισιν, *Il.* 6.418).

σώματα κοσμήσαντες: "decking out, adorning our bodies."

ἐν ἔντεσι δαιδαλέοισιν: "in well-worked weapons." Early Greek lexicographers gloss δαιδάλεος as ποικίλος ("intricate, finely-made"); but the adjective can also indicate exoticness. See Morris 1992.

122 Ταῦτ' εἰπὼν ἀνέπεισε καθοπλίζεσθαι ἅπαντας: This line is the same as 160; some MSS omit it and the following line.

123-31   *The arming of the mice draws on the sequencing and general imagery of conventional arming scenes in Homer. For the arming-scene as a traditional type-scene with recognizable characteristics, see Arend 1975 and Edwards 1992. For arming scenes in the BM, see Kelly 2009. The humor of this scene depends only in part upon the audience knowing the convention of Homeric arming; the mice also make novel use of objects-at-hand for their armament.*

123   καὶ τοὺς μὲν ῥ' ἐκόρυσσεν: κορύσσω in the middle voice generally means to arm oneself, but in the active can mean "to arm, array." Here, the meaning is probably metaphorical (i.e. "to marshal," as in *Il.* 2.273 (πόλεμόν τε κορύσσων). The verb appears in Homer without augment.

Ἄρης πολέμοιο μεμηλώς: The combination πτολέμοιο μεμηλώς "who cares for war" appears in Homer (*Il.* 13.469). The verb can take a genitive or accusative object, cf. *Od.* 1.151.

124   κνημῖδας μὲν πρῶτον ἐφήρμοσαν εἰς δύο μηρούς: "And they fitted the greaves to their two thighs." Greaves are typically put on shins instead of thighs. Some scholars (e.g. Ludwich) have imagined this confusion as resulting from interpolation and corruption. It is possible, however, that the poet is making a joke that mouse legs are too small to accommodate a distinction between shin and thigh or, perhaps, including a bit of nonsense to bring into relief the unreality of many typical Homeric arming and battle scenes. The absurdity of the subsequent arming sequence supports such a reading. On the parody's sophisticated reading of epic precedents, see Kelly 2009. This version of the line appears only in two MSS.

κνημῖδας μὲν πρῶτον: This is close to the Homeric κνημῖδας μὲν πρῶτα ... (see *Il.* 3.330; 11.17; 16.131; 19.369).

125   The arming sequence has multiple variations in the MSS. This line has variants that are closer to 161: φύλλοις μὲν μαλαχῶν κνήμας ἑὰς ἀμφεκάλυψαν ("they covered their shins with mallow leaves").

ῥήξαντες κυάμους χλωρούς: "After breaking pale/yellow beans."

εὖ δ᾽ ἀσκήσαντες: For this second half of the line, some MSS have instead κνήμῃσι καλύπτρην. The verb ἀσκέω often appears with arms in Homer (e.g. *Il.* 14.240) and appears later in this text at 163.

126 ἐπιστάντες: "working on"; the form occurs in Aesop (*Fable* 28 v3.6). Ludwich offers ἐπισπῶντ᾽ ἐς κατάτρωξιν which would mean "who hurry for the gnawing of . . ."

κατέτρωξαν: "nibbled clean" from κατατρώγω.

127 θώρηκας: "chest-piece," common in Homer, e.g. *Il.* 2.544.

καλαμοστεφέων ἀπὸ βυρσῶν: "from reed-bound hides." Ludwich provides the alternate καλαμοραφέων "reed-woven."

128 οὓς γαλέην δείραντες: "After flaying a weasel/cat"; this participle occurs in the accusative at *Od.* 10.533. One might assume that the murine killing of a weasel would require explanation. The passage most likely refers to a tale like that of the *Galeomuomakhia* (see the Introduction). Ludwich (1896, *ad loc.*) supposes that animals so adept at arming for war would obviously be able to kill a weasel. The parody may also be styling the mouse as a mythical hero like Herakles who kills a beast (e.g. lion) and wears its skin.

ἐπισταμένως ἐποίησαν: "They made it skillfully" (see *Il.* 7.317 for preparing dinner; *Od.* 5.245 for the building of the raft).

129 ἀσπὶς δ᾽ ἦν λύχνου τὸ μεσόμφαλον: "their shield was the middle piece of a lamp." The MSS have the dative possessor αὐτοῖς but this renders the line unmetrical.

ἡ . . . λόγχη: "spear."

130 εὐμήκης βελόνη: "well-measured needle"; βελόνη is often used for a spear or arrow point after Homer.

παγχάλκεον ἔργον Ἄρηος: "all-bronze work of Ares." Ares does not actually make weapons—the association here is a metonym for the use of the tool. ἔργον Ἄρηος often indicates the effects of war in general, see *Il.* 11.734. For the adjective with a weapon, see *Od.* 8.408.

131   ἡ δὲ κόρυς: "helmet"; frequent in the *Iliad*.

τὸ λέπυρον . . . ἐρεβίνθου: "husk of a chick pea." A variant has the mice using a nut shell: κροτάφοισι καρύου.

ἐπὶ κροτάφοις: "on the temples"; for the helmet being fitted to temples, see *Il.* 13.188 (Ἕκτωρ δ᾽ ὁρμήθη κόρυθα κροτάφοις ἀραρυῖαν). This image appears four times in the *Iliad* and the *Odyssey*; cf. *Il.* 18.611, *Od.* 13.378 and 22.102.

132–59 The frogs notice the arming of the mice and gather into an assembly where they are approached by a herald who announces the coming war. Physignathos prevaricates and denies his guilt. Then he proposes a specific military strategy for coping with the mouse attack. The frog assembly is less clearly established the previous mouse assembly which may echo political differences between the Achaeans and the Trojans in their assembly practice in the Iliad *(on which, see Mackie 1996: 15–26 and Christensen 2015). If the parody does create this tension, this is another indication of sophisticated engagement with the Homeric tradition. In addition, the fact that the frogs gather suddenly to contemplate dealing with a dangerous threat echoes the Trojans assembly outside the walls after Achilles has appeared suddenly on the battlefield (18.243– 313). Note the initial genitive absolute of the first line describing the Trojan assembly in the* Iliad *(ὀρθῶν δ᾽ ἑσταότων ἀγορὴ γένετ᾽, οὐδέ τις ἔτλη).*

132   ἔνοπλοι: "armed"; a variant in some MSS for ἐν ὅπλοις which Ludwich prefers since the adjective is post-Homeric.

ὡς δ᾽ ἐνόησαν: "when they noticed"; ἐνόησαν ends the line several times in Homer; e.g. *Il.* 12.143.

133   ἐξανέδυσαν ἀφ᾽ ὕδατος: "they rose up from the water." The combination is available in Homer: κύματος ἐξαναδύς, τά τ᾽ ἐρεύγεται ἤπειρόνδε, *Od.* 5.438. Cf. 4.405.

ἐς δ' ἕνα χῶρον: "into one place," a rather bland description for assembly formation. At *Il.* 4.446, a similar phrase is used to describe joining in battle (ἐς χῶρον ἕνα).

134 βουλὴν ξύναγον: "They summoned a council for wicked war." This combination is not archaic, but the objective genitive with βουλὴν is easy to understand. It is unclear whether the line is reflecting the convening of a council regarding war or the creation of a plan about the war. It must also be noted that the narrative is a bit proleptic, the frogs do not yet know that the mice have armed against them.

πολέμοιο κακοῖο: A Homeric formula repeated at 201. Cf. e.g. *Il.* 1.284 (ἕρκος Ἀχαιοῖσιν πέλεται πολέμοιο κακοῖο; "he will be a bulwark against terrible war for the Achaeans").

135 σκεπτομένων δ' αὐτῶν: Genitive absolute ("as they were examining").

πόθεν ἡ στάσις ἢ τίς: Indirect question: "where the chaos was from or what the noise was ..." στάσις is a typical word for civil conflict or strife cf. Theog. 717: καὶ στάσιν Ἑλλήνων λαοφθόρον. ἀλλὰ σύ, Φοῖβε.

ὁ θρύλλος: "noise"; some MSS have μῦθος instead.

136 It is rather un-Homeric for a herald to announce war; see Glei (*ad loc.*).

ῥάβδον: "staff"; not typically used in Homer except by gods, e.g. Hermes (*Il.* 24.343 and Kirke (*Od.* 10.293); Athena (*Od.* 13.429). In Homer, this wand is usually magical, but here it is a gloss for the herald's *kêrukeion*. In later Greek, it stands for all types of rods etc. (scepter, shepherd's staff, etc.).

137 Τυρογλύφου: "Cheeseborer" (i.e. "one who puts holes in cheese").

μεγαλήτορος: "great-hearted," a common Homeric epithet. For this position, see *Il.* 17.299.

Ἐμβασίχυτρος: "Bowldiver."

138   ἀγγέλλων: for the participle with a form of ἔρχομαι (as here with ἦλθε, 136) see *Od.* 13.94 (ἔρχεται ἀγγέλλων φάος Ἡοῦς ἠριγενείης). But note the severe separation here.

φάτιν: "rumor, report," see *Od.* 21.323; some MSS have ἔριν "strife" instead.

εἶπέ τε τοῖα: Again, less specific than Homeric speech introductions. On this combination, see above line 12. Some MSS have μῦθον like line 109 (εἶπέ τε μῦθον).

139   ὕμμιν: Lengthened form of ὑμῖν.

ἀπειλήσαντες: "threatening"; this is a common form of speech in Homer, see *Il.* 2.665 (βῆ φεύγων ἐπὶ πόντον· ἀπείλησαν γάρ οἱ ἄλλοι). The sense is unclear, however: typically the verb correlates with a specific threat, not general menace.

ἔπεμψαν: supply με as subject of the infinitive εἰπεῖν and ὑμεῖς for object.

140   ἐπὶ πτόλεμόν τε μάχην τε: for ἐπὶ + accusative as "for" (as in purpose) see Smyth §1689.3a. For the combination πτόλεμόν τε μάχην see *Il.* 13.11 (καὶ γὰρ ὁ θαυμάζων ἧστο πτόλεμόν τε μάχην τε). The repetitive combination is traditional.

141   ὅν περ: ὅσπερ; this could simply be printed as ὅνπερ, effectively an extra emphatic form of the relative (e.g. "the very man whom . . .").

ἔπεφνεν: "kill, slay"; a common Homeric form (a reduplicated aorist; cf. *Il.* 21.96: ὅς τοι ἑταῖρον ἔπεφνεν ἐνηέα τε κρατερόν τε) related to the noun φόνος. The present φένω is assumed (but does not occur). Some MSS have κατέπεφνεν.

142   ἀλλὰ μάχεσθε: "But fight!" This seems like it might be typical of Homeric battle exhortations, but it is not.

143 οἵ τινες ἐν βατράχοισιν ἀριστῆες: Several MSS have εἴ τινες instead of οἵ τινες. For the motif of calling out the "best" of a group, see book 7 of the *Iliad*. (*Il.* 7.73: ὑμῖν δ' ἐν γὰρ ἔασιν ἀριστῆες Παναχαιῶν and *Il.* 7.159 ὑμέων δ' οἵ περ ἔασιν ἀριστῆες Παναχαιῶν; cf. *Od.* 6.34).

γεγάατε: from γίγνομαι. The epic perfect γέγαα is a variation for γέγονα. This is the only extant occurrence of this form in Greek literature and some MSS propose γεγόνατε while Ludwich has γεγάα[σιν]. This is likely a hyper-archaism.

144 ἀπέφηνε: from ἀποφαίνω: "to speak out."

λόγος δ' εἰς οὔατα πάντων: Homer does describe a sound as striking the ears (*Il.*10.535: ἵππων μ' ὠκυπόδων ἀμφὶ κτύπος οὔατα βάλλει). Compare the *BM*'s programmatic statement in line 5, that the purpose of the poem is to "hit upon everyone's ears" . . . ἐς οὔατα πᾶσι βαλέσθαι. The image of words coming upon the ears is common in Hellenistic Greek. Cf. Apollonius Rhodes 3.904 . . . μὴ πατρὸς ἐς οὔατα μῦθος ἵκηται. Also, see Callimachus *Epigrams* 27.4: ὅρκους μὴ δύνειν οὔατ' ἐς ἀθανάτων. Notice that the poet uses λόγος here interchangeably with μῦθος (138) to refer to the same speech.

πάντων: Many MSS have μυῶν instead but it would make little sense for the mice to be frightened by their own messenger's announcement to the frogs.

145 ἐτάραξε φρένας: from ταράσσω, "stir up, confuse"; used frequently of gods causing descruction and gods are often said to influence human φρένες (see *Il.* 6.234; 7.360; and 9.377).

ἀγερώχων: "arrogant, lordly, gathered" This same epithet is applied to the Rhodians in *Iliad* 2.654. In Homer, the adjective has a positive meaning which is roughly equivalent to "lordly," but it later acquires the meaning "arrogant." (Cf. Plutarch *On Brotherly Love* 492A: . . . ἀγέρωχον ὄντα καὶ ὑβριστήν . . .).

146 μεμφομένων δ' αὐτῶν: The genitive absolute does not clearly indicate whether the frogs were upbraiding the herald Embasikhutros

or their own king Physignathos (they may be doing both). It becomes clear that they are critcizing the king for his actions. In Homer, one may question a king's judgment (Diomedes asserts his right to question Agamemnon in the *agorê*, 9.32–3). If the frogs were criticizing their king, rather than the herald's statements, the genitive absolute may have a causative force which motivates the lie: "*Because* the frogs were reproaching him, Physignathos got up and said ..." It is possible that in creating a scene where the king has risked his own people by acting impetuously, the poet has *Iliad* 1 in mind (or, perhaps, the general motif of a tyrannical king acting against his people's best interests).

εἶπεν ἀναστάς: For a king standing up to address the assembly, see *Iliad* 19.77 (where Agamemnon *does not* stand: αὐτόθεν ἐξ ἕδρης, οὐδ᾽ ἐν μέσσοισιν ἀναστάς). There is no clear indication that the frogs sat in assembly in the text (pushed too far, the image is nonsensical: frogs customarily rest on four limbs). But it is conventional for the army to sit or for new speakers to "stand forward" during assemblies in Homer; see Beck 2005: 221–4.

147   ᾯ φίλοι οὐκ ἔκτεινον ἐγὼ μῦν, οὐδὲ κατεῖδον: Physignathus' protest is reminiscent of Hermes' claim in the Homeric *H. Hermes*: "I didn't see [the cows], nor learn of them, nor hear a story from anyone else" (οὐκ ἴδον, οὐ πυθόμην, οὐκ ἄλλου μῦθον ἄκουσα, 263). The external audiences in both cases know that the speaker is lying.

148   ὀλλύμενον: A temporal participle showing contemporaneous action, "I didn't look on as he was dying."

πάντως δ᾽ ἐπνίγη: πνίγω, "to choke, drown." The aorist is passive, ἐπνίγην like ἔβην (from βαίνω). Note the alliteration of p-sounds (πάντως δ᾽ ἐπνίγη παίζων παρὰ λίμνην) perhaps echoing the sound of a sputtering or panting mouse.

παίζων: The dismissive tone of παίζων, coupled with the reproach which Physignathos leveled against Psicharpax (λίην αὐχεῖς ἐπὶ γαστέρι) suggests that the frogs entertained a rather slighting attitude toward mice, perhaps reflecting human beliefs about the frivolity of a mouse's life.

149   νήξεις: "the swimmings"; cf. line 68 νήξει.

μιμούμενος: The participle μιμούμενος has a certain pathetic conative force: Psicharpax died *trying to imitate* the swimming of the frogs.

150   νῦν ἐμὲ μέμφονται τὸν ἀναίτιον: Assertions that someone is "blaming the blameless" occur with reference to Achilles (*Il.* 11.654) and Hektor (13.775) using the cognate accusative ἀναίτιον αἰτιάασθαι; cf. the reference to Odysseus at *Od.* 20.135). The use of μέμφονται here may be conditioned by the narrative μεμφομένων δ' αὐτῶν (146). In Homer, this verb only appears in compound, e.g. ἐπιμέμφομαι. Blame-negotiation is an essential part of epic. At the beginning of the *Odyssey*, Zeus complains: 1.35–7:

> Mortals, they are always blaming the gods and saying that their evils come from us. But they suffer grief beyond their allotment thanks to their own recklessness.

> "ὢ πόποι, οἷον δή νυ θεοὺς βροτοὶ αἰτιόωνται.
> ἐξ ἡμέων γάρ φασι κάκ' ἔμμεναι· οἱ δὲ καὶ αὐτοὶ
> σφῇσιν ἀτασθαλίῃσιν ὑπὲρ μόρον ἄλγε' ἔχουσιν

See also Agamemnon at *Iliad* 19.86–7: "and they were criticizing me, but I am not to blame, no Zeus, Fate and the Fury who walks on air [are]" (καὶ τέ με νεικείεσκον· ἐγὼ δ' οὐκ αἴτιός εἰμι / ἀλλὰ Ζεὺς καὶ Μοῖρα καὶ ἠεροφοῖτις Ἐρινύς ...). For the expression of blame in Homer, see Vodoklys 1992; Nagy 1979: 211–75; and Martin 1989: 30–5.

151   ζητήσωμεν: Aorist subjunctive, hortatory. The use of ζήτειν for abstract searching is post-Homeric. For this use, cf. Aesch. *Prom. Bound* ... ἄθλου δ' ἔκλυσιν ζήτει τινά. See above, note 25.

ὅπως δολίους μύας ἐξολέσωμεν: Object clause of effort. Some MSS have the adverb δολίως instead of the adjective. The mice, who are actually victims here, have not exhibited any trickiness whereas Physignathos, whose recent denial makes him seem at least a little shifty, is actually formulating a deceptive battle strategy. In defense of the adjective, the frog may attribute to the mice the very quality he is exercising. It is entirely possible as well that mice had a conventional association with cleverness.

ἐξολέσωμεν: from ὄλλυμι, Aorist subjunctive. This compound appears once in Homer (τοὺς Ζεὺς ἐξολέσειε πρὶν ἥμιν πῆμα γενέσθαι, *Od.* 17.597).

152   τοιγὰρ ἐγὼν ἐρέω ὥς μοι δοκεῖ εἶναι ἄριστα: This line is common in Homeric council-scenes. Cf. *Iliad* 9.103 αὐτὰρ ἐγὼν ἐρέω ὥς μοι δοκεῖ εἶναι ἄριστα. When advisors speak what "seems best to them" and are ignored, it signals disfunction or danger in Homer as when Polydamas gives his best advice to Hektor (*Il.*12.315; 13.735). Generally, the contention that something "seems best" is supported by the narrative as when Zeus proposes a plan in the *Odyssey* (13.365).

ἐγών: This is a typical Homeric form for ἐγώ. Of the eight occurences of the first-person pronoun in the *BM* this is the only instance.

153   σώματα κοσμήσαντες ἐν ὅπλοις: essentially, "after arming." Instead of ἐν ὅπλοις, the phrase could end with ἔνοπλοι (simply "armed").

στῶμεν ἄπαντες: The subsequent strategy is for the frogs to stand on the edge of the bank and to capitalize on the forward momentum of the mice's charge to drown as many of them as possible.

154   ἄκροις πὰρ χείλεσσιν: "on the highest part of the bank." Χεῖλος often refers to the lip of a cup, but is also the highest part of a furrow or riverbed (ἐπ᾽ ἄκρῳ / χείλει) as at *Il.* 12.51–2 (τόλμων ὠκύποδες, μάλα δὲ χρεμέτιζον ἐπ᾽ ἄκρῳ / χείλει ἐφεσταότες).

ὅπου κατάκρημνος: "very steep, precipitous."

155 ἡνίκα: "when, at the time when".

ὁρμηθέντες: Aorist passive, but active in meaning.

156 δραξάμενοι κορύθων: "after grabbing them by the helmet." κορύθων occurs in Homer, 13.341 (... κορύθων ἄπο λαμπομενάων.)

ὅς τις σχεδὸν ἀντίος ἔλθῃ: Some MSS have ὅποτε or ὅππως for ὅς τις and others have ἦλθον ἐφ᾽ ἡμᾶς instead of ἀντίος ἔλθῃ. The latter is Homeric phrase; early editors or copyists may have been uncomfortable with the switch from plural to singular.

157 ἐς λίμνην αὐτοὺς σὺν: Variations include σὺν ἔντεσιν / σὺν (metrically problematic) or σὺν ἐκείνῳ which could refer back to Psicharpax. The passage could be requesting that they allow the other mice to join their fallen comrade. Here the feminine ἐκείναις does not have a clear antecedent.

158 πνίξαντες: It is not clear whether drowning was the default mode of murder employed by frogs, or inherited from the fable. There is, at any rate, a certain grim irony in Physignathos' plan to drown the rest of the mice, since he claims to have been wholly innocent in the drowning of Psicharpax. In extolling the virtues of the amphibious life in line 60, Physignathos notes that frogs have the power ἐν ὕδασι σῶμα καλύψαι; if we do not take this reflexively, it may be a grim foreshadowing.

ἀκολύμβους: "Unable to swim." This language may be drawn from a variant of the Aesopic fable in the *Life of Aesop* where the mouse, when invited to swim, declares "I do not know how to swim" (κολυμβῆσαι οὐκ ἐπίσταμαι).

159 στήσομεν: Aorist short-vowel subjunctive; cf. *Il.* 18.278 (στησόμεθ᾽ ἄμ πύργους ...).

τὸ μυοκτόνον ὧδε τρόπαιον: The μυοκτόνον τρόπαιον may be a meta-poetic conceit: the lasting monument to mouse-murder is the poem itself.

τρόπαιον: "trophy." Greeks set up trophies after victories made up of panoplies of captured goods and armor. The term is related to τρέπω: the site was to mark the spot where the enemy turned to retreat. In historical cases, these temporary monuments were replaced by permanent ones. See Steinbock 2013: 84; cf. Paus. 1.32.5.

160–7   The frog arming scence matches the mouse arming sequence. The similar content and contrast adds both to the earlier description and also parodies the type of balance evident in Homeric scenes. See Kelly 2014 for a recent re-evaluation of this scene.

160   Ὣς εἰπών: A typical formula in Homeric speech-framing, e.g. *Il.* 1.326, sometimes expanded to the caesura as Ἤτοι ὅ γ᾽ ὣς εἰπὼν . . . (e.g. *Il.* 7.354).

ἀνέπεισε: This compound is common in authors from Herodotus on. Homer uses παραπείθω and ἐπιπείθω with some frequency.

καθοπλίζεσθαι ἅπαντας: See on 122.

161   φύλλοις μὲν μαλαχῶν: "leaves of of mallow." Mallow may describe many different types of the family *Malvaceae*. The genus native to Europe and Asia Minor, *Althaea*, grows on river banks. The plants reach maturity at between three and six feet with soft flowers whose qualities helped give the name to marshmallows. Greeks and Romans prized the plants for alleged healing properties; the leaves were often eaten in salads.

κνήμας ἑάς: "their own shins"; ἑάς:, reflexive personal pronoun.

ἀμφεκάλυψαν: This compound (unaugmented) ends the line at *Od.* 5.493, 13.152 and 158 and elsewhere.

162   θώρηκας δ᾽ εἶχον καλῶν χλοερῶν ἀπὸ σεύτλων: "they had breastplates from yellow beets."

σεύτλων: This vegetable (beets) appears in one of the lives of Aesop (Life W) along with the μαλαχῶν.

163   φύλλα δὲ τῶν κραμβῶν: "leaves of cabbage."

εἰς ἀσπίδας εὖ ἤσκησαν: cf. *Il.* 23.742: πολλόν, ἐπεὶ Σιδόνες πολυδαίδαλοι εὖ ἤσκησαν ("when the very-talented Sidonians made them well").

164   ἔγχος δ' ὀξύσχοινος ἑκάστῳ μακρὸς ἀρήρει: An awkward sentence with a Homeric parallel: εἵλετο δ' ἄλκιμα δοῦρε, τά οἱ παλάμηφιν ἀρήρει, 16.139 ("he took two strong spears which were fitted to his palms"). Following the pattern of the previous passage, it may be best to consider this as predicative: "For each a sharp reed was fitted as a great spear." ὀξύσχοινος: "sharp reed," may refer to a specific plant.

165   καί ῥα κέρα κοχλιῶν λεπτῶν ἐκάλυπτε κάρηνα: This line has several variants, most of which include the same image: snails' shells as helmets (e.g., . . . κοχλίαι κάρην ἀμφεκάλυπτον).

λεπτῶν: "fine, thin, well-wrought." Since the adjective is being applied to snail shells (κοχλιῶν), we translated this as "polished"—but it may refer instead to the appearance of intricate handiwork.

166   φραξάμενοι: φράσσω, in the middle "to arm oneself." This form appears in Mimnermus (ἤ[ϊξ]αν κοίληι[ς ἀ]σπίσι φραξάμενοι, fr. 13a2).

ἐπ' ὄχθαις ὑψηλαῖσι: "on the high banks"; the adjective appears in Homer and Hesiod for homes (e.g. *Il.* 6.503) and chairs (e.g. *Od.* 8.422).

167   σείοντες λόγχας: "brandishing spears," λόγχη is a post-Homeric noun but the combination is similar to *Il.* (σείοντ' ἐγχείας. 3.345). Likely another literary adaptation.

θυμοῦ δ' ἔμπλητο ἕκαστος: The syntax here is a little strange. Typically in Homer, πίμπλημι signals the filling of a bodypart (in the accusative) with a substance in the genitive as at *Il.* 22.312 when Achilles "filled his heart with eagerness" (μένεος δ' ἐμπλήσατο θυμὸν) cf. *Il.* 1.102–3. In the passive, the verb can simply take a genitive as here if we understand *thumos* metonymically, e.g. "each was filled with enthusiasm." Such a use of *thumos* appears in Isocrates (ἀλλ' ὀργῆς καὶ θυμοῦ καὶ φθόνου καὶ φιλοτιμίας μεστοὺς, 12.81.8). One manuscript has the accusative θυμόν, which would also be non-Homeric without a genitive complement.

168–93:   Zeus calls a council of the gods to consider the severity of the threat. The scene parodies divine concern in the Homeric epics where even the works of men can bring them no real danger. In addition, the parody imitates the actual divine assemblies that occur in Greek epic at Iliad *4, 8, 24; and* Odyssey *1. Athena responds to Zeus and complains that she cannot support either side. The depiction of the goddess contrasts with Homeric epic or Attic tragedy where she is frightening and serious. Here, Athena is rather pathetic, complaining about how the mice have ruined her clothing and that the frogs keep her awake. It is not impossible that Athena would receive such an irreverant treatment in a satyrical context (e.g. satyr plays or comedy), but the patron goddess is not a common target of the classical period.*

168   Ζεὺς δὲ θεοὺς καλέσας: the verb of speech (ἐρέεινε, 172) is rather separated from the subject for Homeric standards.

εἰς οὐρανὸν ἀστερόεντα: A Homeric formula, e.g. *Od.* 12.380.

169   καὶ πολέμου πληθύν: The substantive πληθὺν typically appears unqualified in Homer, but here has a descriptive genitive.

κρατερούς τε μαχητάς: "strong warriors," more hyperbole. The combination is likely modeled on *Il.* 3.179 (... κρατερός τ᾽ αἰχμητής).

170   πολλοὺς καὶ μεγάλους: Hendiadys, "many great and strong warriors."

ἠδ᾽ ἔγχεα μακρὰ φέροντας: cf. *Il.* 3.135 (ἀσπίσι κεκλιμένοι, παρὰ δ᾽ ἔγχεα μακρὰ πέπηγεν).

171   οἶος Κενταύρων στρατὸς ἔρχεται ἠὲ Γιγάντων: This responds to other comparisons in the poem; the mice are compared to giants at line 7 and the battle is compared to the hubris of the giants at 283. Both centaurs and giants are shown in myth to challenge the natural order of affairs. Variants seem to push the comparison to another level

of absurdity (170a–b). The Byzantine edition has ὡς βατράχων στρατὸς ἔβρεμεν εὖτε γιγάντων and καὶ μῦες κενταύρων μεγαλαύχων ἦσαν ὁμοῖοι."The army of frogs roars like the giants and the mice are just like the boasting centaurs." The images paired here (and in the following segment) may show knowledge of Athenian ritual and art on the Acropolis. As Bliquez (1977: 17–18) emphasizes, the Parthenon showed both the Gigantomachy and the Centauromachy; in addition, the robe (*peplos*) offered to Athena each year was decorated with an image of the Gigantomachy.

172   ἡδὺ γελῶν: This form is not found in Homer, where instead we find ἡδὺ γελάσσας· (cf. *Il.* 21.508). This phrase at first appears to introduce a speech in the middle of a line, but it is more likely that this is an indirect description of speech.

τίνες βατράχοισιν ἀρωγοὶ / ἢ μυσὶν ἀθανάτων: Perhaps better understood as indirect question rather than a quotation.

ἀρωγοί: "helpers, assistants," used in the *Iliad* of gods who aid one side or the other, see *Il.* 8.205 (εἴ περ γάρ κ᾽ ἐθέλοιμεν, ὅσοι Δαναοῖσιν ἀρωγοί) which occurs in another divine assembly.

173   ἢ μυσὶν ἀθανάτων: Some manuscripts anticipate 178 with τειρομένοισιν in this line ("who will help the frogs and mice who are being worn down"). Instead, the text has a separation between the partitive genitive and the interrogative, i.e. "Who of the gods will be helpers for the mice or frogs?" In the context we prefer the latter.

174   μυσὶν ἦ ῥα βοηθήσουσα: Zeus expects his daughter to help the mice since they are often in her temple. His image of the playful and happy mice stands in contrast to their described bellicosity.

βοηθήσουσα: Future participle of purpose. Some manuscripts have ἐπαλεξήσουσα; in the *Iliad*, Zeus sends Athena down to defend Herakles (ἐπαλεξήσουσαν, 8.365).

πορεύσῃ: Deliberative subjunctive.

175 ἀεὶ σκιρτῶσιν ἅπαντες: "They are all always dancing." σκιρτάω, perhaps appropriate to the skittish movement of mice (as in Aratus, 1134–5: Ἀλλὰ γὰρ οὐδὲ μύες, τετριγότες εἴ ποτε μᾶλλον / εὔδιοι ἐσκίρτησαν ἐοικότες ὀρχηθμοῖσιν), is applied to the movement of Bacchae (Eur. *Bacchae* 446) and members of a chorus (Ar., *Wealth*, 761); the image of dancing in the temple of Athena may have humorous echoes of ritual practice. A war-dance was performed in honor of Athena's birth in full-armor at the Panathenaean festival (*pyrrhiche*), see Burkert 1985: 102.

176 κνίσῃ τερπόμενοι: The gods are the ones who enjoy the smoke from sacrifices; it may be natural for a god to imagine that the mice would enjoy the things he himself does. For "smoke" in a mouse name, see Κνισσοδιώκτην, line 232. Cf. the "Daughter of Smokey" (Κν]ισέωνος θ[υ]γάτη[ρ], line 8) who appears in the fragmentary *GM*.

ἐδέσμασι παντοδαποῖσιν: Zeus echoes what Psicharpax says about himself at line 31.

177 Ὣς ἄρ᾽ ἔφη Κρονίδης· τὸν δὲ προσέειπεν Ἀθήνη: Rather typical lines of speech conclusion and introduction. It is less common to have an expression of speech conclusion and introduction in the same line. See line 277 below. This combination is probably a literary adaptation.

178 ὦ πάτερ οὐκ ἄν πώ ποτ᾽ ἐγὼ μυσὶ τειρομένοισιν: A future less vivid (using the optative with ἄν in the apodosis) with the protasis in the participle τειρομένοισιν (i.e. "I would never go as a helper to the mice even if they are being worn down"). According to Plutarch (*de Invidia et odio*, 537a) many nations hate mice and kill them to keep them out of the temples (whose gods similarly despise them).

179 ἐπεὶ κακὰ πολλά μ᾽ ἔοργαν: Some MSS have ἐρέξαν instead of ἔοργαν. In either case, the sense is "they've done me many bad things."

180 στέμματα βλάπτοντες καὶ λύχνους εἵνεκ᾽ ἐλαίου: The garlands were most likely made of olive-leaves (Athena is accusing the mice of

eating her sacred objects). The lanterns (λύχνους) also have ritual use and burned olive oil; earlier in the poem the mice use them for their shields (129).

181 ἔδακε φρένας: The use of ἔδακε is rather playful. It is not uncommonly used for psychic phenomena (cf. *Iliad* 5.493 ... δάκε δὲ φρένας Ἕκτορι μῦθος). However, it is perhaps intended to evoke the mouse's characteristic nibbling. (cf. line 45 ... ἄκρον δάκτυλον δάκνω).

182 πέπλον μου κατέτρωξαν ὃν ἐξύφηνα καμοῦσα: This toys with the ritual tradition of Athena's *peplos*. Part of annual offerings to Athena involved the dressing of her cult image in the Parthenon with a new robe (allegedly decorated with images of the Gigantomachy). Presenting Athena as weaving one for herself makes her like the women depicted in Homer but rather unlike a divine entity. The mice's eating of the robe may be another allusion to Callimachus, whose Molorchus suffers a similar fate (fr. 177.29–31; see Scodel 2008: 232).

ἐξύφηνα καμοῦσα: Sequential use of the participle in Greek is often opposite of English sense, here "I wore myself out weaving" instead of the Greek order "I wove, wearing myself out." ἐξύφηνα is a root aorist of ὑφαίνω. The compound ἐξύφηνα does not appear until Herodotus.

183 ἐκ ῥοδάνης λεπτῆς: "from tender weft".

καὶ στήμονα μακρὸν ἔνησα: Athena spins her own wool too!

ἔνησα: νέω, "to spin."

184 τρώγλας τ' ἐμποίησαν: "they made holes in [my robes]."

ἠπητής: A "mender," from ἠπήσασθαι, "to mend."

ἐπέστη: from ἐφίστημι, middle intransitive meaning, "to await, spring upon, pay attention to."

185 καὶ πράσσει με τόκον: "and he makes me a debtor." Ludwich (376) notes that the placement of this line is uncertain, sometimes appearing before 186, sometimes after. The explanatory γὰρ in 186 may provide

some grounds for retaining 185 in its current position. Some scholars have questioned Athena's debt for her robe as absurd. The absurdity is clearly humorous and not out of line with the Homeric tradition where, as Xenophanes claims, the gods appear worse than men (fr. 11 Diehl-Krantz):

> Homer and Hesiod attribute to the gods
> Everything that is reproachful and blameworthy among men:
> Stealing, committing adultery, and deceiving one another.

> πάντα θεοῖσ᾽ ἀνέθηκαν Ὅμηρός θ᾽ Ἡσίοδός τε,
> ὅσσα παρ᾽ ἀνθρώποισιν ὀνείδεα καὶ ψόγος ἐστίν,
> κλέπτειν μοιχεύειν τε καὶ ἀλλήλους ἀπατεύειν.

The undignified depiction of Athena, however, may militate against an Athenian composition for the poem.

τὸ δὲ ῥίγιον ἀθανάτοισιν: ῥίγιον ("more horrible, chilly," from ῥιγέω, "to shiver") appears throughout Archaic poetry and should be prefered to the variant τό γε ῥίπον / γ᾽ ἔριπον.

186　χρησαμένη: from χράομαι, "to borrow."

ἔνησα: See above, note 183.

ἀνταποδοῦναι: ἀνταποδίδωμι, "to repay."

οὐκ ἔχω: sc. οὐ δύναμαι. With infinitives ἔχω can mean "to be able to."

187　ἀλλ᾽ οὐδ᾽ ὣς βατράχοισιν ἀρηγέμεναι βουλήσω. Cf. *Od.* 1.6: ἀλλ᾽ οὐδ᾽ ὣς ἑτάρους ἐρρύσατο, ἱέμενός περ·

ἀρηγέμεναι: from ἀρήγω, "to help"; cf. *Il.* 8.11: ἐλθόντ᾽ ἢ Τρώεσσιν ἀρηγέμεν ἢ Δαναοῖσι. The lengthened infinitive ἀρηγέμεναι does not occur in Homer, but does in Quintus Smyrnaeus. Multiple active infinitive variants often coexist: Consider Homeric ἀμύνειν, ἀμυνέμεν, ἀμυνέμεναι ("to defend").

188　εἰσὶ γὰρ οὐδ᾽ αὐτοὶ φρένας ἔμπεδοι, ἀλλά με πρῴην: for the expression, see *Il.* 6.352: τούτῳ δ᾽ οὔτ᾽ ἄρ νῦν φρένες ἔμπεδοι ... The *BM* adapts the *Iliad*'s "his thoughts are not sound" to "they are not sound in their thoughts"; cf. the conjecture αὐτοῖς φρένες (Ludwich *ad loc.*).

189 ἐκ πολέμου ἀνιοῦσαν: cf. *Il.* 6.480 ἐκ πολέμου ἀνιόντα·

ἐκοπώθην: from κοπόω [κοπιάω] "to weary." Probably the first occurance of this denominative verb from κόπος, "beating, striking." The English "I am beaten down" is perhaps apt. Athena then complains that the frogs' noise annoys her and has kept her from sleeping. Similarly, in Aristophanes' *Frogs*, the eponymous chorus is depicted as "croaking" both during the chorus and the stichomythic exchange. Dionysus complains "I wish this 'croak' would go to hell! There's nothing left but croaking!" ('Αλλ' ἐξόλοισθ' αὐτῷ κοαξ / οὐδὲν γάρ ἐστ' ἀλλ' ἢ κοαξ, 226–7). Frog noise may have been a common complaint in Classical Athens, but the parodist is likely engaging with Aristophanes. For the frog-sounds and possible identification of a local species, see on line 213 below.

190 οὐκ εἴασαν: For the 3rd plural aorist termination in -αν and its bearing on the date of the poem, see the note on line 179.

θορυβοῦντες: "making an uproar." Forms of this verb do not appear in Homer, but they do appear in Pindar to describe the noise of assembled people, in Plato, especially of judicial assemblies.

δευομένην: modifies με in line 188 along with ἀνιοῦσαν (189). The alternation of indirect discourse and first-person verbs would be out of character for archaic hexameters.

191 καταμῦσαι: καταμύειν literally means "to close one's eyes." A reader might see in the form καταμῦσαι a pun on the murine theme of the work, or an echo of the similar-sounding *Katamyomachia* ("battle of cats and mice").

192 ἀλγοῦσαν: Some MSS have this form, following the accusative participles in 189 and 190. Others have the nominative ἀλγοῦσα using τὴν κεφαλὴν as an internal accusative. The sense of the accusative in indirect statement might be better construed if we move this line after 189 (or, without moving it, change to the nominative, following Ludwich, Glei et al. accepting the resulting hiatus ἀλγοῦσα, ἕως.)

ἀλέκτωρ: "cock, rooster."

193   ἀλλ' ἄγε παυσώμεσθα θεοὶ τούτοισιν ἀρήγειν: Several scholars
have objected to the reading of παυσώμεσθα on the grounds that
one cannot stop what one has not yet begun (cf. Ludwich 379 *ad loc.*).
This debate may too severely constrain the meanings of παυσώμεσθα
and ἀρήγειν which are here, more consistent with Hellenistic usage,
functioning more abstractly to indicate reluctance and side-taking
rather than specific assistance.

194   μή κέ τις ὑμείων τρωθῇ βέλει ὀξυόεντι· Byzantine variants
include μή τις καὶ λόγχῃ τυπῇ δέμας ἠὲ μαχαίρῃ and μή κέ τις τρωθῇ
λόγχῃ. Both lines use λόγχῃ (which is post-Homeric, see above) whereas
the first also includes the Homeric short-sword, (cf. 11.844: ἔνθά μιν
ἐκτανύσας ἐκ μηροῦ τάμνε μαχαίρῃ).

τρωθῇ: ("wound") aorist of τιτρώσκω, cf. τρώω.

ὑμείων: Lengthened form of ὑμῶν which appears four times in Homer
(e.g. *Il.* 19.153).

βέλει ὀξυόεντι: "sharp shaft" built analogically on the Homeric formula
ἔγχεϊ ὀξυόεντι. The form βέλει occurs once in the *Iliad* when Athena
encourages Pandaros to shoot at the Achaeans (σῷ βέλεϊ δμηθέντα
πυρῆς ἐπιβάντ' ἀλεγεινῆς, 4.99).

The sentiment here plays upon the wounding of gods in the *Iliad* (e.g.
Aphrodite in book 5) and that epic's separation between the worlds of
gods and men expressed most clearly by Apollo in book 21 (462–7)
where he argues that it is foolish for *immortal* gods to fight for mortals.

195   ἀγχέμαχοι: "near-fighters," "fierce." This Homeric epithet may be
odd here: often it applies not to those you might fight against, but
instead those who fight alongside (near) you, as at *Il.* 16.272 and 17.165.
For line 195, some MSS have instead the full line εἰσὶ γὰρ ἀγέρωχοι
ἄλκιμοι ἀγκιμαχηταί: "They are haughty, stalwart, close-fighters." Both
adjectives (ἀγχέμαχοι and ἀγέρωχοι) are applied to the Mysians in
Homer (Μυσῶν τ' ἀγχεμάχων καὶ ἀγαυῶν ἱππημολγῶν, *Il.* 13.5; πρὸς

Θύμβρης δ' ἔλαχον Λύκιοι Μυσοί τ' ἀγέρωχοι, 10.430). It may be a stretch to imagine play on the sound of Greek *mûs* in the Homeric *Mûsoi* affecting the epithet selection. Close collocation, however, with καταμῦσαι (191) may strengthen the association.

196 πάντες δ' οὐρανόθεν τερπώμεθα δῆριν ὁρῶντες: Compare Athena's sentiments in 193–6 to the speech delivered by Apollo to Poseidon at *Iliad* 21.466–7: ἄλλοτε δὲ φθινύθουσιν ἀκήριοι. ἀλλὰ τάχιστα / παυώμεσθα μάχης· οἳ δ' αὐτοὶ δηριαάσθων. Note as well that δῆριν refers to the topic announced for the poem at line 4.

197 Ὣς ἄρ' ἔφη: A formulaic speech-conclusion line, see above at line 65.

καὶ τῇ γε θεοὶ ἐπεπείθοντ' ἄλλοι: "The rest of the gods agreed with her." In the *Iliad*, the consent of the other gods is often balanced against Zeus' desires (as in book 4 where Hera tells Zeus to do what he wants even though the other gods will not praise it: ἔρδ'· ἀτὰρ οὔ τοι πάντες ἐπαινέομεν θεοὶ ἄλλοι, 4.29). On the importance of praise and consent among the gods, see Martin 1989: 55–6 and Elmer 2013. In the *Odyssey*, however, Zeus and Athena operate primarily without the participation of the other gods. Here, the parodist allows Zeus to convene over the divine assembly, Athena to propose a course of action, and the other gods to follow her.

ἐπεπείθοντ': In Homer, the middle of πείθω often means "to assent to" rather than "obey." On this distinction, see Stensgaard 2003.

198–259 The gods watch the clash of the armies. They direct the audience's attention as an internal audience gazing upon the slaughter of war. The parodist makes this even more explicit after the gods move together as a crowd thronging into a theater for a spectacle. For the gods as an audience in Homer, see Griffin 1980: 179–201. For a more theoretical treatment, see Pucci 2002: 21. What the gods gaze upon is a rather confusing and hectic series of deaths. The text has problems throughout. The last 100 lines of the poem are more formulaic and "Homeric" than the first two-thirds. This formulaic section presents action that is not altogether clear with prominent characters who die only to appear again later. Typically, scholars have interpreted the confusion as resulting from a combination of poor poetic skill and textual corruption. Following Kelly's argument (2009) that the confusion and lack of clarity is an intentional parody of Homeric style, we can view this section as a generic critique. It is clear from the manuscript tradition that there are significant confusions from textual transmission; on the other hand, the sophistication of the poem from the beginning to this point should make us wary of dismissing Kelly's suggestion to take the parody seriously (on which, see also Most 1993 and Sens 2005). It is possible to accomodate both the conventional and the theoretical interpretations of the poem.

198   ἀολλέες: "in throngs, gathered together," Homeric.

εἰς ἕνα χῶρον: Cf. line 133.

199   καὶ τότε: A common Homeric phrase coordinating action among different characters as at *Il.* 1.92 (Καὶ τότε δὴ θάρσησε καὶ ηὔδα μάντις ἀμύμων).

κώνωπες: from κώνωψ, "gnat, mosquito." Here, probably "mosquitoes." The σάλπιγξ was a war trumpet. According to Aristotle (*de Mundo* 399b), the σάλπιγξ was sounded prior to the soldiers' assumption of their arms. Presumably, the mosquitoes were bearing these trumpets for the mice, as it seems unlikely that they would serve the frogs in any function other than a source of sustenance.

200   ἐσάλπιγξαν: Denominative verb from σάλπιγξ.

δεινὸν ... κτύπον: This might typically signal a percussive sound, whereas in Homer trumpets "scream" (ὡς δ' ὅτ' ἀριζήλη φωνή, ὅτε τ' ἴαχε σάλπιγξ, 18.219).

201   Ζεὺς Κρονίδης βρόντησε, τέρας πολέμοιο κακοῖο. Cf. *Il.* 20.56 (δεινὸν δὲ βρόντησε πατὴρ ἀνδρῶν τε θεῶν τε) and 17.548 (Ζεὺς ἐξ οὐρανόθεν τέρας ἔμμεναι ἢ πολέμοιο). For πολέμοιο κακοῖο (Homeric genitive) see 1.284 (ἕρκος Ἀχαιοῖσιν πέλεται πολέμοιο κακοῖο). The appositive use of τέρας—generally associated with Zeus—is a bit odd,

but see *Il.* 5.741–2 ("on it was the Gorgon-head of the terrible monster, dread and terrifying, a symbol of Aegis-bearing Zeus"; ἐν δέ τε Γοργείη κεφαλὴ δεινοῖο πελώρου / δεινή τε σμερδνή τε, Διὸς τέρας αἰγιόχοιο).

202 Πρῶτος δ': δὲ πρῶτος often starts sequences of action. The δέ is not adversative (i.e. anticipating a contrast, cf. Eng. "but"), but instead copulative (close to "and").

Ὑψιβόας: "Shouts-on-high."

Λειχήνορα: "Manlicker." Cf. line 216 below.

οὔτασε δουρί: A common sequence in the *Iliad*, cf. *Il.* 5.56 and 7.258

203 ἑσταότ': Perfect passive particple of ἵστημι. ἑσταότ' is common at the beginning of lines (e.g. *Il.* 4.366).

κατὰ γαστέρα: Some MSS have the genitive κατὰ γαστέρος instead, meaning "through the stomach, he struck the middle of the liver with the spear." The accusative with κατά (meaning "down into" or simply "into") is Homeric (16.465) but the specification "down into the stomach into the liver" seems a bit strained. For κατὰ γαστέρος see on line 71. See also line 235 below. Both are likely literary adaptations, see Camerotto 1992: 12.

ἐς μέσον ἧπαρ: "in the middle of the liver" not in Homeric battle scenes (but cf. . . . μέσην κατὰ γαστέρα τύψε, 17.313), but instead when Hecuba wishes she could eat Achilles' liver (. . . τοῦ ἐγὼ μέσον ἧπαρ ἔχοιμι / ἐσθέμεναι προσφῦσα . . ., 24.212–13).

204 κὰδ: κατά, a common assimilation with δ' ἔπεσεν see *Il.* 11.676: δ' ἔπεσεν πρηνής: "He fell down face forward." In battle language, πρηνής contrasts with ὕπτιος, on one's back ἁπαλὰς δ' ἐκόνισεν ἐθείρας: For κονίω as a transitive, see *Il.*21.207. For falling in dust, cf. 16.469: κὰδ δ' ἔπεσ' ἐν κονίῃσι μακών, ἀπὸ δ' ἔπτατο θυμός.

205 δούπησεν δὲ πεσών: Homeric, see *Il.* 16.599 (δούπησεν δὲ πεσών· πυκινὸν δ' ἄχος ἔλλαβ' Ἀχαιούς). This line is suspect to some: for Glei 1984 (*ad loc.*) it is a variation on a previous line; West 2003 considers it

an interpolation. Its repetitive nature is in line with the tone of the unfolding battle scene.

ἀράβησε δὲ τεύχε' ἐπ' αὐτῷ: this whole line is Homeric, see *Il.* 5.42 (δούπησεν δὲ πεσών, ἀράβησε δὲ τεύχε' ἐπ' αὐτῷ).

206   Τρωγλοδύτης δὲ μετ' αὐτὸν ἀκόντισε Πηλείωνος: The verb here can take the genitive, but some MSS have the accusative πηλείωνα. The addition of μετ' αὐτὸν obscures the matter. For the general sense, perhaps take μετ' αὐτὸν merely temporally (i.e. "after that/him Holedweller hurled at the son of Peleus and his strong spear stuck in his chest").

Πηλείωνος: "The son of Peleus." Physignathos, the frog at the center of the war, dies an understated death here (if this patronymic indicates the same frog). On the name, see Physignathos' speech above at line 19. Note, however, that Physignathos is alive to be struck on the foot at line 250. (And there is likely extra humor that a son of Peleus is struck on the foot as Achilles is in the tradition). The dead mouse-prince, Psicharpax, appears alive at 234.

207   πῆξεν: Unaugmented aorist of πήγνυμι; στιβαρὸν δόρυ is the subject.

τὸν δὲ πεσόντα: object of εἷλε.

208   μέλας θάνατος: "black death" occurs at line 16.687 the phrase is closely based on the common κῆρα μέλαιναν (e.g. 21.66). Cf. Camerotto (1992: 16) and line 236 below. Sens (2005: 233–4) sees a sophisticated engagement with Homeric and Hesiodic models in the adaptation of this line.

ἔπτη: The syncopated, defective aorist of πέτομαι does not appear until after the Hellenistic period.

209   Ἐμβασίχυτρος: "someone who enters dishes" (we suggest "Bowldiver"); he is the herald who announces the war to the frogs at line 137.

Σευτλαῖον: from σεῦτλον, "beet."

ἔπεφνε: See on 141.

210 Ἀρτοφάγος: "Breadeater" from ἄρτος "loaf" and φαγέω, used as a second aorist of ἐσθίω.

Πολύφωνον: "of much voice" e.g. noisy, chatterer; see the note at line 12.

κατὰ γαστέρα: See discussion on 203.

τύψε: unaugmented, 3rd person singular.

210-22: In his edition, Allen suggests that 210, 213a and 217 are "clearly Byzantine" and that the other lines "stand with them" and should be rejected. Several of the lines have metrical issues and present somewhat ungainly repetitions from earlier lines. The first part of 213a does not fit the meter (πέτρῳ μυλοειδέϊ) and the close final repetition of ὡς δ᾽ ἐνόησε at 215 and 217 seems inelegant. There are also several rare words and formulae seemingly lifted from Homer which imply later "authorship." (See the comments on each line below.) West 2003 cuts out some of the lines but preserves most. Glei preserves the bulk while Ludwich agrees that 213, 213a are out of place. 216 and 217 are also absent in some manuscripts.

211 ἤριπε δὲ πρηνής, ψυχὴ δὲ μελέων ἐξέπτη: This line is similar to 204 (κὰδ δ᾽ ἔπεσεν πρηνής) and 208 (ψυχὴ δ᾽ ἐκ σώματος ἔπτη). The first half is similar to *Il.*5.58 (ἤριπε δὲ πρηνής, ἀράβησε δὲ τεύχε᾽ ἐπ᾽ αὐτῷ.). The notion is similar to *Il.* 23.880 (ὠκὺς δ᾽ ἐκ μελέων θυμὸς πτάτο, τῆλε δ᾽ ἀπ᾽ αὐτοῦ).

μελέων: Uncontracted genitive plural of μέλος, μέλεος ("limb").

ἐξέπτη: See on line 208.

212 Λιμνόχαρις: "Delights-in-the-Pond."

ὡς εἶδεν: "When he saw that"; ὡς often follows the clause's subject.

ἀπολλύμενον: Note the present tense of the participle, for progressive force, i.e. "When he saw that Polyphônos was being destroyed."

213   Τρωγλοδύτην ἁπαλοῖο δι' αὐχένος τρῶσεν ἐπιφθάς: There are two lines included in this section in some MSS: 213a and 213b below. In addition, there is a variant for 213: Τρωγλίτην ἁπαλοῖο δι' αὐχένος ἤριπε δ' εὐθύς: 208–9 repeated ἁπαλοῖο δι' αὐχένος.

213a πέτρῳ μυλοειδέϊ· τὸν δὲ σκότος ὄσσε κάλυψε· πέτρῳ μυλοειδέϊ: this appears in the *Iliad* (7.270: εἴσω δ' ἀσπίδ' ἔαξε βαλὼν μυλοειδέϊ πέτρῳ) during the dual of Ajax and Hektor. τὸν δὲ σκότος ὄσσε κάλυψε: A common Homeric formula, e.g. *Il.* 6.11; see line 231 below.

213b   Τρωγλήτης δ' ἄρ ἔπεφνε Βρεκαίκιγα ἐσθλόν ἀίξας: This line also has formulaic aspects. On ἔπεφνε see 141, 209.

Βρεκαίκιγα ἐσθλὸν: The novel compound may echo Aristophanes' frog call (*brekekkex koax koax*; Βρεκεκεκεξ κοαξ κοαξ from the *Frogs*) or derive from the root βρέχω ("to moisten, or to be wet") and ἀίσσω ("to leap"), so: "Waterdarter." Thus, the line-ending participle ἀίξας, by modifying the mouse, not the frog, engages in a bit of linguistic play. For the call *brekekkex koax koax,* see Dover 1993: 219 who draws on Campbell 1984 in proposing that the frog species in question in the Marsh Frog, *Rana ridibunda.*

214   εἷλε: Aorist of αἱρέω.

ἤλασεν ὀξέϊ σχοίνῳ: "with a sharp reed." The final two words adapt a common Homeric line-final adjective-noun pairing: ὀξέϊ χαλκῷ (e.g. *Il.* 10.35), ὀξέϊ δουρὶ (e.g. *Il.* 11.95) and ὀξέϊ λᾶϊ (once, 16.739). The humorous adaptation of Heroic bronze on a spear to the reed would certainly be clear to an audience familiar with Homeric poetry.

214a   ἀλλ' ὁ μὲν ἔσπασεν ἔγκος: This line is similar to the first half of 215.

ἐφωρμήθησαν δ' ἐκ αὐτῷ: This plural aorist passive exists nowhere else in Greek literature. The singular appears in the *Odyssey* (4.713).

ἀλλ' ὁ μὲν ἔσπασεν ἔγκος: This line is similar to the first half of 215 (οὐδ' ἐξέσπασεν ἔγχος ἐναντίον).

215 ἐξέσπασεν: from σπάω, "to draw out."

216 Λειχήνωρ δ' αὐτοῖο τιτύσκετο δουρὶ φαεινῷ: This line is almost identical to Il. 13.159 (Μηριόνης δ' αὐτοῖο τιτύσκετο δουρὶ φαεινῷ). A "Manlicker" was killed as one of the first casualties at line 202. With the apparent resurrections of Physignathos and Psicharpax (see the appearance of the former at 206), the return of the same Leikhênôr may contribute to the parody.

τιτύσκετο: from τιτύσκομαι which can mean "obtain or hit" like τεύχω, τυγχάνω with the genitive object.

217 καὶ βάλεν, οὐδ' ἀφάμαρτε καθ' ἧπαρ· ὡς δ' ἐνόησε: The combination appears in Il. 11.350 (καὶ βάλεν, οὐδ' ἀφάμαρτε τιτυσκόμενος κεφαλῆφιν, 11.350). The tautology of "hitting" and "not missing," is somewhat formulaic.

ἀφάμαρτε: second aorist of ἀφαρματάνω: "to miss."

ὡς δ' ἐνόησε: This is repeated throughout this section as a transition from one action to another. This concept appears in Homer (e.g. Il. 11.248; Od. 24.232) but not in this combination to end a line.

218 Κοστοφάγον: "Spice-eater"; the lexicographer Hesychius glosses κόστος as εἶδος ἀρώματος (a type of aromatic spice).

ἔμπεσεν: aorist from ἐμπίπτω. The subject remains Λειχήνωρ.

219 ἀλλ' οὐδ' ὡς ἀπέληγε μάχης ἀλλ' ἤλασεν αὐτόν: The first part of this line is identical to a repeated line in the Iliad (e.g. ἀλλ' οὐδ' ὡς ἀπέληγε μάχης κορυθαίολος Ἕκτωρ, 7.263). The doubling of ἀλλά in the line is un-Homeric.

ἀπέληγε: from ἀπολήγω, "to leave off," and takes a genitive object.

ἤλασεν: Aorist of ἐλαύνω which can mean "to cut and wound" instead of simply "to drive."

220 κάππεσε: syncope for καταπίπτω.

ἐβάπτετο: βάπτω, "to dip, to dye." In tragedy, this verb is commonly used for scenes of slaughter (e.g. Aesch. *Pr.* 863). With the pond as subject, however, the image is clear but strange.

221 πορφυρέῳ: "dark red"; purple.

παρ' ἠιόν': "along the shore."

ἐξετανύσθη: From ἐκτανύω "to stretch out." This form occurs in the *Iliad* (7.271: βλάψε δέ οἱ φίλα γούναθ'· ὃ δ' ὕπτιος ἐξετανύσθη).

222 χορδῇσιν: "intestines."

λιπαρῇσι: "thin, tender" or, as we prefer, "trailing [as in drawn-out] intestines."

ἐπορνύμενος: Some MSS have genitive ἐπορνύμενου instead. In both cases the lines are hard to construe. The nominative works better; the subject changes at αὐτὸς δέ. Kostophagos is trying to rise up again as his intestines trail out of him. West (2003) believes that this line is out of place.

λαγόνεσσιν: "loins." From λαγών, λαγόνος.

223 Τυροφάγον δ' αὐτῇσιν ἐπ' ὄχθαις ἐξενάριξεν: For this line to make sense, the subject would be Platelicker again, which seems to indicate a mouse killing another mouse (unless this is a frog with a murine name).

Τυροφάγον: "Cheeseeater," a name appropriate for a mouse. Cf. English *tyrophile* ("cheeselover").

ἐξενάριξεν: "to despoil" from ἐξεναρίζω, common ending the line in Homer (e.g. *Il.* 5.151).

αὐτῇσιν ἐπ' ὄχθαις: "the same banks."

224 Πτερνογλύφον: "Hamborer."

Καλαμίνθιος: "Minty."

ἰδών: see ὁράω.

ἦλθεν: Aorist of ἔρχομαι. The idiom ἐς φόβον ἦλθεν appears to be periphrasis for "they fled because of fear." This seems conceptually related to a Homeric "he drove fear into them" (cf. *Il.* 14.522: ἀνδρῶν τρεσσάντων, ὅτε τε Ζεὺς ἐν φόβον ὄρσῃ).

225 ἤλατο: Aorist passive of ἐλαύνω.

τὴν ἀσπίδα ῥίψας: "after abandoning the shield." The shield-abandoning poem is a motif in early Greek literature, and this line seems to draw on lyric fragments (cf. Anacreon fr. 36b ἀσπίδα ῥίψας ποταμοῦ καλλιρόου παρ᾽ ὄχθας). The most famous articulation of this anti-heroic sentiment is Archilochus fr. 5.1–4.

226 Λιτραῖον ("worth a *litra*," i.e. a pound"): Other options for this noun: Λιστραῖον ("digger" from λιστραίνω), φυτραῖον, φιλτραῖον ("of a love-charm"), χυτραῖον ("earthen-pot"), φιτραῖον.

Βορβοροκοίτης: "Sleeps in the mud"; some MSS have the accusative form instead.

227 Ὑδρόχαρις δ᾽ ἔπεφνεν Πτερνοφάγον βασιλῆα: This line is unmetrical and is missing from many MSS.

Ὑδρόχαρις: "Watergrace."

ἔπεφνεν: See above, note 141.

Πτερνοφάγον: "Hameater."

βασιλῆα: accusative singular of βασιλεύς.

228 χερμαδίῳ: "stone"; this word begins the line 5x in the *Iliad* (e.g. 4.518). Sens (2005: 232–233) sees important engagement between lines 228–229 and *Od.* 9.290 (where Odysseus' men have their brains smashed by Polyphemos) among others.

πλήξας: Aorist of πλήσσω, "to strike" (in this form 1x in the *Iliad*).

βρέγματος: "forehead" from βρέγμα, which does not appear before tragedy and comedy (Aesch., fr. 496.8; Strattis, fr. 34: οἶσθ' ᾧ προσέοικεν, ὦ Κρέων, τὸ βρέγμα σου;).

ἐγκέφαλος: "brains," in Homeric battle scenes in this position (e.g. 12.185).

229   ἐκ ῥινῶν: from ῥίς, "nose"; in the plural, "nostrils."

ἔσταξε: from στάζω "to drip." This verb occurs without an augment once in the *Iliad* (19.39) and in a Hesiodic fragment, but popular in tragedy. With ῥινῶν: στάξε κατὰ ῥινῶν, ἵνα οἱ χρὼς ἔμπεδος εἴη, *Il.* 19.39.

παλάσσετο δ' αἵματι: "to be dyed with blood" appears in the *Iliad* (e.g. 5.100) but not with γαῖα. Instead, in Homer has the earth "flowing with blood" (ῥέε δ' αἵματι γαῖα, *Il.* 4.451). This line, then, is likely a composite of the two Homeric images.

230   ἀμύμονα Βορβοροκοίτην: the metrical shape of Borborokoitês is the same as Bellerophontes which shares the same epithet at *Il.* 6.216 (Οἰνεὺς γάρ ποτε δῖος ἀμύμονα Βελλεροφόντην). Some MSS have Leikhopinax in the accusative and Borborokoitês in the nominative (ἀμύμων Βορβοροκοίτης). Some MSS have Ἐμβασίχυτρος instead of Βορβοροκοίτης, although the former is a mouse-name. The accusative Λειχοπίναχα would be unmetrical. The simplest MSS solution, then, is to retain the accusative Βορβοροκοίτην and nominative Λειχοπίναξ.

231   ἔγχει ἐπαΐξας: from ἐπαίσσω, common in Homer, e.g. *Il.* 5.235. Some editors put a comma after Βορβοροκοίτην in line 230, thus construing ἔγχει as a dative instrument with ἐπαΐξας relying on Homeric usage as at *Il.* 5.81 and 5.584. In both cases, however, the dative instruments are probably better with the main verbs. At 5.81, Eurypylos strikes the shoulder "with a sword after he leaps" (ἔλασ' ὦμον / φασγάνῳ ἀΐξας; as opposed to "strikes the shoulder after he leaps with a sword"). Similarly, at 5.584, Antilokhos "struck his temple with a sword after leaping upon him" rather than "struck him after leaping upon him with a sword" (Ἀντίλοχος δ' ἄρ' ἐπαΐξας ξίφει ἤλασε κόρσην). The poet of

this parody has retained the shape of the line and the formula (dative instrument plus participle) with a less comprehensive grasp of the sense.

τὸν δὲ σκότος ὄσσε κάλυψεν: A formulaic passage for death from Homer (see e.g., 6.11) "Darkness covered his eyes." ὄσσε is dual.

[231a] The MSS also have a full line from Homer: δούπησεν δὲ πεσών, ἀράβησε δὲ τεύχε' ἐπ' αὐτῷ, Il. 13.187. But this line also appears at 205.

232 Πρασσαῖος: "Greenstalk" (cf. πρασίνος, "leek"), most likely a frog name. The variant Πρασσοφάγος ("stalk-eater") strengthens the identification with a frog-diet; yet, phage-compounds are more common among the mice: See Ἀρτοφάγος, 210; Κοστοφάγον, 217; Τυρόφαγος, line 223; Πτερνοφάγον, 227.

ποδός: here, "by the foot."

Κνισσοδιώκτην: "Smokehunter" an appropriate name for vermin lurking near sacrifices. The double-sigma is likely a hyper-archaism for κνίση. Some MSS offer νεκρὸν ἐόντα. Syntactically, νεκρὸν ἐόντα would refer back to the last object, in this case Βορβοροκοίτην and would seem to imply frog-on-frog violence; or, this could refer to an unnamed mouse without grammatical antecedent (following Kelly 2009: 47). This reading would have Prassaios leaping upon and drowning a corpse, an image other commentators have found absurd. Perhaps the absurdity characterizes the ferocity of the frog's attack? The reading νεκρὸν ἐόντα would effect a rhyme with the following line (χειρὶ τένοντα) which is typically avoided in hexameter poetry. Ludwich, who has Ἐμβασίχυτρος instead of Βορβοροκοίτης at line 230, offers the variant νεκρόσαντα, providing the sense that Prassaios, once he has witnessed Leikhopinax in the act of making someone else into a corpse, drags *him* by the foot to his drowning death. This works well in a battle where frogs kill mice by drowning.

233 ἀπέπνιξε: On this verb, see above lines 99 and 119. Some MSS present the rather bland variant ἀπέθηκε.

κρατήσας: "to overpower"; κρατέω often takes a genitive object but can function absolutely ("to prevail") or with an accusative of the person prevailed against. In this case "he overpowered [him] as he reached out with his hand."

234 Ψιχάρπαξ: "Crumbthief" here makes a reappearance (he died at line 99). We are left to assume (1) a manuscript problem or artistic error (see Glei 1983, *ad loc.*), (2) that another mouse-hero shares this name, as in the two Ajaxes (in which case, one might disambiguate using patronyms) or (3) that the dead mouse prince has been resurrected (see Kelly's (2009) note on how the parody here takes the ambiguity of Homeric battle scenes to task). MSS variants to solve this problem include: (1) a variant Λειχάρπαξ (a compound of two verbs, meaning "Licksnatch"); (2) Ludwich's conjecture Λυχνάρπαξ ("Oilthief"), for a the lacuna in th text (Λ[...]άρπαξ) and the content of line 180 (στέμματα βλάπτοντες καὶ λύχνους εἵνεκ᾽ ἐλαίου). For (1), we have already the compound Λειχομύλη: "Millstone licker"—but here the combination of two verbal-roots generates a name with little sense; (2) is attractive enough, but still conjecture.

ἑτάρου περὶ τεθνειῶτος: Some MSS have the plural ἑτάρων... τεθνειώτων ἤμυν᾽: The augmented form of ἀμύνω is less common in Homer (see Christensen 2013). The verb can "ward off" danger from an object in the genitive as at *Il.*13.109–10 whereas the use of the preposition περὶ is more common as at 18.173 (οἳ μὲν ἀμυνόμενοι νέκυος πέρι τεθνηῶτος).

235 βάλε: unaugmented, "he struck."

κατὰ νηδύος ἐς μέσον ἧπαρ: on this see above note 203 (κατὰ γαστέρα ἐς μέσον ἧπαρ). Here we have the genitive instead of accusative, but the noun has changed: νηδύς can mean "womb" or just a cavity in the stomach. For a wound in the νηδύς, see *Il.* 20.486 (τὸν βάλε μέσσον ἄκοντι, πάγη δ᾽ ἐν νηδύϊ χαλκός). Instead of ἧπαρ, some MSS have ἦτορ.

236 πῖπτε: Unaugmented imperfect.

οἱ πρόσθεν: οἱ is likely the dative singular 3rd person pronoun. This passage probably means "he fell before him".

ψυχὴ δ' ᾽Αϊδόσδε βεβήκει: This line is most likely influenced by Homeric images, as at 22.362 (ψυχὴ δ' ἐκ ῥεθέων πταμένη ᾽Άϊδος δὲ βεβήκει).

237 Κραμβοβάτης δὲ ἰδών: The triple anaphora in this battle section (name + δὲ ἰδὼν) is not Homeric. The epics often have the sequence τὸν δὲ ἰδὼν.

Κραμβοβάτης: "Cabbagetreader"; some MSS have Πηλοβάτης ("Mudwalker"). We should probably assume that this is a frog; some have suggested that Κραμβοβάτης might denote a mouse (though Psicharpax claims he does not eat cabbages at 53); the sense of the passage would have a mouse attacking a mouse (here Ψιχάρπαξ from line 234) unless we provide another object-pronoun without antecedant.

πηλοῦ δράκα: "Handful of mud"; cf. *drakhma*, "a handful."

238 καὶ τὸ μέτωπον: here, "face."

ἔχρισε: χρίω, "to rub on, annoint"; one manuscript has ἔπληξε instead. The sense with ἔχρισε is more vivid.

ἐξετύφλου: Other MSS have ἐξετύφλωσε ("to blind") instead.

παρὰ μικρόν: Adverbial: "more than a little" which comes to mean "almost." μικρόν as an adverb is not Homeric. This phrase appears in Eur. *Heracl.* 295 (ὡς δεῖν' ἔπαθεν καὶ παρὰ μικρόν), Isocrates 4.59. See the LSJ entry III.5.b. See Smyth §1692.3c παρὰ μικρόν for "narrowly" or almost. This phrase seems gains in popularity during the classical period, appearing in tragedy, oratory, and then philosophy (e.g. Aristotle *Phy.* 1.97.92).

239 ὠργίσθη: from ὀργίζω: "to make angry." Some MSS have ὀργισθείς instead. Others have θυμώθη, μουνώθη, γουνώθη, and συνώθη.

χειρὶ παχείῃ: "with a thick hand," Homeric; see e.g. 21.424: καί ῥ' ἐπιεισαμένη πρὸς στήθεα χειρὶ παχείῃ.

240   ἐν δαπέδῳ: "earth." Some variants include γαίη and πεδίῳ. This is Homeric, see *Od.* 11.577: κείμενον ἐν δαπέδῳ. ὃ δ᾽ ἐπ᾽ ἐννέα κεῖτο πέλεθρα.

λίθον ὄβριμον: "Strong rock." The adjective is most often combined with spear (ἔγχος).

ἄχθος ἀρούρης: "a burden of the earth"; a Homeric formula which is used by Achilles to describe his uselessness while out of battle (ἀλλ᾽ ἧμαι παρὰ νηυσὶν ἐτώσιον ἄχθος ἀρούρης, 18.104). Cf. *Od.* 20.379 (ἔμπαιον οὐδὲ βίης, ἀλλ᾽ αὔτως ἄχθος ἀρούρης) where it insultingly refers Odysseus. The allusion may humorously trivialize the Homeric scenes.

241   Κραμβοβάτην: There is also the variant Πηλοβάτην. The scene is describing the blinding of a mouse who, in rage, hurls the first thing at hand against his assaillant.

ὑπὸ γούνατα: "under the knees."

ἐκλάσθη: "sounded out" from κλάγγω. This form appears once in Homer (*Il.* 11.584)

242   κνήμη δεξιτερή: "Right greave."

πέσε δ᾽ ὕπτιος ἐν κονίῃσι: "He fell face up into the dust." The image and language is taken from Homer (ἑσταότ᾽ ἄγχ᾽ Αἴαντος· ὃ δ᾽ ὕπτιος ἐν κονίῃσι, *Il.* 15.434) but the verb is often enjambed into the next line (νηὸς ἄπο πρυμνῆς χαμάδις πέσε . . .).

243   Κραυγασίδης: A patronymic without any clear antecedant or noun.

ἤμυνε: see above on line 234.

αὖθις: "in turn."

ἐπ᾽ αὐτόν: Another object without a clear antecedant, but it must refer to the subject of 234 (here Ψιχάρπαξ) who kills there and is attacked in 237 (ἐπ᾽ αὐτόν). Once angered (ὠργίσθη δ᾽ ἄρ᾽ ἐκεῖνος), he picks up his boulder and strikes his adversary (241). The new subject at 243 can only have that adversary to strike in 244.

244 κατὰ γαστέρα: On this phrase, see on line 203.

245 ὀξύσχοινος: "sharp reed" (see above, 164) is modified by πᾶς (244).

ἔκχυντο: "poured out"; the subject is in the next line.

246 ἔγκατ': "Innards, guts."

ἐφελκομένῳ: dative of possession "all his guts poured out because of the spear from the stout hand."

ὑπὸ δούρατι: With ὑπὸ, the dative can mean "under the force of" or merely "under."

χειρὶ παχείῃ: The repeition so close to 239 is a little suspect.

247 Τρωγλοδύτης: "Holedweller"; see above on 52.

παρ' ὄχθῃσιν ποταμοῖο: Note the use of a n-moveable before a consonant; Janko (1982; 2012: 29) includes this as an archaism. This is the only instance (other than line-ending n-moveables at 31, 100, 121, 136, and 185) in the epic. This phrase is Homeric, see *Od.* 6.97: δεῖπνον ἔπειθ' εἵλοντο παρ' ὄχθῃσιν ποταμοῖο.

ὡς εἶδεν: "When he noticed," cf. *Il.* 4.149 (ὡς εἶδεν μέλαν αἷμα καταρρέον ἐξ ὠτειλῆς).

248 σκάζων ἐκ πολέμου ἀνεχάζετο, τείρετο δ' αἰνῶς: This line seems like "cut-and-paste" poetry. Each of the three parts appears in Homer in exactly the same position; but only all together here.

σκάζων ἐκ πολέμου: "limping from battle" σκάζω. This phrase occurs only at *Il.* 11.811 (σκάζων ἐκ πολέμου· κατὰ δὲ νότιος ῥέεν ἱδρὼς).

ἀνεχάζετο: "to retreat" from ἀναχάζω "to cause to retreat"; this verb appears frequently in Homer, e.g. *Il.* 5.600, 11.461, 16.710, 17.108

τείρετο δ' αἰνῶς: from τείρω "to wear down"; here "to suffer." αἰνῶς "dreadfully, terribly." Cf. *Il.* 5.352 Ὡς ἔφαθ', ἣ δ' ἀλύουσ' ἀπεβήσετο, τείρετο δ' αἰνῶς·

249 ἥλατο δ' ἐς τάφρους: Some MSS have ἐς τάφρον, Ludwich shows ἐς λίμνην as well, but it would not make sense for a mouse to retreat to the pond. In Homer, the plural never occurs. The singular appears at *Il.* 18.215 (στῆ δ' ἐπὶ τάφρον ἰὼν ἀπὸ τείχεος, οὐδ' ἐς Ἀχαιοὺς).

250 Τρωξάρτης: This is Psicharpax' father who speaks at 109.

ἐς ποδὸς ἄκρον: "Top of his foot." This scene may play upon Paris' wounding of Diomedes' foot in the *Iliad* 11.377ff. The scene probably also resonates with the death of Achilles at Paris' hand in the mythical tradition. The use of the preposition ἐς with ἔβαλεν is odd, but it is not without some precedent: intensifying or directional prepositions are used with βάλλω, see *Il.* 17.517 (καὶ βάλεν Ἀρήτοιο κατ' ἀσπίδα πάντοσ' ἐΐσην). Earlier, at line 209, Physignathos the son of Πηλείωνος dies. This wounding in the foot may indicate (1) an unresolved manuscript conflict; (2) different frogs in the two scenes; (3) intentional literary play with conventional Homeric battle scenes; see Kelly 2009.

251 ἔσχατος δ' ἐκ λίμνης ἀνεδύσετο, τείρετο δ' αἰνῶς: This line is unmetrical; for the first word to scan as a dactyl, we would have to lose the δ' (as Glei does); but the line would be odd without a connective. There are several MSS variants for this line including:

ὦκα δὲ λίμνην ἥλατο τειρόμενός περ δεινῶς
ὦκα δὲ τειρόμενος ἐς λίμνην ἥλατο φεύγων
ὦκα δ' ἐς λίμνην εἰσᾶλτο τειρόμενον δ' αἰνῶς

None of the variants seems more convincing than the others. When it comes to content, this line does not really contribute to the order of the action which would have Physignathos exiting the pond in suffering. Instead, there is logic in having Prassaios noticing his fall and then entering into action. In addition, there are elements repeated from line 248.

252   Πρασσαῖος: Ludwich has Τρωξάρτης instead. Prassaios here makes more sense because the other has just been wounded.

ὡς εἶδεν: A typical Homeric phrase for a character noticing something; see *Il.* 15.484: Ἕκτωρ δ᾽ ὡς εἶδεν Τεύκρου βλαφθέντα βέλεμνα.

ἡμίπνουν: "half-alive."

προπεσόντα: from πίπτω.

252a   καὶ οἱ ἐκέδραμεν αὖθις, ἀποκτάμεναι μενεαίνων: Ludwich includes this variant; Glei does not.

ἀποκτάμεναι μενεαίνων: This phrase is similar to *Il.* 20.165 (σίντης, ὅν τε καὶ ἄνδρες ἀποκτάμεναι μεμάασιν). ἀποκτάμεναι: from ἀποκτείνω. μενεαίνων: "longing for."

253   ἦλθε διὰ προμάχων: "He went through the forefighters"; this is similar to *Il.* 17.88 (βῆ δὲ διὰ προμάχων κεκορυθμένος αἴθοπι χαλκῷ).

ἀκόντισεν: from ἀκοντίζω "to hurl a spear." This form appears in this position at *Il.* 4.490 (Πριαμίδης καθ᾽ ὅμιλον ἀκόντισεν ὀξέϊ δουρί).

ὀξύσχοινον: on this, see line 164.

253–6: Various MSS omit these lines.

254   ἔρρηξε: ῥήγνυμι "to break."

σάκος: "shield."

δουρὸς ἀκωκή: "Tip of the spear," often at the end of the line, cf. *Il.* 23.821 (αἰὲν ἐπ᾽ αὐχένι κῦρε φαεινοῦ δουρὸς ἀκωκῇ).

σχέτο: intransitive aorist of ἔχω, cf. *Il.* 7.248 (ἐν τῇ δ᾽ ἑβδομάτῃ ῥινῷ σχέτο· δεύτερος αὖτε).

255   Some MSS omit both 255 and 256. The sense of line 255 (οὐδ᾽ ἔβαλε τρυφάλειαν ἀμύμονα καὶ τετράχυτρον) is difficult in context. With 254: "He didn't break the shield, but the tip of the spear stuck in it / and he also didn't hit the helment, blameless and four-pots-thick."

Switching the order of the two lines might make more sense. However, there is probably a subject change at 255 with the nominative δῖος Ὀριγανίων postponed to 256. According to a scholiast, these objects are actually names, Tetrakhutros and Truphaleios, of the victims here (the "strong heroes" reflected in ἥρωας κρατερούς at 259).

τετράχυτρον: "Four-pots thick," modifying τρυφάλειαν, "helmet." The epithet τετράχυτρον only appears here in all of Greek literature, a clear parodic neologism. Cf. the similar form at A.R. 2.920 (τετράφαλος φοίνικι λόφῳ ἐπελάμπετο πήληξ). In addition, this form may also be built on the "four-layered" shield that appears at *Il.* 15.479 (αὐτὰρ ὅ γ' ἀμφ' ὤμοισι σάκος θέτο τετραθέλυμνον).

256 δῖος Ὀριγανίων: "Shining/Glorious Oregano;" the common Homeric epithet here is humorous and functional.

μιμούμενος αὐτὸν Ἄρηα: μιμούμενος: see on line 7 and 149. The participle of μιμέεσθαι here and at line 7 highlights the parodic detachment between the world of myth and the ridiculous mice. This is underscored by the fact that we encounter Zeus ἡδὺ γελῶν in line 172, but also is discordant with the fears expressed by Athena (194) and even Zeus himself (272–3).

257 ὃς μόνος ἐν βατράχοισιν ἀρίστευεν καθ' ὅμιλον: "he alone among the frogs had his aristeia through the throng." In Homer, καθ' ὅμιλον usually indicates movement (e.g. *Il.* 12.468: κέκλετο δὲ Τρώεσσιν ἐλιξάμενος καθ' ὅμιλον); here this makes more sense if the verb ἀρίστευεν is understood as having a sense of motion, i.e. "he had his aristeia all through that crowd." This turns out to be funny shortly—he is said to be the only one who has an *aristeia* but then jumps into the water when he notices that everyone else is fleeing!

ἀρίστευεν: "to have an *aristeia*," "to be the best"; this verb appears in Homer, e.g. 11.784 (αἰὲν ἀριστεύειν καὶ ὑπείροχον ἔμμεναι ἄλλων).

καθ' ὅμιλον: "Throughout the throng."

258   ὥρμησεν: ὁρμάω is comparatively rare in Homer but common in prose authors after the fifth century BCE.

δ' ὡς ἴδεν: Note the unaugmented form instead of the earlier ὡς εἶδεν at 247.

259   This line is left out by several MSS. There is a metrical problem midline (ἀλλ' ἔδυνε seems to be missing a syllable). The previous line needs some corresponding or continuing action—the action is a bit abrupt with a character seemingly changing his mind and retreating into the pond. This line is probably corrupt, but we find the representation of altered action attractive.

ἥρωας: In early epic poetry, the term "hero" can refer, as in Hesiod's *Works and Days*, to the race of heroes (ἀνδρῶν ἡρώων θεῖον γένος, 159) who perish fighting around Thebes and Troy (159–65). From Hesiod's perspective, the word "Hero" is restricted to this generation (see Nagy 1979: 159). In the *Iliad*, all participants are referred to generically as heroes, see *Iliad* 1.3–4. Obviously, it is parodic to depict mice as heroes in a mythical—even Homeric sense—but there is another possible level of meaning. More than once in this poem, the combatants are compared to mythical beasts such as giants (line 7), centaurs (170–1) or kosmic threats like the Titans (280–3). Here, they are compared to men: this may indicate interpolation (insofar as it doesn't conform to the earlier strategy) or amplifies and complicates the parodic move.

ἥρωας κρατερούς: The adjective κρατερούς in the masc. accusative plural is not found typically in Homer (but is in later authos such as Ap. Rhodes and Quintus Smyrnaeus). One MS preserves κραταιούς.

ἔδυνε: from δύνω (cf. δύω; the former is a parallel formation with the present infix -n-) lit. "to put on," but used frequently in Homer to describe putting on clothing (e.g. *Il.* 11.19: δεύτερον αὖ θώρηκα περὶ στήθεσσιν ἔδυνε) but also of entering water (cf. *Od.* 4.425: ὡς εἰποῦσ' ὑπὸ πόντον ἐδύσετο κυμαίνοντα·). The dative object we accept here (βένθεσι λίμνης) is probably also evidence of corruption.

βένθεσι λίμνης: "in the depths of the pond." This is a Homeric formula, see *Il.* 13.21: Αἰγάς, ἔνθα δέ οἱ κλυτὰ δώματα βένθεσι λίμνης.

260-8: The Aristeia of Meridarpax has several MŚS variants and difficulties in sense. The basic narrative is that this young, exceptional hero threatens to wreak such destruction that Zeus takes pity on the frogs and sends crabs to defend them.

260 Ἦν δέ τις: The phrase Ἦν δέ τις recalls the language and style of fable.

παῖς Μεριδάρπαξ ἔξοχος ἄλλων: The conjunction of παῖς and ἔξοχος ἄλλων, as well as the terror which Meridarpax instills in the frogs, may be a parodic joke on the overwhelming awe and fear which young warriors such as Achilles and Neoptolemus could inspire. For the sense of ἔξοχος ἄλλων, cf. αἰὲν ἀριστεύειν καὶ ὑπείροχον ἔμμεναι ἄλλων, *Il.* 6.208 and τῆς ἧ μιν παρὰ νηυσὶν ἐτίομεν ἔξοχον ἄλλων, 9.631).

Μεριδάρπαξ: μερίς (from μερίς, μερίδος) + ἅρπαξ: A scholiast glosses this name as "the one who seizes the portions" (ὁ τὰς μερίδας ἁρπάζων).

261 Κναίσωνος: perhaps from κνάω, "to scrape or grate," an appropriate name for a rodent. A scholiast glosses this as "one who eats meat" (τοῦ τρώγοντος τὰ κρέα).

ἀρτεπιβούλου: ("bread-conspirer"). The epithet ἀρτεπιβούλου is unique, found only here in Greek literature. It is compounded from ἄρτος (bread or cake) and ἐπιβουλεύω (to purpose, plot, or design).

Three variants for this line present different difficulties. 261a (μεριδάρπαξ ὄρχαμος μιμούμενος αὐτὸν ἄρηα) replicates the naming in 260 and begins with two short syllables; 261b (ὃς μόνος ἐν μύεσσιν ἀρίστευεν καθ᾿ ὅμιλον) may expand excessively on his description, but such expansiveness is both in accord with epic description and with the parody; 261c, however, seems thoroughly out of place, insofar as it describes the wounding of the character named as Meridarpax's father (Κναίσων μέν, βατράχοιο βέλει πληγεὶς κατὰ χεῖρα). Nevertheless, 261a echoes line 7 (μιμούμενοι ἔργα Γιγάντων) and repeats the sense of 256 (δῖος Ὀριγανίων, μιμούμενος αὐτὸν Ἄρηα).

262   οἴκαδ' ἴεν: The beginning of the line is a typical position for οἴκαδε in Homer (13x *Iliad*; 20x *Odyssey*) and with forms of εἶμι as at *Iliad* 1.170 (οἴκαδ' ἴμεν σὺν νηυσὶ κορωνίσιν, οὐδέ σ' ὀίω). ἴεν occurs in the *Iliad* and the *Odyssey*; it is the epic imperfect third singular of εἶμι where Attic has ᾔει(ν).

μετασχεῖν: "To join in" (from μετέχω), taking a genitive direct object (here, πολέμου).

The sense of this line is off: It seems to describe the father (Knaisôn) going home and ordering his son to join the battle. This is a bit of a strain for a Homeric parallel—the arming is late, and the motif of having a father order a son to go to war is out of place. This scene is similar both to Nestor's encouragement for Patroklos to go to war in *Iliad* 11 and Nestor's own tale of his own father's command that *he* not join battle in his youth (618–804).

In addition, the syntactical link with the earlier lines is unclear. In the abrupt and compact style presented in the battle section, it is possible that a subject change is implied by the δέ. However, it is likely that 262 is an interpolation. We suggest reading 260, 261a, 261b, 263 for the following logic:

> There was a certain child among the mice exceptional among the rest, Meridarpax
> The dear son of the blameless bread-conspirer Knaisôn
> Who had an aristeia among the mice through the throng.
> And he stood boasting along the shore
> And was threatending that he would eradicate the race of frogs.

> Ἦν δέ τις ἐν μυσὶ παῖς Μεριδάρπαξ ἔξοχος ἄλλων,
> Κναίσωνος φίλος υἱὸς ἀμύμονος ἀρτεπιβούλου·
> ὃς μόνος ἐν μύεσσιν ἀρίστευεν καθ' ὅμιλον.
> αὐτὸς δ' ἑστήκει γαυρούμενος κατὰ λίμνην
> οὗτος ἀναρπάξαι βατράχων γενεὴν ἐπαπείλει·

262a   is most probably an addition that makes sense with the inclusion of 261c (Κναίσων μέν, βρατράχοιο βέλει πληγεὶς κατὰ χεῖρα). The final line is missing any sort of connective.

263–9: Several MSS omit some or all of these lines.

263   ἀναρπάξαι: "To extirpate, eradicate." The mouse declares his genocidal intentions. This infinitive only occurs here. The verb ἀναρπάξαι is a play on Merdiarpax's (as well as Psicharpax's) name. The noun ἅρπαξ appears below at line 274.

ἐπαπείλει: "to threaten."

263a   στεῦτο δὲ πορθήσειν βρατράχων γένος αἰχμητάων: this is identical to line 291 with the exception of the initial verb (στεῦτο for "he promised/threatened"). Most editors see it as more appropriate for the latter context.

264   ἀγχοῦ δ᾽ ἔστηκεν μενεαίνων ἶφι μάχεσθαι: Only one MS has this line.

ἔστηκεν: intransitive perfect of ἵστημι.

μενεαίνων ἶφι μάχεσθαι: "eager to fight with force." This is a modified Homeric phrase (e.g. *Il.* 5.606, εἴκετε, μηδὲ θεοῖς μενεαινέμεν ἶφι μάχεσθαι).

265   καὶ ῥήξας καρύοιο μέσην ῥάχιν εἰς δύο μοίρας. This line is omitted by a handful of MSS. Its tone is certainly humorous: "he breaks the middle spine of the chestnut into two portions" for the mouse version of brass-knuckles.

ῥήξας: from ῥήγνυμι, "Break."

καρύοιο: "nut," from κάρυον, "nut tree."

ῥάχιν: "spine or outer edge," from ῥάχις. A form occurs in Soph. *Ajax* 56.

εἰς δύο μοίρας: "into two parts"; in Archaic Greek, μοῖρα can denote "portion" as when the night is split into three segments *(Il.* 10.253: τῶν δύο μοιράων, τριτάτη δ᾽ ἔτι μοῖρα λέλειπται).

266 Meridarpax is the only character to be treated in an individual arming scene in order to highlight his importance as the greatest warrior on the field.

φράγδην: "piece-by-piece."

κενώμασι: From κένωμα, a later noun related to κένος, "empty parts."

267 οἱ δὲ τάχος δείσαντες ἔβαν πάντες κατὰ λίμνην· Some MSS omit this line.

τάχος: The normal adverb ταχέως is supplanted by this adverbial neuter. Cf. Il. 406: νῦν ὤρεξε τάχος καὶ ἐπ' αὐτῷ κῦδος ἔθηκεν·

δείσαντες: Aorist from δείδω "to fear."

ἔβαν: From βαίνω, occuring in this position with some frequency in Homer (cf. the similar structure of Il. 7.432: ἐν δὲ πυρὶ πρήσαντες ἔβαν κοίλας ἐπὶ νῆας).

268 Several MSS omit this line.

ἐξετέλεσσεν: aorist of τελέω. One manuscript has ἐξετέλεσσαν, but the plural would not make sense here. Cf. Od. 11.317 (καί νύ κεν ἐξετέλεσσαν, εἰ ἥβης μέτρον ἵκοντο). In that case, the antecedent of the action "and they would have completed it" is the previously described act. Here, the verb's notional antecedent is the extirpation of the frogs threatened at line 263 (οὗτος ἀναρπάξαι βατράχων γενεὴν ἐπαπείλει).

ἐπεὶ μέγα οἱ σθένος ἦεν: ἐπεί can be used temporally and causally as here: "since he had great strength." These contrafactual scenes are typical in Homer, referred to as "*if* not-situations" by de Jong 1987; "pivotal contrafactuals" by Louden 1993; and "reversal passages" by Morrison 1992.

269–303 The gods note the demise of the frogs and Zeus pities them. He convenes another council. Ares is afraid to face a threat as dangerous as the frogs, so Zeus himself decides to intervene. When even his intervention appears in vain, he sends in an army of crabs to relieve the beleagured frogs. The absurdity and hyperbole in this section is obvious. There is, however, a good deal of imagination and poetic skill in the final segment.

269   εἰ μὴ ἄρ᾿ ὀξὺ νόησε πατὴρ ἀνδρῶν τε θεῶν τε. This line is repeated entirely from the *Iliad* (e.g. 8.132 εἰ μὴ ἄρ᾿ ὀξὺ νόησε πατὴρ ἀνδρῶν τε θεῶν τε·) from a scene prefacing divine intervention.

270   ἀπολλυμένους: "in the process of being destroyed."

ᾤκτειρε: from οἰκτείρω, "to pity." cf. *Iliad* 7.27: δῷς; ἐπεὶ οὔ τι Τρῶας ἀπολλυμένους ἐλεαίρεις.

271   κινήσας δὲ κάρη: "moving his head" see *Odyssey* 5.285: κινήσας δὲ κάρη προτὶ ὃν μυθήσατο θυμόν· cf. line 92 above: ὕδασι δ᾿ ὀλλύμενος τοίους ἐφθέγξατο μύθους·

272   This entire line is repeated from *Iliad* 13.99, 15.289, 21.344, 22.54; cf. *Od.* 19.36.

῍Ω πόποι: The phrase ῍Ω πόποι, like many Greek exclamations, does not admit of direct translation into English; the sense to be conveyed is one of anger or vexation. Cf. *Odyssey* 1.32, where Zeus angrily complains of the accusations which humans make against the gods: ὢ πόποι, οἷον δή νυ θεοὺς βροτοὶ αἰτιόωνται.

μέγα θαῦμα: "A great wonder." Some MSS have πένθος or ἔργον, either of which might constitute an interesting variation on the formulaic line.

273   οὐ μικρόν με πλήσσει Μεριδάρπαξ ὃς κατὰ λίμνην: This line appears in most MSS but is questioned by Allen. Some MSS omit the με to preserve the line in this form με would have to be scanned as a long syllable with μικρόν as two shorts. Ludwich presents the emendation οὐ μ᾿ ὀλίγον πλήσσει, which preserves the sense of the line.

274   This line is difficult to construe unless ἅρπαξ refers to Meridarpax (either as a nickname or as a predicate) or we take the

rather bland translation of ἀμείβεται as "take turn" as at *Il.* 15.684 (θρῴσκων ἄλλοτ᾽ ἐπ᾽ ἄλλον ἀμείβεται, οἳ δὲ πέτονται). So, we suggest: "He is taking his turn as a destroyer among the frogs." There are several variants for the line, including ἐνναίρειν, ἐναίρων, αἴρειν, and ἤλασε for the beginning.

ἅρπαξ: The scholia gloss this as φθορεύς, "destroyer"

275   πέμψωμεν: hortatory subjunctive (aorist).

πολεμόκλονον: see on line 4 above. The epithet πολεμόκλονον ("raising the din of war") while suited to both Athena and Ares, is ironic here, since their purpose is to *detain* Meridarpax from the battle.

276   οἵ μιν ἐπισχήσουσι: "they will restrain" *something* in the accusative from someone/something in the genitive (hence, "they will restrain him from battle"). This form is not well attested in early poetry.

κρατερόν περ ἐόντα: "though he is strong." ἐόντα: uncontracted, epic form. This particular phrase does not appear in Homer, but κρατερόν περ appears in the same possition (*Il.* 21.63) and ἐόντα typically ends a line (cf. the similar phrase ἀγαθόν περ ἐόντα. 9.627 or ἴφθιμόν περ ἐόντα, 16.620).

277   Ὣς ἄρ᾽ ἔφη: An answering formula, see on line 65.

Ἄρης δ᾽ ἀπαμείβετο μύθῳ: Part of an answering formula cf. *Il.*24.200 (...καὶ ἀμείβετο μύθῳ). Essentially just "Ares answered." The conversation between Zeus and Ares (with Athena present) may recall *Iliad* 5.871–899 where Ares tries to complain about Athena's behavior to their father only to have Zeus express his hatred for his own son.

278   οὔτε Ἄρηος: It is strange that Ares refers to himself in the third person (which happens at times in early Greek poetry). Some MSS take issue; Ludwich offers the conjecture ἐμεῖο; and West suggests instead that Hera should be the speaker. The form may in part be conditioned by the position: Ἄρηος ends the line over twenty times in the *Iliad* alone).

Κρονίδη: vocative, "Son of Kronos."

279 ἀμυνέμεν αἰπὺν ὄλεθρον: "To ward off dread ruin"; cf. *Il.* 18.129 (τειρομένοις ἑτάροισιν ἀμυνέμεν αἰπὺν ὄλεθρον). On ἀμύνω see 234 above. It can take a dative of advantage as it does here. Some MSS have ἀρηγέμεν instead of ἀμυνέμεν.

ἰσχύει: Here "to be able" or "has enough strength to . . ."; the verb ἰσχύω (from ἰσχύς) appears in Classical poetry and prose, but is comparatively rare with an infinitive.

280 ἴωμεν: "Let us go"; Homer typically has the short-vowel subjunctive ἴομεν. The lengthened form ἴωμεν is typical of tragedy and Classical prose.

ἀρηγόνες: "helpers, aids," from ἀρηγών (ἀρήγω). This is typically used of gods helping mortals. Cf. *Il.* 4.8 (δοιαὶ μὲν Μενελάῳ ἀρηγόνες εἰσὶ θεάων / Ἥρη τ᾽ Ἀργείη καὶ Ἀλαλκομενηῒς Ἀθήνη).

281 κινείσθω· οὕτω γὰρ ἁλώσεται ὅς τις ἄριστος: In some MSS this line occurs at 284. There is an unmetrical variant: κινείσθω τιτανοκτόνον ὀβριμοεργόν ("let him send in the Titan-killing, strong-worker"). ὀβριμοεργόν: In the *Iliad*, ὀβριμοεργόν is an epithet for Diomedes (5.403) in Hesiod, it is applied to Pelias (*Th.* 997). There is also an additional line recorded by some MSS: (281a).

281a ᾧ Τιτᾶνας πέφνες ἀρίστους ἔξοχα πάντων): "with which you killed the best of the Titans." This makes some sense with the examples of the giants and Capaneus. But the syntactical flow is awkward.

κινείσθω: This imperative does not appear in Homer but the verb κινέω does (e.g. *Il.* 10.158; 16.298).

ἁλώσεται: from ἁλίσκομαι, a defective verb overlapping with αἱρέω. The meaning here seems: "Whoever is best will be destroyed." See Demosthenes (*On the* Crown 45.5) and Herodotus (7.102.4) for "caught" in the sense of "detected."

282 ὥς ποτε: anticipating a comparison or story from the past.

Καπανῆα: Capaneus is the father of Sthenelos, Diomedes' the friend in the *Iliad*. He is one of the leaders in the traditional tale of the Seven against Thebes. During the battle he was struck by Zeus' lightning as he boasted that not even the gods could stop him (see Aesch., *Septem* 440 ff.; Pausanias 9.8.7).

κατέκτανες: "to kill"; similar to *Od.* 22.29 (καὶ γὰρ δὴ νῦν φῶτα κατέκτανες, ὃς μέγ' ἄριστος).

ὄβριμον ἄνδρα:"powerful man"; the diction, from the divine perspective, may signal impiety or hubris. In the *Iliad*, ὀβριμοεργόν is an epithet for Diomedes during his aristeia (5.403); in Hesiod, it is applied to Pelias in his treatment of Jason (*Th.* 997).

283 Ἐγκελάδοντα: Enkelados was one of the giants. According to Vergil (*Aen.* 3.578–83) his entombed body formed Mt. Aetna. Cf. Eur., *Herakles* 908. Both Kapaneus and Enkelados are appropriate figures since they exhibit hubris. As in other mythical comparisons in the poem, this is obviously parodic.

ἄγρια φῦλα Γιγάντων: For giants, see also lines 7 and 171. In the first, the narrator anticipates that his traditional tale (ὡς λόγος) will feature frogs "mimicking the deeds of the giants." In the latter, the narrator has Zeus describes the gathering of the armies, "like the army or centaurs or giants" (οἷος Κενταύρων στρατὸς ἔρχεται ἠὲ Γιγάντων). Cf. *Od.* 7.206: ὥς περ Κύκλωπές τε καὶ ἄγρια φῦλα Γιγάντων.

ἄγρια φῦλα: "savage tribes," see *Il.* 19.30–1 where Thetis promises Achilles that she will ward the "savage race of flies" (ἄγρια φῦλα / μυίας) from Patroklos' body.

284 Ὣς ἄρ' ἔφη: See above on line 277.

βαλὼν ἀργῆτα κεραυνόν: "bright lightning," cf. *Il.* 8.133 (βροντήσας δ' ἄρα δεινὸν ἀφῆκ' ἀργῆτα κεραυνόν). Cf. Ar. *Birds* 1747.

285 ἐβρόντησε: "To thunder," see Hes. *Theogony*, 839 (σκληρὸν δ' ἐβρόντησε καὶ ὄβριμον, ἀμφὶ δὲ γαῖα).

μέγαν δ' ἐλέλιξεν Ὄλυμπον: "he shook great Olympos"; from Homer (*Il.* 1.530: κρατὸς ἀπ' ἀθανάτοιο· μέγαν δ' ἐλέλιξεν Ὄλυμπον).

286   αὐτὰρ ἔπειτα κεραυνὸν δειμαλέον Διὸς ὅπλον: This line is considered an interpolation by most editors. Ludwich supposes that αὐτὰρ ἔπειτα was inserted to answer the πρῶτα μὲν of 285. The appositive string "Lightning, the frightening weapon of Zeus," is a bit repetitive (cf. ὅπλον in 280; κεραυνόν in 284).

δειμαλέον: "frightening" or "horrible," a post-Hellenistic Greek adjective.

287   ἧκ' ἐπιδινήσας: "he threw it, whirling it down." This combination begins a line in Homer, cf. *Il.* 7.269: ἧκ' ἐπιδινήσας, ἐπέρεισε δὲ ἶν' ἀπέλεθρον.

ἔπτατο: Aorist from πέτομαι, "it flew from the hand of the god." The subject changes awkwardly to the lightning bolt and then in the next line back to Zeus (clear from the active particple βαλών). This form is used of a missile in motion in Homer (θώρηκος γύαλον, ἀπὸ δ' ἔπτατο πικρὸς ὀϊστός, *Il.*13.287).

288   πάντας μέν ῥ' ἐφόβησε βαλὼν βατράχους τε μύας τε: This text is superior to the alternative which ends ἐπὶ τούσδε τε μύας—the sense of the demonstrative here is unclear. Only one manuscript, however, presents our preferred reading.

289   οὐδ' ὣς ἀπέληγε: This occurs at *Il.* 7.263 (ἀλλ' οὐδ' ὣς ἀπέληγε μάχης κορυθαίολος Ἕκτωρ).

ἀπέληγε: imp. "the army of mice *was not relenting*" from ἀπολήγω.

ἀλλ' ἔτι μᾶλλον: This combination ends the line in Homer, cf. *Il.* 9.678: κεῖνός γ' οὐκ ἐθέλει σβέσσαι χόλον, ἀλλ' ἔτι μᾶλλον.

290   ἔλπετο πορθήσειν: "the army of mice was expecting/hoping to uproot the race of spear-bearing frogs." This is not the first time a genocidal wish has been expressed by the mice: see 263a and 264. For the sense of expectation of future outcomes with ἔλπομαι, see *Il.* 10.355–6. Cf. Aesch. Fr. 99.19: αὐχεῖν δὲ Τρώων ἄστυ πορθήσειν βίᾳ.

αἰχμητάων: "spearmen, warriors." Uncontracted genitive plural; this form occurs only at the end of the line in Homer and Hesiod and is one of Janko's (2012: 29; cf 1982) markers for relative age in dating Homeric epic. The *Iliad* has 224 occurrences of this form (for a ratio of 1:70.5 lines) while Hesiod shows a ratio of 1:85 lines in the *Theogony* and 1:92 lines in the *Works and Days*.

291   ἀπ᾽ Οὐλύμπου: "down from Olympos." The description makes sense (Zeus is pitying the frogs from the vantage point of Olympus) but in Homer (e.g. *Il.* 1.532) this combination of preposition and adjective nearly always describes motion. This lengthened form appears in Homer in this metrical position (*Il.* 16.364: Ὡς δ᾽ ὅτ᾽ ἀπ᾽ Οὐλύμπου νέφος ἔρχεται οὐρανὸν εἴσω).

ἐλέησε Κρονίων: for this combination, cf. *Il.* 17.411 (Μυρομένω δ᾽ ἄρα τώ γε ἰδὼν ἐλέησε Κρονίων). ἐλέησε is from ἐλεέω ("to pity"). Many MSS have ᾤκτειρε instead. See above on line 270 for ᾤκτειρε Κρονίων

292   ἀρωγούς: "helpers"; see above on line 172 (ἡδὺ γελῶν ἐρέεινε· τίνες βατράχοισιν ἀρωγοί) in Homer, the gods can be "helpers" to men *Il.*8.205 (εἴ περ γάρ κ᾽ ἐθέλοιμεν, ὅσοι Δαναοῖσιν ἀρωγοί, cf. 21.428). Mortals can be helpers too (οἵδε κακὰ φρονέοντες, ἐμοὶ δ᾽ οὐκ εἰσὶν ἀρωγοί, 18.232).

ἐν βατράχοισιν: "among the frogs"; some MSS have instead ῥα φθειρομένοισιν ("he sent helpers to those who were being destroyed . . .").

293   For the next six lines we have a somewhat absurd listing of epithets for the crabs who are sent to defeat the mice. The image, without the elaboration, is humorous enough: crabs would be cataphracts among the lightly armored frogs and mice. But the accumulation of epithets—most of which are neologisms—might amount to a type of artistic gaming as the artist stretches the meaning and the conventions of epic poetry. (We imagine that performers and even amateurs might have competed in composing humorous and absurdist hexameters. Even at this extreme, the list attests to a type of virtuosity.) Parody is often excessive; the excessive excess here marks the end of the poem with a vivid, memorable, and

humorous *deus ex machina*. The scholarly tradition attributes something analogous to the poet Lykophron who took very seriously the play of integrating obscure diction, references and possible innovations into his poetry. For this as a parody of the "extreme allusiveness" of Hellenistic poetry, see Fusillo 1988: 134; cf. Scodel 2008: 233.

νωτάκμονες: νωτ-άκμονες "anvil-backs" (LSJ "mail-backs," i.e. "armor-backed"; the surface can take a pounding.)

ἀγκυλοχεῖλαι: "with twisted lips (or claws)" χεῖλος, "lip" (often used metaphorically for "lip of a drinking vessel"), while the alternate spelling χηλή can mean "claws." Glei supports the latter spelling. Aristotle uses the latter to describe to a crab specifically (*Historia Animalium* 527b5) in astronomy χηλαί. This epithet is used in Homer of vultures in the same position (*Il.* 16.428).

294   λοξοβάται: "side-ways walker"; "walking at a slant," cf. λοξός "sideways" ἀεροβάτης ("air-walker").

στρεβλοί: "twisted or crooked," sometimes "squint-eyed." Many crabs have eyes on the end of antennae. Some species, however, have eyes or eye-like holes on the main part of their bodies. The freshwater crab *Potamon fluviatile*—whose eyes are situated thus—is native to rivers and lakes near the Mediterranean basin in Europe and still found in many islands in the Aegean. Nevertheless, the epithet here may be more apropos of the contour of the crabs' eyes, cf. the *ankulotoksoi* ("curved bows").

ψαλιδόστομοι: "scissor-mouthed"; ψαλίδον: "scissor." The word can also mean "vault or arch" but in line 298 the crabs use their mouths to dismember the mice.

ὀστρακόδερμοι: "pottery-skinned"; "hard-shelled."

295   ὀστοφυεῖς: "bony."

πλατύνωτοι: "wide-backed."

ἀποστίλβοντες ἐν ὤμοις: "shining in the shoulders" ἀποστίλβοντες appears in Homer, see *Od.* 3.408 (λευκοί, ἀποστίλβοντες ἀλείφατος· οἷσ' ἔπι μὲν πρὶν).

296 βλαισοί: "knock-kneed" or simply knees that knock together.

χειλοτένοντες: "holding mouths-out"; a *hapax legomenon*; some MSS have χειροτένοντες instead, but the next line describes the crabs as "handless." Repetition would certainly not be a problem here.

ἀπὸ στέρνων ἐσορῶντες: "They see from their chests." This confirms that the species of crab imagined most likely did not have eyes on antennae (see note 294 above).

297 ὀκτάποδες: "eight-footed."

δικάρηνοι: "two headed." Cf. Nonnus at 13.131 where he uses the epithet to describe Parnassus.

ἀχειρέες: "handless."

οἱ δὲ καλεῦνται: "who are called."

298 καρκίνοι: "crabs," note the postponement of this noun.

οὐράς: "tails"; the crabs immediately strike at the unarmored, exposed extremities of the mice.

στομάτεσσιν: Dative of instrument. Early Greek poetry would be more likely to use the shorter form, see στόμασιν (e.g. Theognis, 240 ἐν πάσαις πολλῶν κείμενος ἐν στόμασιν).

299 ἠδὲ πόδας καὶ χεῖρας: After disfiguring the mice, the crabs now immobilize them. It is not clear how the mice were able to flee after the crabs deprived them of their appendages, unless we are to understand that the phrase δειλοὶ μύες in 298 refers to those who had been holding back from the battle, in contrast to the πρόμαχοι.

ἀνεγνάμπτοντο δὲ λόγχαι: "the spears were bent back," i.e. they were bent and broken on the armor of the crabs. The mice struggle against their mutilators, but their weapons founder on the crabs' natural defenses.

300 ὑπέδεισαν: Aorist, third person plural of ὑποδείδω "to cower before," "shrink in fear," a not un-mouselike thing to do (from a human perspective). This appears in the same position in the *Iliad* (1.406 τὸν καὶ ὑπέδεισαν μάκαρες θεοὶ οὐδ' ἔτ' ἔδησαν).

δειλοί: "cowards," prior to the advent of the crabs, the mice were certainly not cowardly. This is an early pejorative in Greek poetry, see *Il.* 11.816 *Od.* 10.431; cf. Theogn. 58.

301 ἐς δὲ φυγὴν ἐτράποντο: "They were routed"; "They turned to flight," a common phrase in historiography, see Herodotus 3.13.1 (Οἱ δὲ Αἰγύπτιοι ἐκ τῆς μάχης ὡς ἐτράποντο, ἔφευγον οὐδενὶ κόσμῳ. "After the Egyptians were routed from battle. They were fleeing in disorder").

ἐδύετο δ' ἥλιος ἤδη: "the sun was already going down"; the image is possibly Homeric, see *Il.* 7.465 (δύσετο δ' ἠέλιος, τετέλεστο δὲ ἔργον Ἀχαιῶν; "the sun went down and the work of the Achaeans came to an end").

302 πολέμου τελετή: "end of the war"; the form τελευτή appears in Homer (e.g. 16.787: ἔνθ' ἄρα τοι Πάτροκλε φάνη βιότοιο τελευτή; "There then the end of your life came clear, Patroklos"). This shorter form occurs as early as Herodotus: "The end of his life came most illiustriously" (τελευτὴ τοῦ βίου λαμπροτάτη ἐπεγένετο, 1.30.22). For possible connections between this language and mystery cult, see Glei *ad loc.*

μονοήμερος: "single-day," "of a day." This may be the earliest instance of this compound. Cf. Theogn. 52 μούναρχοι δὲ πόλει μήποτε τῇδε ἅδοι; and Hes. *Th* 426: μουνογενής. Μοῦνος (the Ionic form of Attic μόνος) is preferred in early poetry.

ἐξετελέσθη: "was completed, was effected"; this form appears at the end of the line in Theocr., *Id.* 17: ὧδε καὶ ἀθανάτων ἱερὸς γάμος ἐξετελέσθη ("In this way too the sacred marriage of the gods was completed").

Glossary

A

ἀγαπητός: desirable, beloved

ἀγγέλλω: announce, report, bring news

ἄγε: come on! *Imperative form of* **ἄγω**; *plural imp.* **ἄγεθ'** (120)

ἀγέρωχος: high-minded, lordly, noble

ἀγκυλοχήλης: with crooked claws (293)

ἀγορεύω: speak in the assembly, speak, say, declare, proclaim

ἀγορήνδε: to the assembly, to the market

ἄγριος, -α, -ον: wild, savage, uncultivated, fierce

ἀγχέμαχος, -ον: fighting hand to hand

ἀγχοῦ: near (*adv.*)

ἄγω: lead, draw, carry, convey

ἀεί: always, forever

ἀηθείη, ἡ: novelty, unaccustomedness, inexperience

ἀθάνατος, -η, -ον: immortal, undying; *used substantively* = "the undying ones," i.e. "the gods"

Ἀθηναίην, Ἀθηναίης: *see* **Ἀθήνη** *below*

Ἀθήνη, ἡ: Athena

αἶα, ἡ: earth/land (*epic form of* **γαῖα**)

Ἀϊδόσδε: to Hades (*adv.*)

αἷμα, -ατος, τό: blood

αἰνός, -ή, -όν: dread, dire, horrible; *adv.* **αἰνῶς** = terribly, exceedingly

αἰπύς, εῖα, ύ: high, steep, towering; *used with* **ὄλεθρος**

αἱρέω: grasp, seize, take away

αἰχμητής, -οῦ, ὁ: spearman, warrior

ἀκόλυμβος, -ον: unable to swim

ἀκοντίζω: to hit or strike with a javelin

ἄκρος, -α, -ον: highest, topmost

ἀκωκή, ἡ: point (often of a spear or missile weapon)

ἀλγέω: feel pain, suffer

ἀλγοῦσαν: *fem. acc. sing. participle of* **ἀλγέω**

ἀλέκτωρ, -ορος, ὁ: rooster, cock

ἀλέομαι: avoid, shun, flee for one's life; ἀλεύατο (86)

ἀληθεύω: speak truth; imp. form ἀλήθευσον (14)

ἁλίσκομαι: be taken, be conquered, fall into enemy hands

ἄλκιμος, -η, -ον: stout, brave

ἀλλά: but, otherwise, still, at least

ἄλλος, -η, -ο: other, another, a different one; οἱ ἄλλοι = the others, the rest

ἀλύξας: *participle – sg. aor. act. of* ἀλύσκω

ἀλύσκω: flee, avoid, shun

ἁλώσεται: *3rd sing. fut. of* ἁλίσκομαι

ἅμα (*shortened form* ἅμ'): at once, at the same time

ἀμείβω: exchange, repay; surpass, outdo

ἀμείνων, -ον: *comparative form of* ἀγαθός, better

ἄμμα, -ατος, τό: knot, cord, noose, halter

ἀμύμων, -ον (*gen.* -ονος): blameless, noble, excellent

ἀμύνω: keep off, ward off, protect, defend

ἀμφίβιος, -ον: living a double life

ἀμφικαλύπτω: enwrap, enfold, cover with a veil

ἀμφότερος -α, -ον: either, both (of two)

ἄν: *modal particle serving to limit verbs; this does not admit of ready translation into English*

ἀνάγκη, ἡ: force, constraint, necessity

ἀναγνάμπτω: bend back

ἀναδύνω: come to the top of the water

ἀναδύομαι: shrink back, withdraw

ἀναίτιος, -α, -ον: not guilty, blameless, guiltless

ἀνανεύω: throw the head back, reject, deny

ἄναξ, ἄνακτος, ὁ: lord, master

ἀναπείθω: persuade, convince

ἀναρπάζω: snatch, carry off, take by storm

ἀναστάς: *nom. masc. sg. aor. act. part. of* ἀνίστημι

ἀναφαίνω: bring to light, make known, display; *in passive*, ἀνεφαίνετο = "appeared"

ἀναχάζομαι: draw back, give way, retire

ἀνεθρέψατο: *3rd sg. aor. act. ind. of* ἀνατρέφω = bring up, rear, educate

ἄνειμι: go back, go up, approach

ἀνέστη: *3rd sing. aor. of* ἀνίστημι

ἀνήρ, ἀνδρός, ὁ: man

ἄνθρωπος, ὁ: man; *in plural,* humankind, humans

ἀνιοῦσαν: *acc. sing. aor. act. part. of* **ἄνειμι**

ἀνίστημι: stand up, raise up, rise

ἀνταποδίδωμι: give back, repay

ἀνταποδοῦναι: *aorist. act. inf. of* **ἀνταποδίδωμι**

ἀνέκτισις, -εως, ἡ: revenge, requital, retribution

ἀντίον: *as adv.* against, in front of all, in response

ἀντίος, -ία, -ιον: against, opposite, contrary, in opposition

ἄξας: *nom. sg. aor. act. part. of* **ἄγω**

ἄξιος, -ία, -ιον: worthy, estimable, deserving

ἀοιδή, ἡ: song, the act of singing

ἀολλής, -ές: all together, in crowds

ἀπαλός, -ή, -όν: soft, tender

ἀπαμείβομαι: answer, reply, respond

ἅπας, ἅπασα, ἅπαν: all, the whole, entire

ἀπειλέω: promise, threaten

ἀπειλήσαντες: *nom. pl. aor. act. part. of* **ἀπειλέω**

ἀπειρέσιος, -α, -ον: boundless, immense

ἀπέφηνε: *3rd sg. aor. ind. of* **ἀποφαίνω**

ἀπηνής, -ές: rough, cruel, merciless

ἀπλόω: spread out, unfold

ἀπλώσας: *nom. sg. aor. act. part.* **ἀπλόω**

ἀπό: from, out of

ἀποδίδωμι: repay, give back, restore

ἀποδώσει: *3rd sg. fut. act. ind. of* **ἀποδίδωμι**

ἀπολήγω: leave off, desist from

ἀπόλλυμι: destroy, kill, ruin

ἀποπνέω: breathe out, exhale, breathe one's last breath

ἀποπνίγω: choke, suffocate

ἀποστίλβω: shine brightly

ἀποφαίνω: show forth, display, make known, declare

ἀποφεύγω: flee from, escape *cf.* ἀπέφυγον (42) ἀπέφυγεν (47)

ἄρα: then (*denoting consequence or temporal succession*)

ἀραβέω: rattle, ring, clang

ἀραρίσκω: fit together, construct

ἀργής, -ῆτος, ὁ, ἡ: bright, shining

ἀρήγω: aid, assist, succor (*w. dat.*)

ἀρηγών -όνος, ὁ, ἡ: helper, one who brings aid

ἀρήρει: *see* **ἀραρίσκω**

Ἄρης, ὁ: Ares, god of war

ἀριστεύς, -έως, ὁ: chief, noble man, prince

ἀριστεύω: be the best, noblest, finest

ἄριστος, -η, -ον: best, noblest, finest

ἄρουρα, ἡ: arable land, earth, ground

ἁρπάζω: seize, grasp, take swiftly

ἁρπάξ-αγος, ὁ, ἡ: robbing, rapacious

ἁρπάξασα: *nom. sing. aor. fem. part. from* **ἁρπάζω**

Ἀρτεπίβουλος, ὁ: Breadthief, literally, "one who contrives plans for [taking] bread"

ἄρτος, ὁ: cake or bread

Ἀρτοφάγος, ὁ: Breadeater

ἄρτυμα, -ατος, τό: condiment, seasoning

ἀρχή, ἡ: beginning, origin

ἄρχω: make a beginning, begin from

ἀρωγός, -όν: helper (*from* **ἀρήγω**)

ἀσκέω: form by art or skill, fashion, dress, deck out

ἀσκήσαντες: *nom. pl. aor. act. masc. part. from* **ἀσκέω**

ἀσπίς, -ίδος, ἡ: shield

ἀστερόεις, -εσσα, -εν: starry, like a star, sparkling

αὖ: again, further, once more

αὖθις: back, back again, anew

ἄϋπνος, -ον: sleepless, wakeful

αὐτάρ: but, besides, moreover

αὖτε: again, furthermore

ἀϋτή, ἡ: cry, shout

αὐτός, αὐτή, αὐτό: himself/herself/itself; he, she, it

αὐχέω: boast, assert confidently

αὐχήν, -ενος, ὁ: neck, throat

ἀφαμαρτάνω: miss the mark

ἀφέθη: *3rd sg. aor. act. ind. of* **ἀφίημι**

ἀχειρ-ής, -ές: without hands

ἄχθος, -εος, τό: burden, load

ἄχος, -εος, τό: pain, distress

ἄχρηστος, -ον: useless, unprofitable

B

βάθος, -εος, τό: depth
βαθύς, βαθεῖα, βαθύ: deep, stout, thick
βαίνω: walk, step, mount
βάλλω: throw, cast, hurl
βάπτω: dip, dye, sink
βάρος, -ους/-εος, τό: weight, burden, oppressiveness
βασιλεύς, -ῆος, ὁ: king
βαστάζω: lift, carry, bear
βάτραχος, ὁ: frog
βεβήκει: *3rd sg. plupf. of* βαίνω
βέλος, -εος, τό: missile, projectile weapon, javelin
βελόνη, ἡ: needle
βένθος, -εος, τό: depth
βίος, ὁ: life
βλαισός, -ή, -όν: bent, distorted, bandy-legged
βλάπτω: disable, hinder, harm
βλέπω: look upon, see
βοάω: cry out, shout
βοηθέω: aid, assist, rescue
βοηθήσουσα: *nom. fem. sg. fut. act. part. of* βοηθέω
Βορβοροκοίτης, -ου, ὁ: Mudbedder/Mudcoucher
βουλεύω: take counsel, plan, devise
βουλή, ἡ: counsel, plan; Council, Senate, assembly
βρέγμα, -ατος, τό: the forehead
βροντάω: thunder
βρωτός, -ή, -όν: to be eaten
βυθός, ὁ: the depth
βύρσα, ἡ: hide, leather
βωστρέω: call on (for aid)

Γ

γαῖα, ἡ: earth, land
γάλα, γάλακτος, τό: milk

γαλέη, ἡ: weasel

γάρ: for (*often used in an explanatory sense to clarify what has just been stated*)

γαστήρ, **γαστέρος**, ἡ: belly, stomach

γαυρόμαι: exult, pride oneself in

γαυρούμενος: *nom. sing. masc. pres. part. of* **γαυρόομαι**

γε: at least, at any rate, in any case

γεγάατε: *2nd pl. pf. act. ind. of* **γίγνομαι** = come into being, be born

γείνομαι: bring forth

γείτων, **-ονος**, ὁ, ἡ: neighbor, borderer

γελάω, Ep. **γελόω**: laugh

γενεή, ῆς, ἡ: race, family, birth

γένειον, τό: chin

γένος, **-εος/-ους**, τό: race, offspring, clan

γηγενής, **-ές**: born of the earth, earthborn

γηθόσυνος, **-η**, **-ον**: glad, joyful

Γίγας, **-αντος**, ὁ: a giant

γλυκερός, **-ά**, **-όν**: sweet

γνοίην: *1st sg. aor. act. opt. of* **γιγνώσκω** = come to know

γόνυ, **γόνατος/γούνατος**, τό: knee

Δ

δαήμεναι: *aor. inf. of* **δάω,** to learn

δαιδάλεος, **-α**, **-ον**: carefully wrought, intricately fashioned

δάκνοντος: *gen. sing. pres. act. part. of* **δάκνω**

δάκνω: bite, sting

δάκρυ, τό: tear, drop

δάκτυλος, ὁ: finger, toe

δάπεδον, τό: level surface, plain

δέ: *adversative particle meaning* but (*in several contexts; sometimes untranslated*)

δέδια, **δείδια**: *variant forms of the 1st sg. perf. act. indic. of* **δείδω**

δείδω: fear

δείκνυμι: point out, show, demonstrate

δειλός, -ή, -όν: cowardly, wretched

δειμαλέος, -α, -ον: timid, fearful

δεινός, -ή, -όν: terrible, dreadful, wonderful, marvelous

δείξας: *nom. masc. sing. aor. part. of* **δείκνυμι**

δείραντες: *nom. masc. pl. aor. part. of* **δέρω**

δείσαντες: *nom. masc. pl. aor. part. of* **δείδω**

δέλτος, ἡ: writing-tablet

δέμας, τό: body, bodily structure

δεξιτερός, -ή, -όν: on the right hand/right side

δέρω: skin, flay

δεύω: wet, drench; δευόμεναι (91) δευομένην (190)

δή: now, then, finally; indeed, truly, in fact

δῆλος, -η, -ον: visible, conspicuous, famous

δῆρις, ἡ: battle, contest

διά: through (*w. gen.*)

δίδωμι: give, grant, assign

δικάρηνος, -ον: two-headed

Διός: *gen. of* Ζεύς

δῖος, δῖα, δῖον: divine, godlike, heavenly

δισσός/διττός, -ή, -όν: double, twofold, duplicated

διψαλέος, -α, -ον: thirsty

δοκέω: appear, seem

δόλιος, -α, -ον: deceitful, tricky, treacherous

δολόεις, -εσσα, -εν: tricky, subtle, crafty

δόλος, ὁ: trap, trick, stratagem

δόμος, ὁ: house, abode, dwelling

δόρυ, δούρατος, τό: spear shaft

δουπέω: fall with a thud or heavy sound

δράξ, -ἄκός, ἡ: handful

δραμών: *nom. masc. sing. aor. act. part. of* **τρέχω**

δράσσομαι: grasp, take a handful

δραμών: *nom. masc. pl. aor. act. part. of* **δράσσομαι**

δρόμος, ὁ: course, footrace

δῦ: *3rd sg. aor. act. ind. of* **δύω**

δύο: two

δύστηνος, -ον: wretched, unfortunate, suffering

δύω: sink, plunge into

δῶμα, -ατος, τό: home, dwelling, household

δῶρον, τό: gift, present
δώσω: *1st sg. fut. act. ind. of* δίδωμι

E

ἐάω: permit, allow
ἔβαινε: *3rd sg. impf. act. ind. of* βαίνω
ἔβαλε: *3rd. sg. aor. act. ind. of* βάλλω
ἔβαν: *3rd pl. aor. act. ind. of* βαίνω
ἐβάπτετο: *see* βάπτω
ἐβάστασε: *3rd sg. aor. act. ind. of* βαστάζω
ἔβησαν: *3rd pl. aor. act. ind. of* βαίνω
ἔβλεπε: *3rd sg. imp. act. ind. of* βλέπω
ἐβόησεν: *3rd sg. aor. act. ind. of* βοάω
ἐβρόντησε: *3rd sg. aor. act. ind. of* βροντάω
ἐβώστρει: *3rd sg. imp. act. ind. of* βωστρέω
ἐγγύθεν: from nearby; ἐγγύθεν ἐλθεῖν = approach
ἔγκατα, τά: innards, guts, entrails
Ἐγκελάδος, ὁ: the name of one of the Giants
ἐγκέφαλος, -ον: within the head; *used subst.* = the brain
ἔγχος, -εος, τό: spear, lance
ἐγὼ/ἐγὼν: I (*1st sg. pronoun*)
ἔδακε: *3rd sg. aor. act. ind. of* δάκνω
ἔδεσμα, -ατος, τό: food
ἐδίδου: *3rd sg. imp. act. ind. of* δίδωμι
ἔδυ: *3rd sg. aor. act. ind. of* δύω
ἐδύετο: *3rd sg. aor. m/p ind. of* δύω
ἔδυνε: *3rd sg. aor. act. ind. of* δύω
ἔδωκε: *3rd sg. aor. act. ind. of* δίδωμι
ἔην: *3rd. sg. imp. act. ind. of* εἰμί
ἔθειρα, ἡ: hair
ἐθέλω: wish, will
ἔθηκεν: *3rd sg. aor. act. ind. of* τίθημι
ἔθος, -εος, τό: custom, habit
εἰ: if
εἶ: *2nd sg. pres. act. ind. of* εἰμί

εἴασαν: *3rd. pl. aor. act. ind. of* ἐάω

εἶδον: see ὁράω

εἷλε: *3rd sg. aor. act. ind. of* αἱρέω

εἷλκον: *3rd pl. imp. act. ind. of* ἕλκω

εἵλκυσε: *3rd sg. aor. act. ind. of* ἕλκω

εἷλξαν: *3rd pl. aor. act. ind. of* ἕλκω = draw out, drag

εἰμί: I am

εἶναι: *pres. act. inf. of* εἰμὶ

εἵνεκα: for the sake of, on account of

εἶπον: say (*aorist of* λέγω)

εἶπε: *present imperative of* εἶπον

εἰς: to, toward; against; in respect to, regarding

εἷς, μία, ἕν: one

εἰσαφικνέομαι: come to, arrive at

εἰσαφίκηαι: *2nd sg. aor. act. ind. of* εἰσαφικνέομαι

εἰσελθών: *nom. masc. sg. aor. act. part. of* εἰσέρχομαι

εἰσέρχομαι: come into, enter

εἰσῆλθον: *3rd pl. aor. act. ind. of* εἰσέρχομαι

εἴσω: into, to the inside

εἶχε (83): *3rd sing. imp. act. of* ἔχω

εἶχον (127, 162): *3rd pl. imp. act. of* ἔχω

ἐκ/ἐξ: out of, from

ἐκάλυπτε: see καλύπτω

ἕκαστος, -η, -ον: each one

ἔκδικος, -ον: avenging

ἐκεῖνος, ἐκείνη, ἐκεῖνο: that one/that person/that thing

ἐκέλευεν: *3rd sg. imp. act. ind. of* κελεύω

ἐκέλευσαν: *3rd pl. aor. act. ind. of* κελεύω

ἐκλάσθη: *3rd sg. aor. pass. ind. of* κλάω

ἐκλύζετο: *3rd sg. imp. m.p. ind. of* κλύζω

ἐκόνισεν: *see* κονίω

ἔκοπτον: *3rd pl. aor. act. ind. of* κόπτω

ἐκοπώθην: *see note on 189*

ἐκόρυσσεν: *3rd sg. imp. act. ind. of* κορύσσω

ἔκτεινεν, ἔκτεινον: *see* κτείνω

ἐκτελέω: bring to an end, accomplish, fulfill

ἔκτοσθεν: outside

ἐκχέω: pour away, spill

ἔκχυντο: *3rd pl. aor. mid. indic. of* ἐκχέω
ἔλαιος, ὁ: olive
ἐλεέω: have pity, show compassion
ἐλέησε: *3rd sg. aor. act. ind. of* ἐλεέω
ἐλέλιξεν: *3rd sg. aor. act. of* ἐλελίζω = to shake or quiver
ἐλθεῖν: *pres. act. infin. of* ἔρχομαι
ἔλθῃ: *3rd sg. aor. act. subj. of* ἔρχομαι
ἔλθοι: *3rd sg. aor. act. opt. of* ἔρχομαι
ἐλθοίμην: *1st sg. aor. act. opt. of* ἔρχομαι
ἐλθόντες: *nom. masc. pl. aor. act. part. of* ἔρχομαι
Ἑλικών, Ἑλικῶνος, ὁ: Mount Helicon, the home of the Muses
ἕλκω: draw, drag away
ἐλοῦσα: *fem. nom. aor. act. part. of* αἱρέω
ἔλπομαι: hope, expect
ἑλών: *masc. nom. aor. act. part. of* αἱρέω
ἔμαθον: *3rd pl. aor. act. ind. of* μανθάνω
Ἐμβασίχυτρος, ὁ: Bowldiver
ἐμέ: *acc. sing. of* ἐγώ
ἔμειναν: *3rd pl. aor act. ind. of* μένω = stay, remain
ἐμεῖο: *gen. sing. of* ἐγώ
ἔμελλεν: *3rd sg. imp. act. ind. of* μέλλω
ἐμίχθην: *3rd sg. aor. ind. of* μίγνυμι
ἔμμεναι: = εἶναι
ἐμοί: *dat. sg. of* ἐγώ
ἐμός, -ή, -όν: mine
ἔμπεδος, -ον: firm, steadfast, sure
ἔμπεσεν: *3rd sg. aor. act. ind. of* ἐμπίπτω
ἐμπίπλημι: fill up
ἐμπίπτω: fall in, fall upon
ἔμπλητο: *3rd sg. aor. act. ind. of* ἐμπίπλημι
ἐμποιέω: make in, fashion, produce upon; ἐμποίησαν (184)
ἐν: in
ἕνα: *acc. sing. of* εἷς
ἐναντίος, -α, -ον: opposite
ἔνησα: *1st sg. aor. act. ind. of* νέω, to spin fabric
ἐνόησαν: *3rd pl. aor act. ind. of* νοέω
ἐνόησε: *3rd pl. aor act. ind. of* νοέω
ἔνοπλος, -ον: armed, in arms

ἔντεα, τά: arms, armor, weapons

ἐξαίφνης: suddenly, on a sudden

ἐξανέδυσαν: *3rd pl. aor. act. of* ἐξαναδύομαι = rise out, emerge from

ἐξεθρέψατο: *3rd sg. aor. mid. of* ἐκτρέφω = raise, rear, bring up

ἐξέλθωμεν: *1st sg. pres. act. subj. of* ἐξέρχομαι

ἐξέλθωσι: *3rd pl. aor. act. subj. of* ἐξέρχομαι

ἐξενάριξεν: *3rd sg. aor. act. ind. of* ἐξεναρίζω = strip of armor, despoil

ἐξέπτη: *3rd sg. aor act. ind. of* ἐκπέτομαι = fly out, escape from

ἐξέρχομαι: go out from, come out of

ἐξέσπασεν: *3rd sg. aor. act. ind. of* ἐκσπάω = draw out, remove by force

ἐξετανύσθη: *3rd sg. aor. pass. ind. of* ἐκτανύω = stretch out

ἐξετελέσθη: *3rd sg. aor. pass. ind. of* ἐκτελέω

ἐξετέλεσσεν: *3rd sg. aor. act. ind. of* ἐκτελέω

ἐξετύφλου: *3rd sg. imp. pass. ind. of* ἐκτυφλόω = make blind

ἐξευρόντες: *nom. masc. pl. aor. act. part.* ἐξευρίσκω = find out, discover

ἐξήπλωτο: *3rd sg. imp. pass. ind. of* ἐξαπλόω = spread out

ἐξολέσωμεν: *1st pl. aor. act. subj. of* ὄλλυμι = kill, destroy

ἐξολόλυξε: *3rd sg. aor. act. ind. of* ἐξολολύζω =howl aloud

ἐξύφηνα: *1st sg. aor. act. ind. of* ἐξυφαίνω = weave, finish weaving

ἔξοχος, -ον: towering above, excellent, eminent

ἐόντα: *acc. masc. sing. pres. part. of* εἰμὶ

ἔοργαν: *3rd pl. aor. act. ind. of* ἔρδω = do, fashion, work

ἑός, ἑή, ἑόν: their own; his/her/its own

ἐοῦσαν: *acc. fem. pres. sing. part. of* εἰμὶ

ἐπαΐξας: *nom. masc. sg. aor. act. part. of* ἐπαΐσσω = jump at, rush at

ἐπαπειλέω: threaten, guarantee

ἐπαρωγός, ὁ: helper, one who brings aid

ἐπεί: when, since

ἔπειτα: then, thereupon

ἔπεμψαν: *3rd pl. aor. act. ind. of* πέμπω

ἐπενήχετο: *3rd sg. imp. m./p. ind. of* ἐπινήχομαι = swim upon

ἔπεσεν: *3rd sg. aor. act. ind. of* πίπτω

ἐπέστη: *3rd sg. aor. act. ind. of* ἐφίστημι

ἐπεύχομαι: pray

ἔπεφνε: *3rd sg. aor. act. ind. of* θείνω = slay, kill

ἐπέχω: hold out, hold upon, impose, attack

ἐπί: upon (*w. gen.*)

ἐπιβόσκομαι: feed upon, graze upon

ἐπιδινήσας: *nom. masc. sg. aor. act. part. of* ἐπιδινέω = whirl around

ἐπινώτιος, -ον: on the back

ἐπιπείθομαι: be persuaded, comply with

ἐπισταμένως: skillfully, expertly

ἐπιστάντες: *nom. masc. pl. aor. act. part. of* ἐφίστημι

ἐπισχήσουσι: *3rd pl. fut. act. ind. of* ἐπέχω

ἐπιφθάς: *nom. masc. sg. aor. act. part. of* ἐπιφθάνω = outstrip, reach first

ἔπλασε: *3rd sg. aor. act. ind. of* πλάσσω = form/mold/shape into

ἐπνίγη: *3rd sg. aor. pass. ind. of* πνίγω = choke, suffocate

ἐποίησαν: *3rd pl. aor. act. ind. of* ποιέω

ἐπορνύμενος: *nom. masc. sg. pres. m./p. part. of* ἐπόρνυμι

ἔπος, -εος, τό: word, counsel, speech

ἔπτατο: *3rd sg. aor. act. ind. of* πέτομαι

ἔπτη: *3rd sg. aor. act. ind. of* πέτομαι

ἔργον, τό: work, deed

ἐρέβινθος, ὁ: chickpea

ἐρεείνω: ask, inquire

ἔρεξαν: *3rd pl. aor. act. ind. of* ῥέζω

ἐρέω: question, ask, inquire

ἔρρηξε: *3rd sg. aor. act. ind. of* ῥήγνυμι

ἔρριψας: *2nd singular aor. of* ῥίπτω

ἔρχομαι: come, go, approach

ἔρως, -ωτος, ὁ: love

ἐς: *see* εἰς

ἐσάλπιγξαν: *3rd pl. aor. act. ind. of* σαλπίζω = play the trumpet, sound the horn

ἐσθλός, -ή, -όν: brave, stout, good

ἐσορῶντες: *nom. masc. pl. aor. act. part. of* εἰσοράω = look into, look upon

ἐσταότα: *acc. masc. sg. pf. act. part. of* ἵστημι

ἔσταξε: *3rd pl. aor. act. ind. of* στάζω

ἐστήκει: *3rd. sg. plup. act. ind. of* ἵστημι

ἔστηκεν: *3rd sg. pf. act. ind. of* ἵστημι

ἔστησαν: *3rd pl. aor. act. ind. of* ἵστημι

ἔσφιγγε: *3rd sg. imp. act. ind. of* σφίγγω

ἔσχατος, -η, -ον: farthest, extreme, uppermost

ἑταῖρος, ὁ: comrade, companion, friend

ἐτάραξε: *3rd sg. aor. act. ind. of* ταράσσω = stir up, disturb

ἔτι: still, to this point, even now

ἐτράποντο: *3rd pl. aor. ind. mid. of* τρέπω
εὖ: well, thoroughly
εὐθύμως: cheerfully
εὐθύς, -εῖα, -ύ: straight, direct, forthright
εὔκυκλος, -ον: well-rounded
εὐμήκης, -ες: tall, long, of goodly proportion
Εὐρώπη: Europa
εὐχερής, -ές: easy
εὔχομαι: pray, entreat, beseech
εὐχόμενος: *nom. masc. sg. pres. act. part. of* εὔχομαι = pray
ἐφεζόμενος: *nom. masc. sg. pres. act. part. of* ἐφέζομαι: sit upon
ἐφέλκω: lead, draw on, drag
ἔφη: *3rd sg. imp. act. ind. of* φημί = say
ἐφήρμοσαν: *3rd pl. aor act. ind. of* ἐφαρμόζω = fit together, fasten upon
ἐφίστημι: set upon, impose upon
ἔχθιστος, -η, -ον: most hated, most hateful
ἔχρισε: *3rd sg. aor. act. ind. of* χρίω = anoint, rub with oil
ἔχω: have, hold
ἕως: until

Z

Ζεύς, ὁ: Zeus
ζητέω: seek, search, look for

H

ἦ: in truth, to be sure
ἦγ'/ἦγεν: *3rd sg. imp. act. ind. of* ἄγω
ἤγγειλε: *3rd sg. aor. act. ind. of* ἀγγέλλω = announce
ἠδέ: and
ἤδη: already
ἡδύς, ἡδεῖα, ἡδύ: sweet, pleasant
ἠέ: or
ἦεν: *3rd sg. imp. act. ind. of* εἰμί

ἠϊών, ἠϊόνος, ἡ: beach, shore

ἧκε: *3rd sg. aor. act. ind. of* ἵημι

ἤλασεν: *3rd sg. aor. act. ind. of* ἐλαύνω = drive

ἤλατο: *3rd sg. aor. act. ind. of* ἄλλομαι = leap, spring, jump

ἦλθε, ἦλθεν, ἦλθες, ἦλθον: *see* ἔρχομαι

ἥλιος, ὁ: the sun

ἡμίπνοος, -ον: half-breathing/half-alive

ἤμυνε: *3rd sg. aor. act. ind. of* ἀμύνω = guard/ward off

ἦν: *3rd sg. imp. act. ind. of* εἰμί

ἡνίκα: at the time when

ἧπαρ, -ατος, τό: the liver

ἠπητής, -οῦ, ὁ: repairer, mender

Ἠριδανός, ὁ: The Eridanus, a river

ἤριπε: *3rd sg. aor. act. ind. of* ἐρείπω = throw down, cast away

ἥρως, ὁ: a hero

ἦσαν: *3rd pl. imp. act. ind. of* εἰμί

ἦσθα: *2nd sg. imp. act. ind. of* εἰμί

ἤσκησαν: *3rd sg. aor. act. ind. of* ἀσκέω

ἦτορ, τό: heart

ηὔδα: *3rd sg. imp. act. ind. of* αὐδάω = utter, speak

ἠύτε: as, like

ἠώς, ἡ: dawn

Θ

θάνατος, ὁ: death

θᾶσσον: sooner, earlier, more swiftly

θαῦμα, -ατος, τό: a wonder, a marvel, something causing amazement

θεός, ὁ: god

θῆκα: *1st sg. aor. act. ind. of* τίθημι

θνητός, -ή, -όν: mortal

θοίνη, ἡ: meal, dinner, feast

θορυβέω: make a noise, make an uproar

θρύλλος (135) θρῦλος, ὁ: noise, murmur

θυγάτηρ, θυγατρός, ἡ: daughter

θυμός, ὁ: spirit, soul
θώρηξ, -ηκος, ὁ: coat of mail, armor

I

ἰδέσθαι: *aor. mid. inf. of* εἶδον
ἴδεν: *3rd sg. aor. act. ind. of* εἶδον
ἰδών: *masc. nom. sg. aor. act. part. of* εἶδον
ἴεν: *3rd sg. imp. act. ind. of* εἶμι = go
ἵημι: send forth, throw, hurl
ἱκάνω: come, reach, arrive
ἱκνέομαι: come, arrive, reach
ἵστημι: set up, make stand, establish
ἰσχύω: be strong, have the ability to (*w. comp. inf.*)
ἶφι: by force, by power, by might
ἴωμεν: *1st pl. pres. act. subj. of* εἶμι = go
ἰών: *nom. masc. pres. act. part. of* εἶμι = to go

K

κάδ: *poetic form of* κατά
καθοπλίζω: arm, equip, fashion out
καί: and, also
καινός, -ή, -όν: new, fresh, novel
κακός, -ή, -όν: bad, base, wretched, ugly
Καλαμίνθιος, ὁ: Minty
καλαμοστεφής, -ές: covered with reed
καλέω: call, summon
καλέσας: *nom. masc. sg. aor. act. part. of* καλέω
καλός, -ή, -όν: beautiful, noble, excellent, good
καλύβη, ἡ: hut, cabin, a hiding place
καλύπτω: conceal, hide, cover
καλύψαι: *aor. act. inf. of* καλύπτω
καμοῦσα: *nom. fem. pres. act. part. of* κάμνω = work
κάνειον, τό: the lid of a vessel

Καπανεύς (282): Kapaneus

κάππεσε: *3rd sg. aor. act. ind. of* **καταπίπτω** = fall down

κάρη, τό: the head, peak, topmost point

κάρηνον, τό: head

καρκίνος, ὁ: crab

κάρυον, τό: a nut

κατά: *w. acc.* = throughout, on/over a space, down against; *w. gen* = down from, down upon

καταδύω: go down, sink down, plunge into

κατάκειμαι: lie down, lie outstretched; lie hidden, lurk

κατάκρημνος, **-ον**: steep, rugged

κατακτείνω: kill, slay

καταλείπω: leave, behind

καταμῦσαι: *aor. inf. of* **καταμύω** = close the eyes

κατατρίζω: squeak

κατατρώγω: eat, chew

κατεῖδον: look down

κε: *this is a modal limiting particle, and does not admit of simple translation into English (see* **ἄν**)

κέαρ/κῆρ, τό: heart

κεδνός, **-ή**, **-όν**: cared-for, dear, careful, trusty

κεῖμαι: lie down, lie dead

κεῖνος: *see* **ἐκεῖνος**

κελεύω: urge on, drive on, order

Κένταυρος, ὁ: a centaur

κένωμα, **-ατος**, τό: an empty space, void

κέρας, τό: horn

κεραυνός, ὁ: thunderbolt

κεφαλή, ἡ: head

Κήρ, ἡ: death, doom (*acc. in* κῆρα)

κῆρυξ, **-υκος**, ὁ: herald, messenger

κηρύσσω: announce, summon

κικλήσκω: call, address by name

κίνδυνος, ὁ: danger

κινέω: set into motion

κινείσθω: *3rd. sg. imperat. m./p. of* **κινέω**

κινήσας: *nom. masc. sg. aor. act. part. of* **κινέω**

κίρκος, ὁ: hawk, falcon

κλάω: break off, shatter

κλέω: call (= **καλέω**)

κλύζω: wash over

Κναίσων, Κναίσωνος, ὁ: Grater

κνήμη, ἡ: the leg between the ankle and the knee

κνημίς, ῖδος, ἡ: greave, leg-protector

κνίση, -ης, ἡ: the smoke which arises from the fat of a burnt sacrifice

Κνισσοδιώκτης, -ου, ὁ: Smokehunter

κολοκύντη, ἡ: gourd

κόνις, -ιος, ἡ: dust

κονίω: make dusty, cover with dust

κόπτω: cut, chop, strike

κόρυς, -υθος, ἡ: helmet

κορύσσω: equip, muster, marshal

κοσμέω: order, arrange, marshal

κοσμήσαντες: *nom. masc. pl. aor. act. part. of* **κοσμέω**

κοσμοῦντες: *nom. masc. pl. pres. act. part. of* **κοσμέω**

Κοστοφάγος, ὁ: Spice-eater

κοῦρος, ὁ: boy, young man

κοῦφος, -η, -ον: light, easy

κοχλίας, -ου, ὁ: spiral-shelled snail

κράμβη, ἡ: cabbage

Κραμβοβάτης, ὁ: Cabbagetreader

κρατερός, -ά, -όν: strong, stout, mighty

κρατέω: get possession of, hold on

κρατήσας: *nom. masc. sg. aor. act. part. of* **κρᾰτέω**

Κραυγασίδης, ὁ: Croakerson

Κρήτη, ἡ: Crete

Κρονίδης -ου, ὁ: Zeus (son of Kronos)

Κρονίων, -ονος, ὁ: "Son of Kronos," i.e. Zeus

κρόταφος, ὁ: the side of the forehead, the temples (*in pl.*)

κρυόεις, -εσσα, -εν: chilly, ice-cold

κτείνω: kill, slay, put to death

κτύπος, -ου, ὁ: bang, crash, loud striking sound

κύαμος, -ου, ὁ: bean

κῦμα, -ατος, τό: swell, wave, billow

κώνωψ, -ωπος, ὁ: gnat, fly, mosquito
κώπη, ἡ: oar, the handle of an oar

Λ

λαβόμην: *1st sg. aor. mid. ind. of* λαμβάνω = seize, take hold of
λαγών, -όνος, ἡ: flank, hollow beneath the ribs
λακτίζω: kick, struggle
Λειχήνωρ, -ορος, ὁ: Lickman
Λειχομύλη, ἡ: Mill-licker
Λειχοπίναξ, -ακος, ὁ: Platelicker
λέκτρον, τό: couch, bed
λεπτός, -ή, -όν: husked, peeled, fine, small, delicate
λέπυρον, τό: rind, shell, husk
λευκοχίτωνος, -ον: white-coated
λευκός, -ή, -όν: white, light, bright
λήθει: *3rd sg. pres. act. ind. of* λανθάνω/λήθω = escape notice
λήσεις: *2nd sg. fut. act. ind. of* λανθάνω/λήθω
λίην: very much, too much, excessively
λίθος, -ου: stone, rock
λίμνη, ἡ: pond, lake, marsh, body of standing water
λιμνόχαρις, -ιτος, ὁ: Grace of the marsh, pond-loving; as a proper name = Pondlubber
λιπαρός -ά, -όν: oily, shining with oil, unctuous
Λιτραῖος, ὁ: Poundweight
λίχνος, -η, -ον: greedy, gluttonous
λόγος, ὁ: story, rumor, report
λόγχη, ἡ: lance, spear, javelin
λοξοβάτης, -ου, ὁ: walking sideways, walking obliquely
λύχνος, ὁ: lamp, lantern

M

μάγειρος, ὁ: butcher, cook
μάκαρες, οἱ: the blessed (i.e. the dead)

μακρός, -ά, -όν: great, large, long

μάλα: greatly, exceedingly, quite

μαλακός, -ή, -όν: soft, gentle, luxuriant

μαλάχη, ἡ: mallow

μᾶλλον: more, rather

μανθάνω: learn

μάχομαι: battle, strive, contend, fight

μάχη, ἡ: battle, combat

μαχητής, -οῦ, ὁ: combatant, fighter

μέγας, μεγάλη, μέγᾰ: big, great, large

μεγαλήτωρ, -ορος, ὁ/ἡ: great-hearted

μειδήσας: *nom. masc. sg. aor. act. part. of* **μειδάω** = smile

μέλας, μέλαινα, μέλαν: black, dark, murky

μελιηδής: honey-sweet

μελίτωμα, -ατος, τό: honey-cake

μέλλω: to be about to do, on the verge of doing, destined to do (*w. compl. inf.*)

μέλος, -εος, τό: limb

μέμφομαι: blame, censure, upbraid

μεμφομένων: *gen. pl. pres. m/p. part. of* **μέμφομαι**

μὲν: *used absolutely* = indeed; *used with* δέ = "on the one hand … on the other hand" (27, 33, 74, 89, 113, 123, 124, 132, 161, 261c, 285, 288)

μενεαίνω: desire earnestly, long for eagerly

μεμερισμένα: *neut. pl. pf. passive part. of* **μερίζω**

μένω: stay/remain

Μεριδάρπαξ, -ᾰκος, ὁ: Crumbthief

μέροψ, -οπος, ὁ: possessing the power of speech

μεσόμφαλος, -ον: in the middle; mid-navel

μέσος, -η, -ον: middle, intermediate

μετά: *w. acc.* = among, in the middle of; *w. dat.* = between

μετάνοια, ἡ: change of mind, repentance

μετασχεῖν: *aor. act. inf. of* **μετέχω** = to partake, have a share in

μεμηλώς: *nom. masc. pf. act. of* **μέλω**: care for, take an interest

μέτωπον, τό: brow, forehead

μὴ: *w./subj., expressing negative wishes or negative purpose. Also used to express counterfactual statements, as in line 291,* εἰ μὴ … βατράχους ἐλέησε Κρονίων, *if Zeus had not pitied the frogs.*

μήποτε: in no way

μηρός, ὁ: thigh
μήτηρ, ἡ: mother
μίγνυμι: mix, mingle
μικρός -ά, -όν: small, little, tiny
μιμούμενος: *nom. masc. sg. pres. act. part. of* **μιμέομαι** = imitate, mimic
μιν: *3rd sg. masc. acc.* = him
μιχθείς: *nom. masc. sg. aor. pass. part. of* **μίγνυμι**
μοῖρα, -ας: fate, destiny
μονοήμερος, -ον: being completed in one day
μόνος, -η, -ον: singular, alone
μόρος, ὁ: fate, destiny, doom
μοῦνος: *see* **μόνος**
μῦα, ἡ: fly
μῦς, ὁ: mouse
μῦθος, ὁ: word, speech, conversation, account, report
μυλοειδής, -ές: like a millstone
μυοκτόνος, -ον: mouse-slaying
μῶλος, ὁ: the toil of war

N

ναίω: dwell, inhabit
ναυηγός, -όν: shipwrecked
νεκρός, ὁ: corpse, dead body
νέος, **νέα**, **νέον**: new, young
νεόπηκτος, -ον: fresh-curdled
νήδυμος, -ον: sweet, delightful
νηδύς, -ύος, ἡ: stomach, belly,
νηός, ὁ: temple

νῆξις, -εως, ἡ: swimming

νοέω: perceive, apprehend
νοήσας: *nom. masc. sg. aor. act. part. of* **νοέω**
νομή, ἡ: food
νυ: now

νύξ, νυκτός, ἡ: night
νῦν: now
νωτάκμων, -ονος, ὁ: having an armored back
νῶτον, τό: the back

Ξ

ξεῖνος, ὁ: friend, guest, stranger
ξεινήϊον, τό: a gift given by a host to a guest
ξύλινος, -η, -ον: wooden
ξύναγον: *3rd pl. imp. act. ind. of* ξυνάγω = bring together

Ο

ὄβριμος, -ον: mighty, powerful, strong
οἴκαδε: to home, to a house
οἶκος, ὁ: a house, home
οἶος, οἴα, οἶον: of what sort
ὀκτάπους, ὁ: having eight feet
ὄλεθρος, ὁ: death, destruction
ὄλεσσα: *1st sg. aor. act. ind. of* ὄλλυμι = destroy, kill
ὀλέτειρα, ἡ: destroyer
ὀλίγος, -η, -ον: small, little
ὀλίσθης: *2nd sg. aor. act. of* ὀλισθάνω = slip, fall
ὀλλύμενος: *nom. masc. sg. pres. m.p. part. of* ὄλλυμι = perish, die
Ὄλυμπος, ὁ: Mount Olympus
ὅμιλος, ὁ: crowd, throng
ὄμμα, τό: the eye
ὁμοῖος, -α, -ον: the same, similar
ὀξυόεις, -εσσα, -εν: having a sharp point
ὀξύς, -εῖα, -ύ: sharp, keen, piercing; ὀξύ: quickly, swiftly (*neut. adj. used as adv.*)
ὀξύσχοινος, ὁ: Juncus acutus, a spiny type of reed
ὁπλίζω: get ready, equip
ὅπλον, τό: tool, instrument, shield, weapon

ὅπου: where, wherever

ὅπως/ὅππως: in order to (*in final clause w./subj. verb*)

ὅραμα, -ατος, τό: something seen, a sight

ὀρθός, -ή, -όν: straight, upright, just

Ὀριγανίων, ὁ: Mr. Oregano

ὁρμηθέντες: *nom. masc. pl. aor. pass. part. of* ὁρμάω = set in motion, drive on

ὅρμος, ὁ: harbor, shore

ὄρχαμος, ὁ: leader, chief

ὁρῶ: *contracted form of* ὁράω = see

ὁρῶμαι: *1st sg. pres. mid. of* ὁράω = see

ὁρῶντες: *nom. masc. pl. pres. act. part. of* ὁρῶ

ὅσος/ὅσσος, -η, -ον: as great as, how great

ὄσσε, τώ: (*dual form*) the two eyes, both eyes

ὀστοφυής, -ές: possessing a bony nature

ὀστρακόδερμος, -ον: hard-shelled; having a potsherd skin or shell

ὅτε: when

οὐδέ: but not, and not

οὐδέν: *neut. adj. used adverbially* = in no way

οὐδέποτε: never

οὖς, τό: an ear

οὐρά, ἡ: a tail

οὐράνιος, -α, -ον: heavenly, dwelling

οὐρανόθεν: down from heaven

οὐρανός, ὁ: the sky, the heaven

οὔτασε: *3rd sg. aor. act. ind. of* οὐτάζω = to wound

οὔτε: and not; οὔτε ... οὔτε neither, nor

οὗτος, αὕτη, τοῦτο: this (*demonst. pronoun*)

οὕτω: in such a way, in this way

ὀφθαλμός, ὁ: eye

ὄχθη, ἡ: the bank of a river or pond

Π

παγίς, -ίδος, ἡ: trap, snare

παγκράτιον, τό: a contest combining elements of boxing and wrestling

παγχάλκεος, -ον: made entirely of bronze

παίζω: play

παῖς, παιδός, ὁ: child

παλάσσω: besprinkle, bespatter

πάλη ἡ: wrestling

πάλιν: back, again

Παλλάς, -άδος, ἡ: Pallas (epithet of Athena)

πάλλετο: *3rd sg. imp. pass. ind. of* **πάλλω** = quiver, shake

παντοδαπός, -ή, -όν: of every sort, of all kinds

πάντως: absolutely, assuredly, entirely

πάρ: around

παρά: beside, next to; παρὰ μικρόν (238) = nearly

πᾶς, πᾶσα, πᾶν: all, whole, entire

πατήρ, πατρός, ὁ: father

παυσώμεσθα: *1st pl. aor. act. subj. of* **παύω** = make an end, desist, cease from

παχύς, εῖα, ύ: thick, stout, robust

πεῖρα, -ας, ἡ: an attempt against someone

πέλε: *3rd sg. aor. act. ind. of* **πέλω** = come into existence.

πέμπω: send

πένθος, -εος, τό: grief, sorrow

πέπλος, ὁ: sheet, robe

πέπονθα: *1st sg. pf. act. ind. of* **πάσχω** = suffer

περ: *at lines 44, 276, used adversatively* = although; *at line 141, this particle adds force to the assertion*

περί: around (*w. gen.*)

περιδείδια: *1st sg. pf. act. ind. of* **περιδείδω**: fear greatly

πέσε: *3rd sg. aor. act. ind. of* **πίπτω**

πεσών: *nom. masc. sg. aor. act. part. of* **πίπτω**

πετεηνός -ή, -όν: winged, capable of flying

πέτομαι: fly

πέτρη, ἡ: rock, stone

πέτρος, ὁ: rock, stone

πίπτω: fall upon, fall down

Πτερνογλύφος, ὁ: Hamscratcher/Hamcarver

Πηλείων, -ος: Mr. Muddy

Πηλεύς, ὁ: Peleus, *here* "Mudman"

πηλός, ὁ: clay, dirt, mud

πῆξεν: *3rd sg. aor. act. ind. of* **πήγνυμι**

πικρός, -ά, -όν: sharp, pointed, bitter

πλακοῦς, -οῦντος, ὁ: flatcake

πλανήσας: *nom. sg. aor. act. part. of* **πλανάω** = lead astray

πλατύνωτος, -ον: having a broad back

πλεῖος, -η, -ον: full, filled

πλεῖστος, -η, -ον: the most

πληγείς: *nom. masc. sg. aor. pass. part. of* **πλήσσω**

πληθύς, -ύος, ἡ: crowd, large group

πλήξας: *nom. sg. aor. act. part. of* **πλήσσω**

πλησίος, -α, -ον: near, next to

πλήσσω: strike, smite

πνίξαντες: *nom. masc. pl. aor. act. part. of* **πνίγω** = choke, suffocate

ποθέω: desire, crave, require

πόθεν: from where?

ποιήσας: *nom. masc. sg. aor. act. part. of* **ποιέω**

ποιέω: make, do, fashion

ποινή, ἡ: recompense, restitution, requital

πολεμόκλονος, -ον: raising the din of war

πόλεμος, ὁ: war

πολύς, πολλή, πολύ: much, great, large

πολλάκι: many times

πολύφημος, -ον: speaking much, many-voiced

Πολύφωνος, ὁ: Sir Croaks-a-Lot

πόνος, ὁ: work, toil

πόντος, ὁ: the sea

πόποι: *an untranslatable expression of anger or exasperation*

πορεύω: carry, convey

πορθέω: destroy, lay waste, ravage

πορφύρεος, -η, -ον: gushing, bubbling, surging, purple

ποταμός, ὁ: river, stream

ποτε: at one time, once

πότμος, ὁ: destiny, final fortune, death

πούς, ποδός, ὁ: foot

Πρασσαῖος, ὁ: Greenstalk

πράσσω: exact payment from

πρηνής, -ές: stooping, bent forward, prone

πρόμαχος, -ον: champion, fighter at the front

πρός: for, for the purpose of (44); in response to (56)
προσεῖπον: speak to, address
προσέθηκε: *3rd sg. pf. act. ind. of* **προστίθημι**, place upon, place near
πρόσθεν: before, in front of
προπεσόντα: *acc. masc. sing. aor. act. part. of* **προσπίτνω** = fall
forward
πρῴην: early in the morning
πρῶτος, -η, -ον: first of all, foremost, primary
πτέρνη, ἡ: the heel, the butt-end; a ham hock
Πτερνοτρώκτης, -ου, ὁ: Hamnibbler
Πτερνοφάγος, ὁ: Hameater
πώ: yet, up to this point
πῶς: how?

Ρ

ῥα: *shortened form of* **ἄρα**
ῥάβδος, ἡ: rod, wand, scepter
ῥάφανος, ἡ: cabbage
ῥάχις, -ιος, ἡ: backbone, ridge, trunk
ῥέζω: do, act, perform
ῥήγνυμι: break, break out, burst forth
ῥήξαντες: *nom. masc. pl. aor. act. part. of* **ῥήγνυμι**: break, break off
ῥήξας: *nom. masc. sg. aor. act. part. of* **ῥήγνυμι**: break, break off
ῥίγιον: colder, horrible, miserable
ῥῑνός, ὁ: skin, hide
ῥίπτω: throw, cast away, hurl
ῥίψας: *nom. masc. sg. aor. act. part. of* **ῥίπτω** = cast, throw, hurl
ῥίψεν: *3rd sg. aor. act ind. of* **ῥίπτω** = cast, throw, hurl
ῥοδάνη, ἡ: spun thread

Σ

σάκος, -εος, τό: shield
σάλπιγξ, -ιγγος, ἡ: war-trumpet

σείω: shake, brandish

σελίς, -ίδος, ἡ: a column of writing

σέλινον, τό: celery

Σευτλαῖος, ὁ: Beety

σεῦτλον, τό: a beet

σησαμότυρον, τό: cheese blended with sesame

σθένος, -εος, τό: strength, bodily power

σκάζω: limp, halt

σκέπτομαι: look around

σκηπτοῦχος, -ον: holding a scepter (used of a king)

σκιρτάω: jump or leap about

σκιρτῆσαι: *aor. act. inf. of* **σκιρτάω**

σκότος, ὁ: darkness, gloom

σπεύδω: hurry, make haste

στάζω: let fall, drop, drip

στάσις, -εως, ἡ: sedition, tumult, discord

στέμμα, -ατος, τό: garland, wreath

στέρνον, τό: breast, chest

στεῦμαι: promise, threaten

στήμων, -ονος, ὁ: warp

στήσομεν: *1st pl. fut. act. ind. of* **ἵστημι**

στιβαρός, -ά, -όν: strong, sturdy, stout

στοιχεῖον, τό: an element; *pl.* means the elements, elements of knowledge

στόμα, τό: the mouth

στονόεις, -εσσα, -εν: mournful, causing groans

στρατός, ὁ: the army

στρεβλός, -ή, -όν: twisted, crooked

στῶμεν: *1st pl. aor. subj. of* **ἵστημι**

σύ: you

σῦκον, τό: the fig

σύν: with

σύρω: draw, drag along

σφίγγω: clutch, bind, hold together, strangle

σχεδόν: near, close

σχέτο: *3rd sg. aor. mid. ind. of* **ἔχω**

σχοῖνος, ὁ: reed

σῶμα, -ατος, τό: the body

T

τάδε: these things

τανύπεπλος, **-ον**: with a flowing robe

ταῦρος, ὁ: a bull

ταῦτα: these things

τάφρος, ἡ: a ditch, trench

τάχιστα: most quickly

τάχος **-εος**, τό: speed, quickness

τε: *enclitic particle, serving as conjunction* and; τε . . . τε = both . . . and

τεθνειῶτος: *gen. sg. perf. act. part. of* **θνῄσκω** = die

τείρω: wear out, distress

τείσεις: *2nd sg. fut. act. ind. of* **τίνω** = pay back

τελετή, ἡ: *properly,* an initiation into a mystery rite; *here, however, the author uses it as an equivalent of* **τελευτή** = end, fulfillment, completion

τένοντα: *masc. acc. sg. pres. act. part. of* **τείνω** = extend, stretch out

τέρας, τό: something monstrous or wonderful to behold

τέρπω: delight, cheer; (*in mid./pass.* = have enjoyment of, enjoy)

τετράχυτρος, **-ον**: consisting of four pots

τέτυκται: *3rd sg. perf. pass. ind. of* **τεύχω**

τεῦχος, **-εος**, τό: tool, implement, weapon, armor

τεύχω: make, fashion, form

τέχνη, ἡ: skill, craft, art

τίθημι: put, place, draw up (for battle)

τίλλω: pluck, pick out

τίνω: pay back

τίπτε: why?

τις, **τι**: (*indefinite*) anyone, anything; in line 84, **οὔ τι** = not at all

τίς: (*interrogative*) who?

τίσουσι: *dat. pl. fut. act. part. of* **τίνω**

τιτρώσκω: wound

τιτύσκομαι: fashion, prepare, make ready

τλήμων, **-ονος**: steadfast, wretched, suffering

τόδε: this thing

τοι: *dat. form of* **σύ**

τοιγάρ: therefore, accordingly

τοῖος, **τοία**, **τοῖον**: of such a sort, such

τόκος, ὁ: interest

τόμος, ὁ: a slice
τότε: then, at that time
τράχηλος, ὁ: neck, throat
τρεῖς: three
τρέπω: turn around, turn oneself
τρέχω: move quickly, run
τρισκοπάνιστος, -ον: kneaded three times
τρίτος -η, -ον: third
τρίχες: hairs, from θρίξ, ἡ
τρόπαιον, τό: trophy, a monument marking the defeat of
    an enemy
τρυφάλεια, ἡ: a helmet
τρυφερός, -ά, -όν: delicate, soft
τρωθῇ: *3rd sg. aor. pass. subj. of* τιτρώσκω
τρώγλη, ἡ: hole
Τρωξάρτης, ὁ: Breadmuncher
τρωγλοδύνων, -οντος, ὁ: crawling into a hole
Τρωγλοδύτης, ὁ: Holedweller
τρώγω: eat, nibble, gnaw
τρῶσεν: *3rd sg. aor. act. ind. of* τιτρώσκω
τύψε: *3rd sg. aor. act. ind. of* τύπτω = strike
Τῡρογλύφος, ὁ: Cheeseborer
τυρός, ὁ: cheese
Τυροφάγος, ὁ: Cheeseeater

Υ

Ὑδρομέδουσα, ἡ: Waterqueen
ὕδρος, ὁ: watersnake
Ὑδρόχαρις, ὁ: Watergrace
ὕδωρ, ὕδατος τό: water
υἱός, ὁ: son
ὑμεῖς: you (*pl.*); *dat. form in* ὕμμιν
ὑμέτερος, -α, -ον: yours
ὑπαλύξαι: *aor. act. inf. of* ὑπαλύσκω
ὑπαλύξεις: *2nd sg. fut. act. ind. of* ὑπαλύσκω

ὑπέδεισαν: *3rd pl. aor. act. ind. of* ὑποδείδω = to fear/shrink in fear
ὑπέμεινεν: *3rd sg. aor. act. ind. of* ὑπομένω = to stay behind
ὑπέρ: over, above (*w. gen.*)
ὑπεστενάχιζε: *3rd sg. imp. act. ind. of* ὑποστεναχίζω = to groan
  beneath
ὕπνος, ὁ: sleep
ὑπό: under, beneath
ὕπτιος, -α, -ον: backwards, on the back
ὑψηλός, -ή, -όν: lofty, towering
Ὑψιβόας, ὁ: the Loud Shouter
ὑψώσας: *nom. masc. sg. aor. act. part. of* ὑψόω = to lift/raise up

Φ

φαεινός, -ή, -όν: shining, radiant
φάτις, ἡ: saying, report, talk
φάτο: *3rd sg. aor. act. ind. of* φημί
φέρω: bear, carry, wear
φεύγω: flee, run away, take flight
φημί: say
φθέγγομαι: utter a cry
φίλος, -η, -ον: dear, beloved (*used substantively* = friend)
φιλότης, -ητος, ἡ: love, intercourse
φοβέω: terrify, alarm, scare
φόβος, ὁ: fear, terror
φόρτος, ὁ: cargo, burden (*from* φέρω)
φορέω: possess, hold, bear
φράγδην: piece-by-piece
φραξάμενοι: *nom. masc. pl. aor. m./p. participle of* φράσσω = fortify,
  defend
φρήν, φρενός, ἡ: heart, mind
φύγῃ: *3rd sg. aor. act. subj. of* φεύγω
φυγή, ἡ: flight, retreat
φῦλον, τό: race, tribe, class
φύλλον, τό: leaf
φύσας: *nom. masc. sg. aor. act. part of* φύω = beget

Φυσίγναθος, ὁ: Bellowmouth
φύσις, ἡ: nature
φωνή, ἡ: sound, tone
φώνησεν: *3rd sg. aor. act. ind. of* **φωνέω** = make a sound

X

χαίρω: take joy in, rejoice in, be delighted
χαίτη, ἡ: hair
χαμαί: on the ground
χεῖλος -εος, τό: the lip
χειλοτένων, -οντος, ὁ: lip-stretching
χείρ, χειρός, ἡ: hand
χερμάδιον, τό: a boulder
χθών, χθονός, ἡ: the earth, the ground
χλοερός, -ά, -όν: verdant (*poetic form of* **χλωρός**)
χλωρός, -ά, -όν: pale, green or yellow
χόλος, ὁ: wrath, anger
χολόομαι: to be provoked to anger
χορδή, ἡ: guts
χορός, ὁ: chorus, choral dance
χρησαμένη: *nom. fem. sg. aor. mid. part. of* **χράομαι:** be in need, be in debt
χρηστός, -ή, -όν: useful, serviceable
χύτρα, ἡ: a pot
χῶρος, ὁ: land, country

Ψ

ψαλιδόστομος, -ον: scissor-mouthed
ψευδόμενον: *acc. masc. sing. pres. m.p. part. of* **ψεύδω** = lie, cheat
Ψιχάρπαξ, Ψιχάρπαγος, ὁ: Crumbthief
ψυχή, ἡ: the soul, life

Ω

ὦ: O, *as a form of address preceding a vocative*

ὧδε: thus, in this way

ᾤκτειρε: *3rd sg. aor. act. ind. of* **οἰκτείρω** = feel pity upon

Ὠκιμίδης, ὁ: Basilson

ὦμος, ὁ: shoulder

ὠργίσθη: *3rd sg. aor. pass. ind. of* **ὀργίζω** = make angry

ὥρμησεν: *3rd sg. aor. act. ind. of* **ὁρμάω** = set upon

ὡς: as, how, when

ὥς: thus, so, in such a manner

ὠχρός, -ά, -όν: pale

Index

meter
  Homeric 23–7
  and oral-poetic dialects 30
mice (*see also* names of individual
    mice)
  and Athena 122–3
  characterization of 90
  contrast with frogs 90
  as cowards 158
  disfiguring/immobilization of
    157–8
  enemies of 105 (*see also*
    weasel(s))
  genocidal wishes of 154
  as gluttons 89
  Mouse Assembly and Arming—
    commentary 102–10
  Mouse Assembly and Arming—
    translation 56–7
  names of 79–80
  Zeus's image of 121
Mill-licker 54, 176
Millstone Licker 79, 138
Minty 60, 134, 173
morning 103, 183
Morrison, J.V. 149
mortals 67, 84, 115, 126, 152, 155
Moschus 65, 72, 97
mosquito/gnat 128, 176
mousestrap 87
mousetraps 54, 56, 86
Mudbedder 60, 163
Muddy 59, 72, 181
Mudman 53, 76, 181
Mudwalker 139
Muses 63–5
myth 8, 16, 97, 120, 142, 144, 145

nature 54, 81, 90, 188
Nicander 70
Nonnus 21, 33, 157
novelty 95, 159

object clauses 93, 116
Odysseus 71, 76, 78

Odyssey 28, 101, 103, 115 (*see also*
    frequent mentions throughout
    the Commentary)
Oilthief 138
Old and Middle Comedy 83
Olson, S.D. 16
Olympus 6, 65, 179
oral performance, and
    Batrakhomuomakhia 32
oral-poetic dialects, and meter 30

Pallas 18, 61, 181
Panathenaean festival 122
pankration 100
Panyassis 16
Paradeigmata 97
Paris 142
parody
  animal parody 22
  and arming of the mice 102
  Athenian influence on 22
  divine concern 120
  epic 12–23
  excessive 155–6
  and the Homeric tradition 12–14,
    17–18
  and "serious" epic 15
Parry, M. 27, 29
participle, use of 67, 68, 69, 85, 92,
    123
Patroklos 101, 147, 153, 158
Pavese, C.O. 30–1
Peace 16n.32
performance-oriented poetry 64
Pelias 152, 153
Peleus 76, 130, 181
Peplos 121, 123
perna 80, 83
Philostratus 34
Philumenus 70
Physignathos (Bellowmouth)
  accused of killing the mouse 56
  attitude towards mice 115
  characterization of 82
  criticism of 114